INVISIBLE WOUNDS

AN INSIDE STORY

ALEXIS FAERE

MTNWALKER MEDIA, LLC

Invisible Wounds: An Inside Story

Text copyright © 2024 Alexis Faere
Published by MTNWalker Media, LLC

Cover design by Danijela Mijailovic
Book Production and Publishing Services by Miramare Ponte Press

Hardback ISBN-13: 979-8-9902996-0-3
Paperback ISBN-13: 979-8-9902996-1-0
eBook ISBN-13: 979-8-9902996-2-7

Library of Congress Control Number: 2024906505

Faere, Alexis
Invisible Wounds / Alexis Faere
As an awkward music-nerd teenager, with the help of a trusted confidant, Alexis took a
leap of faith to go on a blind date. In an innocent instant, at knifepoint, the landscape of
her life forever changed. Would she ever be able to get on with life after clawing her way
through 23 hours of sheer terror? This is a story about her "big ugly" and how it became
her big amazing.
ISBN-(hc) 13: 979-8-9902996-0-3

For the person I'm still becoming and for people who choose to grow the loving spirit within. Let us live well, be caring, and make loving choices.

CONTENTS

PART THREE

A FEW WORDS ABOUT
THIS BOOK

Let me begin by saying how truly honored I am to be writing this—not as a writer per se, but as someone privileged to have come to know Alexis Faere and her story personally. Few people will ever let you see so deeply inside themselves without reserve. This book is an unadulterated act of public intimacy—more than a rarity, a truly singular treasure, a sacrifice freely offered, a sacred gift of self.

Trauma disorients. The greater the trauma, the greater the disorientation. The unspoken picture of life as we had it secretly framed in our inward parts is suddenly shattered beyond recognition. What we thought we knew as reality loses the landmarks we once used to navigate that reality. Uncertainty prevails. The process of assembling a new reality comes with no user manual. Questions roll in on endless waves:

Will I ever be the same again?

Will life ever be the same?

Who am I now?

Am I still me?

Who or what can I ever trust again?

How do I stop the endless memory loop from replaying the trauma over and over and over in my head?

As a young man, in an act of foolishness, my left foot tangled unsuccessfully with the blades of a power mower. Fifty years later, I cannot see or hear a mower start up without that moment rushing back in. The inward need to put something violent into a safe context is hard-wired into us—even something as simply accidental as the relatively minor injuries I sustained. Years later, when my uncle suffered something similar in an encounter with a snowblower, we talked about how what we experienced remained with us and replayed inwardly so often. In that exchange, we both grew to accept our scars as part of our new reality without bitterness and resentment. We were forever changed. And yet we were still us. In reading *Invisible Wounds*, I realized that all trauma includes certain shared aspects, even though my and my uncle's traumas were nothing compared to what Alexis Faere faced. That is part of why this book is so important, whether your trauma is great or small.

What you have in your hands right now is the closest thing to a roadmap through this unwanted maze as you are ever likely to read, thanks to the unsparing and heroic journey Alexis fearlessly and freely offers to everyone who is crying for the help that eludes so many sufferers.

Invisible Wounds is not an easy read. But astonishingly, it is as hopeful as it is harrowing. Every page drips with a bravery that allows a trauma survivor to safely look into the abyss of their pain with less fear and more hope. It is truly remarkable. It surely is a priceless gift.

What Alexis faced both in her abduction and the unspeakable violations that followed is unimaginable to me. How I wish it were unimaginable to everyone. But I know full well that crimes like she endured are tragically shared by many others as well. And while there are some resources to help, very few (if any) are as personal, comprehensive, practical, and transparent as this book.

If you are a survivor yourself, let Alexis take you by the hand as she retraces the dark and frightening steps of her own story. Join her as she traverses those paths with new light and hope, and without fear. As you join her, you'll find true hope that you can do the same—in time. She is a faithful friend.

Or perhaps you know someone who has suffered the life-shattering, disorienting aftermath of severe trauma. Read this yourself and learn how to understand what your loved one is going through and where you can be a healing party and a place of safety.

As I read (and re-read) *Invisible Wounds*, there were times I audibly groaned and wept. I then reflected on the remarkable woman who so unsparingly cast her eyes over all these events, over and over again, and then thought to place this treasure in the hands of others. Here is more than just hope and help. Here is light—light that dispels the shadows of darkness and fear.

Thank you, Alexis. Thank you.

—Rev. Reid A. Ferguson, Pastor, Author, Speaker

Writing this book was an act of courage. It is an emotional high-wire act, allowing readers to have insight into the thoughts and fears of a young girl as she is forced to endure the nightmare of every woman and parent. It is not an easy read.

For survivors who are ready, this story is a relatable and honest rendering of horrific events and the personal struggles Alexis dealt with in the aftermath of those events. For those fortunate enough to have not been abused, it is a window into the experience, providing a means of understanding the ongoing consequences endured by the survivors of abuse. If you have a friend or family member who has been sexually assaulted (and whether you know it or not, you all do), reading this book will certainly help you understand their thoughts, feelings, and fears. And if you're a survivor still in the throes of abuse recovery, be forewarned. Alexis Faere's personal account could trigger frightening memories.

The ultimate message in Ms. Faere's book is one of healing and hope. She brings the reader into her world, describing not just the trauma but also her heartbreaking desire for a return to normalcy after the assault, her inevitable anger, intense anxiety and fear, depression, and suicidal thoughts. Alexis shares her grief, self-hatred, loneliness, and fears of stigmatization. Her willingness to be vulnerable while navigating her life's journey and her path toward learning to cope and to trust again is shockingly real and raw.

I have known Alexis for almost 30 years. I am a clinical psychologist whose practice (through a series of decisions and their unintended
consequences) has become devoted to the treatment of sexual abusers.
The goal of this treatment is to minimize re-offense risk. As she
describes in this book, Alexis and several other survivors have coura-
geously agreed to meet with small groups of the offenders I treat once
those offenders have overcome their denial and reached the point
where they are open to developing some insight and empathy for
those they have hurt. As an observer of these special group sessions
(which are facilitated largely by Ms. Faere and the other survivors), I
have witnessed her recounting her story on countless occasions.

In addition to the vulnerability she displays during these sessions, I
have seen her attempt to emotionally connect to the offenders as a
means of helping them understand the lifelong consequences of their
selfish actions. Her efforts and those of the other survivors with whom
she leads these groups have had a significant impact on many of the
sexual abusers I have treated over the years. Not all, of course; unfortunately, a percentage of sexual abusers are simply too antisocial or
narcissistic to ever expend energy toward understanding others' feelings. Alexis is well aware of this, yet she continues to be vulnerable
with groups of men similar to the man who raped her in an attempt to
try to reach them. That, too, is an act of bravery.

In the end, it is her will to survive and thrive that dominates Ms.
Faere's memoir. This is not just a personal story of trauma, fear, and
loss; it is a story of survival and personal growth. She offers invaluable
insight and advice to others who are navigating their own personal
journey through abuse recovery. For those of you who have endured
abuse of any type, you are about to be reminded of the resilience of the
human spirit. You, too, are resilient in the same way.

—Pete Henschel, Ph.D., Licensed Psychologist, Licensed Sex
Offender Treatment Provider

PRELUDE

Dear Reader,

I share this personal story with you as one example of how to take a horrific personal experience and use it to carve and shape yourself into the person you want to be. In the years I have lived, I have realized we all have traumatic experiences that make up our personal histories. There is no one trauma that is worse than another. It's all trauma, and it all hurts. I've also come to realize by living with my experience that these dramas in our lives don't have to define us.

When we are born into this world, we become part of a soup that is full of possibility. We have every opportunity to shape ourselves into who and what we want to be. Sometimes, though, people who lack a depth of soul and emotional maturity cross our path. These people often act with no principled awareness. Their unwitting actions create deep, life-altering trauma for the people who are in their path. There is nothing pretty about what they do. Unfortunately, we (as humans) create belief systems around these experiences that are less than helpful.

I've written about my personal experience with rich detail for a couple of reasons.

1. Maybe you have not experienced kidnap and/or rape, but perhaps you know people who have. This will give you some idea of what it was like for me to survive it and give you an understanding of what it was like for the people you know. Every experience is unique. How I handled it is not the *only* way. Another person in the same circumstance might do things differently. That's okay.

2. If you have experienced sexual abuse of any kind, I honor and respect the choices you made to be where you are today. If you've come out of something like that alive, then you made the choices necessary to survive it. My life journey in the aftermath of such horror is just one person's way of walking through it. There are about as many unique ways to process and navigate life after the fact as there are people in this world. I honor them all.

3. Some of you may have other types of horrific experiences in your lives. I also honor and respect the choices you made to be where you are today. Every experience brings with it dynamics that affect our lives, our relationships with others, and how we interact with the world. I share these words with you as a reflection of just one person's journey through her stuff.

4. If you have perpetrated actions upon others with no attention to how those actions impact another person, I share these stories so that you can learn about your choices. I believe you have the power to make different choices if you want to. You have the power to care about another person or to hurt another person. Perhaps sharing my story will help you stop for just one moment to determine what you want—to hurt or to care.

Trigger alerts: The first several sections of this book detail my experience of being kidnapped and raped. Please read those only if it feels safe for you to do so. Listen to your heart, and let it be your guide.

Starting with Chapter 10, the remaining chapters talk about how I navigate integrating these experiences into the whole of who I am;

from being a victim to being a survivor to becoming an integrated person with an experience in her history. Please feel free to only read the stories I've offered here that support what you're looking for. If you prefer not to read the parts about the actual kidnap and rape, please skip to Chapter 10. There's lots of other great content without graphic details to aid you in your own journey.

And don't worry; there are "trigger alerts" noted at the beginning of sections that might be of concern. I make every effort not to surprise you with something that may be triggering.

I offer you my journey so that you might gain insights into your own particular journey.

PART ONE

VICTIM

CHAPTER 1
WHEN THINGS HAPPEN

THERE ARE ABOUT AS many traumas in this world as there are people. We all have a story (or stories) related to big things that happen in our lives. What I failed to realize when my big story event happened was that I was being victimized. There's no word for it when it happens. It is shocking, and it uproots everything that, to that moment, seemed normal.

In my circumstance, I immediately fell into surviving. I didn't know from one moment to the next if I would live or die. That's a normal response, whatever the experience. There's something in our human existence that strives for survival, no matter what the circumstance. We want to live!

Once I got past the survival part and came out of the situation alive, my immediate response was to do what I could to jump back into that which felt normal. I wanted the situation to be over, and I wanted to pick up where I left off. Understanding how to do that was mysterious and elusive. I just wanted it to happen: to get over it and get on with life.

It wasn't until a decent amount of time passed in my journey that I came to realize that I was a victim. No one wants to admit to being victimized. Admitting to that makes us seem weak or incapable somehow; that's how it felt to me. I much preferred to turn a blind eye to it and ramrod myself back into life as I knew it before the massive interruption.

When big life events such as this happen, the aftermath follows much the same path as grief recovery. There is loss, denial, acceptance, and a process for healing that we often prefer to rush through to get over it. One important part of that is stepping back to acknowledge what happened—to name it.

In my case, being a teenager, I just wanted the horror to be over and to get back to my hum-drum life. The idea of acknowledging my victimization was not a concept I grasped or understood. I resorted to my own devices to get back on the proverbial horse and ride.

The moment I grasped my victimization, I unwittingly set myself on a course of healing. This recovery is one that takes a lifetime. There are waves of steps, large and small, that occur in that process. I got stuck on some of those steps, which resulted in what is now my life experience. Some of those steps are big and painful. Some of them are catapults that put the puzzle pieces together that have carried me to be the person I am today.

Everyone processes those steps in their own way. This story outlines my steps. If you can read these words and find wisdom that helps you on your own journey, I share them freely. Perhaps my learning can help you move your own recovery through whatever phase you're in and propel you toward becoming the person you want to be in this world.

I also share these words for those of you who have made choices to disregard a person's general right to be a whole human life. Perhaps my sharing helps you to understand the impact of your choices so that you, too, can grow and learn to make different, more caring choices.

The chapters in this section of the book not only detail my experience, but the very normal and brave initial steps I took to put myself back together again. There are warnings so that you don't have to read the gory details if you choose not to. The reason I've included them here is so there is a context for you to see or experience what it was like for me. I was a person navigating life as a teenager when, suddenly, someone put their caring aside and ripped that away from me.

CHAPTER 2
A BLIND DATE

APART FROM JIMMY JOE'S marriage declaration when he marched down the church aisle with 3-year-old me, dating was unfamiliar. There was John, of course, who stuffed my Valentine's bag with homemade blue notebook paper hearts in elementary school. Oh, and yes, sneaking a kiss with him in the cello closet. Then there was the unforgettable long homecoming kiss goodnight with Mark my freshman year of high school. As a teen, I was curious about dating and had lots of romantic daydreams about being swept off my feet.

In 1977, my junior year of high school, awkward and a misfit in the social ways of the world, I took a liking to one of the youth sponsors at my church. Allison had a warm kindness and understanding toward teens. I felt like we saw eye-to-eye on many issues. She felt like a friend and someone I could relate to. She helped me feel less awkward during my challenging dating endeavors.

As we developed our sponsor/teen relationship, I felt comfortable sharing my frustrations about dating. I loped my way through my pre-teen years without many dating opportunities. Aside from Mark and one other insignificant rendezvous with Lionel (the country-est bumpkin you can imagine), I didn't date. Dates were scarce, and I felt shy about accepting dates on my own, let alone initiating one.

Fate presented itself when Allison's nephew, David, moved into the area. New to town, introverted (like me), and in search of people he could relate to, Allison suggested we meet by phone. She thought if we got along well enough, perhaps David and I could meet for an informal date. Maybe we could at least be friends, widening my circle of friends and helping David get to know some people. He didn't go to church with Allison, and he lived in a suburb east of where I lived. Our opportunities to cross paths were non-existent.

A few weeks after Allison's suggestion, I settled into the idea, and David called me up. We talked about what we liked to do and what we enjoyed in school and did our share of normal, nervous, getting-to-know-you conversations. He phoned me a few times, and topics for chatter were always at the tips of our tongues. Phone conversations were simple. My dialog with David came comfortably, easily, and effortlessly.

Upon a rare break in the conversation, David mustered up the courage to suggest a dinner engagement. Having never met in person, we described ourselves to one another so we could identify each other when we met. We ironed out the logistics and settled for dinner on Sunday evening after youth activities at the church. David had a car and offered to drive. All we had to do was figure out the best way for him to retrieve me at the close of scheduled activities.

I was going to wait in my dad's car, which was parked outside of Cope Cottage, where he led counseling groups at the church. David would swing by the parking lot outside of Cope Cottage, pick me up, and then take us to Chrystal's Pizza for some dinner and conversation.

I was freaking out about our date. But I was also excited about meeting someone new. I wore a cute red, white, and blue suit that I always felt dressed up in. Hand-me-downs and garage sale finds supplied most of my wardrobe. I never looked poor in my clothes, but some outfits made me feel more like the "in crowd" than others. This was one such outfit, and I felt confident wearing it.

The suit was a little more formal than blue jeans and a pullover shirt. I usually wore the latter attire for church youth activities. The suit wasn't so dressy as to draw attention to me. For descriptive purposes, it was a nice outfit for David to recognize me. David had a beard and was going to wear jeans. He was going to drive, so I could identify him in the car when he approached me at Cope Cottage.

As I sat in Dad's car, awaiting David's arrival, I saw someone standing near the chapel doorway just across from Cope Cottage. He seemed a little shabbily dressed, and his hair was unkempt. I watched as he walked toward the car; he had a beard. He was wearing blue jeans and had on a blue jean jacket. My first instinct was that this couldn't possibly be David.

He's walking over here. He looks uncertain. God, I feel so nervous! Maybe I should just get out of the car now. But what if it isn't him? I feel safer in the car. I'll find out if it's him, and then I'll get out of the car.

My heart is pounding! Slow down! It's just a date. Be cool. Everything will be just fine. I don't want to be rude, but just reveal a crack in the window. He must think I'm a wuss. God! I have to find out if it's him. I'll ask him if he's related to Allison. If he says no, then I know it's not him, and I can drive away if I need to. God, he's here.

My heart pounded with such fervor it seemed like a miracle that it could still be in my chest cavity. My body vibrated with uncertainty and excitement all over.

This guy does have a beard; it must be him.

I rolled the window down about two inches and bravely asked the foreboding person standing just outside, "Are you David?"

"Yes."

I started having second thoughts again. My first inclination led me to a certain skepticism. I didn't believe him. Something didn't feel right about this person.

Get a grip! Of course, it's him. After all, he has a beard, and he's standing here where we discussed we'd meet each other.

"Is Allison Donnally your aunt?" I asked.

"Yes."

The butterflies in the pit of my stomach ran amuck! A never-before-met-in-person stood before me. My anxiety about dating, especially with someone I'd never seen before, climbed like a roller coaster at the highest point and then plummeted. He answered my questions correctly. I reasoned my nerves were getting the best of me. It was time to start my date with David.

I grabbed the car keys, my brown purse, and opened the door of the red Datsun wagon to join David and walk to his car. As I rolled the window back up and reached for the door latch to open it, I wondered why he didn't just bring his car over to where Dad's car was situated, like we'd talked about.

Maybe he's unfamiliar with the church grounds and parked in the main lot.

The large Gothic church was a regal sight among the downtown Fort Worth skyscrapers. Around the corner from where I was and across the street from the obvious front face of the building sat the main parking lot. In the middle of the parking lot, there was a big cross made of concrete and stone. In the middle of the landscaped cross, a tall, serene statue of Jesus with outstretched arms welcomed members, visitors, and guests. If David didn't know where to go to find the car I'd described, wouldn't he park his car there?

CHAPTER 3
KIDNAPPED

TRIGGER ALERT: This chapter contains potentially triggering material about being kidnapped. If you prefer to skip this chapter, it's okay. You can skip to Chapter 10.

As I OPENED the car door, I turned to position myself to step out. Fireworks of excitement coursed through my whole being without restraint. I stepped out of my dad's car, trying to appear calm. By all means and measures, my blind date started.

In an instant, he placed a knife at my side. "Wait a minute, baby, you're going with me! Unlock the back door so I can get in, and don't try anything funny!"

This can't be my blind date.

My entire body turned into a bundle of uncontrollable trembling as though overtaken by an involuntary convulsion. Every muscle in my body tensed up as if to create a protective barrier.

He's wearing jeans, has a beard, and answered all my verifying questions correctly. However, this can't be my date. He smells like three-day-old alcohol and needs a shower. Allison would never set me up with someone like this. This can't be her nephew!

Everything felt like it was in slow motion. My clothes were the only insulation between the intensity of the knife and my perceived demise. As I settled back into the driver's seat, my body functioned like a mechanical robot. My body knew what to do but didn't want to move. My arms and legs obeyed my deliberate mental instructions to get back into the car and unlock the back door.

This must be it! I made it into my junior year of high school, and this could very well be the end. Right here, right now. What if he kills me? I don't want to get hurt! I don't want to die!

My enthusiastic, meandering, date-focused, whirling thoughts instantly turned to fear and survival. I grasped at each thought, trying to make sense of the shocking events unfolding before my eyes.

A second ago, I was stepping out of Dad's car to go on a blind date with David! Now I've got a knife pointed at me, and I'm being told to let this scary person into the back seat of the car. Will I live to see the next five minutes, another day, or even tomorrow? I want to be alive tomorrow. I want to be alive in five minutes!

Boom! The subject of my choices churned like a gazelle running from a hungry wildebeest to stay alive. Seconds into my date, I'm fighting for my life.

I thought I would be safe in my dad's car. It's parked right outside of his office. My dad is just inside the little house where the car is, but he does not know what's happening or that I'm in danger. How can I get his attention? What would happen if I honked the horn and someone came running? But he's got a knife. He might kill me! I don't want to get hurt or die. That would be terrible. I just want to stay alive.

Maybe I could run up to his office, but the knife is right here at my side. He's in there counseling people, and I'd have to interrupt him. But that's not fair to his clients. If I jump out of the car, run around to the porch, and up the stairs to the door, what if Dad doesn't open the door when I knock? But the knife is in the way. My legs are so wobbly I'm not sure I can outrun him. He'll stab me. If he gets angry, I might get hurt, and then how would I get inside without him killing me? I want to stay alive. I have to stay alive. There's no way I can make it up there.

Mechanically, I got the back door unlocked. Everything on my body shook as the guy who answered my questions correctly slithered into the back seat, and the knife returned to my side.

God! I just want to live. Just let me come out of this alive!

"Do you want my purse, my money? What do you want?" I asked the creepy guy in the back seat. It was my best attempt to figure out what I was dealing with. If giving him what little money I had in my purse saved my life, it seemed worth it to be alive and in one piece.

He offered no response. My legs trembled uselessly, like a stilted structure, moments from a sure tumble.

Thank goodness for the seat beneath me. I don't think my legs would hold me.

As these thoughts bubbled to the surface, the stranger climbed over the small console between the two front seats into the front passenger seat. "Drive!"

I asked my trembling mechanical arms and hands to put the keys in the ignition and start the car. Then, I mustered enough control of my shaking leg to get my foot placed near the accelerator so that I could start the car.

But Dad. What about Dad? How will he get home from work?

As I got the car started and put the transmission in reverse to back out of the parking spot, I did not know where to go.

"Where should I go?" Getting the words to come out of my mouth seemed like a miracle.

"I've got to get out of Fort Worth! Take me to California!"

With a seemingly impossible target identified, I backed the car out of its parking spot and turned so that I could drive forward out of the parking lot. My trembling legs felt uncertain, but they functioned enough to brake and speed up the vehicle as needed. I looked at the fuel gauge to see how much gas was in the car. California was a long way from Fort Worth, Texas.

"I can't get you to California on half a tank of gas," I said. In the back of my mind, I wanted to find out how reasonable this guy was and try to understand what he was thinking.

I only have $2 in my little brown canvas purse, and I bet he doesn't have any money. David was going to pay, so I didn't grab any money. I don't have *any credit cards. There's no way I can get him to California on half a tank of gas. I wonder where he really wants to go. How do I get to California from here, anyway? I don't have a map, and I don't know how to get there.*

I tried to figure out a more logical destination and expected what might follow.

This can't be my date. It can't be the person Allison told me about, and he doesn't look like the nice person I talked to on the phone. If this isn't my date, then who the hell is he? I don't know who this is. What does he want with me?

My poor dad. He won't know where his car is when he's ready to go home. It's almost dark. Maybe as I drive past the church without my lights on, someone will see me. I forgot to turn the lights on. Maybe one of my friends at church will try to stop me, and I can get some help. How will Dad get home? He'll have to call Mom, and then I'll be in big trouble for taking the car. Someone, please see me. I'm in trouble and need some help. Someone, please flag me down to tell me my lights aren't on.

With a knife pointed at my side, I drove out of the church parking lot and drove away.

Dad, I'll be back. I'll come home. If there's anything to telepathy, now would be a good time for Dad to get the message. Hear me, Dad. I need help. Hopefully, I'll be back. I'll come home. Hear me. Help me.

As long as it didn't threaten my life, I tried anything I could think of to get help. I forced myself to believe in something hopeful. Dad, being who he is, might sense my pleas for help.

As I drove into the street from the parking lot and approached the first nearby traffic light, I prayed for it to turn red.

If I sit at the traffic light, someone in another parking lot can see Dad's car instead of my date's car, and they'll put two and two together.

The car lights were off, and the setting sun turned to darkness.

Please, someone, flag me down!

Every determined will in the universe failed me, and the light stayed green. My plan to be noticed while I sat at the traffic light vanished as quickly as I tried to come up with a plan. My hope of catching someone's attention dwindled as soon as it appeared. I was totally on my own, with no way to draw hopeful, helpful notice. It was just me and my life in someone else's hands. My plan failed.

It's getting too dark to see. I have to turn my lights on.

Shaking and terrified, I had to see to drive.

This can't be David. This is not my date! I wonder which way I should go.

The scary guy in the passenger seat pointed to where he wanted me to go, and soon, I was too far away from Fort Worth to see anything familiar in the rearview mirror. I observed road signs to figure out our general direction and knew enough to understand that going toward Dallas would not get us to California.

I need to find out as much about this guy as I can so I can identify him later.

"What is your name?" I asked. I tried to sound calm, even though my hands and body shook like a leaf desperately clinging to a branch.

"John."

Good! He's not David if he's telling the truth about his name, which he probably isn't.

"How old are you?" he asked, shifting the focus of the conversation back to me.

I'm 17, but if I tell him I'm younger than I really am, maybe he won't hurt me so badly. I'm driving, so I have to be old enough to do that.

"I'm 16. Where are you from?"

"What does that matter?" he hurled back, obviously irritated.

With that response, I uncovered a boundary, a line I better not cross. I didn't want to anger or provoke him in any way that might cause undesirable consequences.

I need to keep him calm whatever I do. If I make him angry, there's no telling what he'll do. I don't want to die.

Out of fear, I decided my fact-finding mission would have to wait for the time being, and I drove in silence. After a pregnant pause, I thought I'd give it another try.

"What do you want with me?" I asked.

I wanted to understand my plight. If I understood his intentions, I might devise a plan to escape or, at the very least, draw attention to myself.

"I want to marry you and take you to California. Doesn't that sound like fun?" he asked.

Ewwwww! He wants to marry me? That would be awful, having to marry him. We're driving east, and California is the other direction. What in God's name is he really up to?

I did my best to keep my mind focused on coming up with a plan for escape and to learn what I could, attempting to anticipate whatever might be next. The prospect of having to marry this stinky, angry guy sent a whole new set of scenarios whirling in my brain. I tried to control my body's tornadic trembling.

If his name is really John, he lied about being David. I can ask him all the questions I want, but he's going to say whatever he wants and not give me any actual information. He may want to go to California, but he's got a funny way of getting there!

My head stepped into high gear, trying to make sense of it all.

He didn't want my purse when I offered it to him, so he must not want to rob me. God, what would he do if he found out I only had $1 or $2? If he's not a thief, then what does he want?

For now, understanding what he wanted was going to remain a mystery for fear of my life.

In the silence, as I drove, the relentless trembling jostled my body around like a rogue jackhammer. My foot rested on the accelerator, and I was driving, but my legs trembled with grave fear. I gripped the steering wheel with my hands, hoping that would stabilize my arms, but to no avail.

Scared to death, I could hardly breathe, taking short, shallow breaths. That probably didn't help the shaking. I wanted to be prepared for anything that might come my way, and breathing was really the furthest thing from my thoughts. But, with this realization, I wanted to do what I could to make my body act normal. It was imperative that I stay alert and responsive to anything that might happen. I felt completely out of control, and my thoughts ran a hundred miles an hour. Looking back, I know my body did what it needed to do to protect itself—mind and all. Now and then, I grasped a good, deep breath, and when I did, my whole torso quivered. That only heightened my awareness of the knife still pointed at my side and my determination to stay alive.

I didn't want him to notice how badly my body was shaking, and I used my mental focus to do what I could to make it stop. Or, at the very least, slow it down a little. I was terrified that if he noticed, he would order me to stop, and I couldn't control it! I thought he would kill me if I couldn't stop it.

If I drive faster than the speed limit, maybe I'll get pulled over. This nightmare would be over if a cop came to the car. I wonder what he's thinking. What's going to happen next? What if I stop the car and get out? But there's no place for me to run to for safety.

Time passed with long pauses in conversation. My thoughts filled the moments when no words eked out of either of us. Then, suddenly, he asked the most bizarre question.

"Do you believe in God?"

What a curious question while my thoughts are pleading with God to let me live.

"Yes." The word fell out of my mouth.

"Well, what do you think of your God now?" he asked.

What is this God thing really all about, anyway? It's a big part of my upbringing, with Dad being a minister. This is part of my life. I go to church every Sunday. Sunday school is a required regular activity. I'm involved in choir and the youth programs. This is my life, but what do I really think about God? I'm sure as hell not thinking about God right now. What God would allow this horrible, terrifying thing to happen to me? How the hell am I supposed to answer that kind of question?

His short patience demanded an answer, so I made something up.

"I still believe in Him," I said.

How am I supposed to feel about a God that allowed this to happen to me? I don't know how I feel about it at the moment! I want to believe in God. After all, I keep asking Him to let me live!

That was the end of that conversation. My thoughts about God would have to wait for another time. All I could think about was what I had to do to stay alive. In the ensuing sporadic conversations, I aspired to learn as much about him as I could. The more I knew about him, the better my chances of reporting him if I ever got away.

~

Will I ever see my family and friends again?

I thought about home and the house I lived in. It was the biggest house I'd ever lived in. We always lived in furnished parsonages in Oklahoma. When my family moved to Fort Worth, we were fortunate to move into a large, furnished, three-bedroom house that had two living rooms and even a fireplace.

Thank you, Barbara, for the opportunity to live in your house. I'm so glad to have the baby grand piano to play.

I remembered how the leader of the small non-denominational church where my dad worked offered us a home to live in when she wanted to move into a smaller house. She knew our family had nothing to speak of in the way of furnishings or a place to live when we moved to Fort Worth. Barbara's husband (the Dean of Fine Arts at Texas Christian University) had recently passed away. Her Tanglewood neighborhood home was more than she wanted, and she was scaling down.

Thank you for your generosity. Our family had little when we moved here, and your graciousness has given us a fine place to live. Thank you!

I earnestly pictured Barbara in my mind and visualized being with her in person to express my gratitude.

Maybe she'll hear me. Maybe if I think about her hard enough, she'll hear my message. Please hear me, Barbara. Please hear that I need some help. Someone has taken me away in my dad's car. I don't know where we are going, but he has a knife at my side, and I need help. Please hear me!

Dad, I'm sorry about your car. I didn't take it on purpose. Maybe Mom can pick you up and take you home. I'm sure she'll come to your aid, aggravated as she may be. Please, Daddy, hear me. I know you're working with people tonight. Thank you for everything you do to provide for our family. I know I didn't want to move to Fort Worth. I know I hated it at first, and I know you're doing the best that you can.

Thank you, Mom, for the clothes to wear. I know I don't always appreciate second-hand clothes, but thank you! Thank you for the food you provide for us. Please hear me. I need your help. I don't know where we're going, but I'm not safe. Please help me. I need your help.

I saw my mom and her short, dark hair and her big winning smile in my mind. When I hit my head as a youngster, Mom would pull me close and cradle my head in her soft, fluffy bosom. I longed to be where she could hold me safely. I thought about how my older brother and I never wanted to be in trouble with Mom. She was a stern disciplinarian, but she was also kind and generous. She always found a little extra something to share with someone else.

Pictures flashed through my head of Dad preaching in all the small churches he served in rural Oklahoma. I remembered when he went back to school, later in life, to become a counselor. That's what brought us to Fort Worth. He was six feet tall. His balding was often the subject of fun family ridicule. Then there was the time he preached a whole sermon about Nicodemus in the tree (instead of Zacheus). I knew he spent quiet time every day in meditation, and I imagined him hearing my notions of gratitude and my pleas for help.

I bet my little sister is coloring. Don't drop the box of crayons! You know how messy that is to pick up, and you know Mom won't be happy about that!

Laci was nine years old, but I enjoyed remembering the spilled crayon incident. She put her little hands on her hips and said, "Oh, cwap!" She was so cute, and Mom didn't even scold her for saying the forbidden word.

Vickie, can you hear me?

I thought about my five-and-a-half-years older sister who didn't live at home. She was severely mentally and physically handicapped and lived in the State School in Pauls Valley, Oklahoma.

I know sometimes people like Vickie are sensitive to things we can't imagine. Vickie, it's your little sister here. Please hear me!

I imagined being with Vickie in her wheelchair and me picking up the squeaky dog or cat toy that was there for guests to play with. When I handed her the dog toy, she took it, chewed on the ear, and then threw it down with all the enthusiasm she could muster. When the toy hit the floor with a thud and a squeak, Vickie laughed and giggled with every fiber of her being. Her joyous entertainment was contagious enough to get everyone to laugh.

If you can hear me, Vickie, tell Mom and Dad I need some help. I love you, Vickie.

I pictured me and Paul, my year-and-a-half older brother, in Jane Park in Ponca City, where we lived before we moved to Fort Worth. We would climb up to the canopy covering the top of the slide and smoke cigarettes. I remembered coughing and hacking on the first few puffs as he taught me how to smoke.

Paul, you're my big brother. I don't know what you're up to this evening, but if you can hear me at all, I need your help!

Thinking about cigarettes, I thought about my good friend Brenda. Two peas in a pod, we did lots of growing up together. She was the first good friend I found when I moved to Fort Worth. Far from the comfort of my familiar life and friends in rural Oklahoma, I came to Fort Worth kicking and screaming. I was determined not to be influenced by the people or perceived as hickish in the ways of Texans. From my first day of school at McLean Middle School through this time at Paschal High School, Brenda and I stuck together like glue.

Our interests were far from similar. I was a total music nerd, and Brenda had a keen interest in adventures outside of "the boundaries." We had fun being "bad girls," smoking cigarettes at school, the library, football games, or roaming around local shopping malls.

As my captor indulged in a cigarette, the distinctive smell reminded me of Brenda and our shenanigans. She came from a strict Christian upbringing and was no stranger to prayer. In my desperation to connect with someone who could hear my cry for help, I thought of Brenda. I saw her sandy blonde hair and her winning, engaging smile. I thought about her gracious laughter and the way she always wanted to say a prayer or blessing before mealtime. With all of my might, I imagined Brenda at church praying. It was Sunday, after all.

Brenda, you are such a good friend. I love having you as a friend. If you can hear me, I need your help right now. I'm in trouble! Please call my mom and tell her I need help.

I imagined the phone ringing, Mom picking up the phone, and Brenda saying, "Is Alexis okay? I was thinking about her, and I think she needs your help." It seemed important to picture everything in as much detail as I could, and I tried to energize my thoughts into action. Maybe someone would respond.

The instant I remembered smoking with Brenda, I also thought about my cousin, Janice. I searched my imaginary address book for church and school friends, family, preachers, and adults. I visualized standing in front of each one, gazing into their eyes, and expressing gratitude for each person. I thought about the nice things each of these people did for me over the short 17 years of my life and pictured my thoughts flying instantly from my heart to theirs. My heart desperately hoped someone would hear my petition for help. I would try anything! If telepathy was real, perhaps the intensity of my thoughts would reach someone.

Distracting myself with driving and reflection took my mind off the knife in my side and the scary passenger in the car. Rain fell off and on, sometimes heavier than others, so my mind got busy crafting a plan to get noticed.

If I drive with my brights on or keep the windshield wipers on when it's not raining, maybe someone will notice something is wrong. Maybe a state trooper or police officer will pull me over. Someone, please notice!

When the rain let up, I turned my brights on, leaving the windshield wipers running. I yearned for my captor to remain unaware of my ploy, so he wouldn't get any more agitated than he already was.

If I drive over the speed limit, a cop will see me and stop me.

It seemed dumb, but my survival and the persistent threat didn't give me much wiggle room. Thinking up plans gave me a sense of hope that maybe I could get out of this situation alive. My wobbly legs made trying to outrun him seem out of the question, even if an opportunity presented itself. Out on the highway, options for places to run appeared to be fewer and farther between. If I stopped the car, safely getting out and running didn't seem the best option. My thoughts about drawing attention to the car derailed when he moved the knife from my ribs to my throat.

"Don't you try anything funny!"

Without a doubt, I knew he meant business. Trembling fiercely, images of the knife piercing my throat only magnified my already fearful state of mind.

I better do exactly what he wants. I don't want to die!

He pulled out the ashtray in the center of the front dash to extinguish his cigarette, and my mind leaped toward my cousin Janice. A forensic chemist for the Oklahoma State Bureau of Investigation, she took me to her workplace during one of our visits. In her eye-opening tour of the facility, Janice took every opportunity to educate people, and I was no exception.

She showed me pictures of crime scenes and explained how she gathered forensic evidence to convict criminals. She worked primarily rape cases. Evidence gathering came from bodily fluids and by looking in the most unsuspected places to locate DNA. With DNA, she could identify criminals and prove someone was at a specific location at a certain point in time.

When he put out his cigarette, I remembered something.

DNA from saliva on the cigarette butt can identify the smoker. Ah ha! I can keep those butts and tell the police that he smoked them. When he's not looking, I'll put that in my purse to save for DNA testing.

My memory of my time with Janice distracted me from the terror of having a knife at my throat and turned me into a criminal investigator. I recalled what I learned from Janice and developed my plan for gathering evidence. Thinking about that changed my immediate concern from whether I would live from one moment to the next to actively watching and learning as much as possible. I turned on an imaginary video recorder to convey information to the police. It was a way for me to survive. I listened carefully to every conversation so I could recall information that might be important. Observing and making mental notes about anything he touched might reveal a fingerprint. I wanted the police to have every opportunity to identify this person, to prove anything he did to me.

What evidence is he leaving behind? He's smoking and leaving his butts in the ashtray. They can identify him with the saliva that he leaves.

It was redundant, but I wanted to ingrain every detail to recall it later. If he touched anything I could save in my purse, I chronicled the information in my head so I could gather things when the opportunity presented itself.

Dad popped into my head. *By now, his groups have ended, and he has probably discovered there's no car for him to get home.* I pictured Mom getting the phone call from Dad to come and rescue him. I worried about how late it was, knowing Mom was the only person at home with my little sister. My older brother was at the church with the other youth, so he couldn't watch her if Mom left the house. Laci was probably already in bed, and Mom would have to wake her up to go get Dad.

I'm going to be in so much trouble! It's not my fault, Mom. This is not David. This is not my date, and... Oh, God! I wonder what's going on in David's mind? He's never going to go out with me again! I never have dates. I'm doomed! David, it's not my fault! Please don't be mad. I wonder what he thinks about me standing him up? How long did he wait for me? I never showed up. He's probably pissed at me. He's never going to go out with me again!

My thoughts kept me occupied as I drove into Dallas. As instructed by the man holding a knife at my throat, I turned onto I-45 toward Corsicana. I didn't know where Corsicana was in relation to where I was, other than it was a long way from home; and directionally, it made little sense to get to California. I knew my directions well enough to know California was west, and we were headed south—away from California.

CHAPTER 4
RAPED

TRIGGER ALERT: This chapter contains potentially triggering material about being raped. It's okay for you to move ahead in this book without reading this chapter. You can skip to Chapter 10 and still read about things I've learned as a result of this experience.

As we neared Corsicana, he commanded me to pull off the highway and onto a dirt road. The rain-soaked earth left a messy, slippery ribbon of mud on the ordinarily crusty dirt road. The knife still held at my throat made me especially alert to drive carefully, navigating bumps in order to keep the blade from puncturing my flesh. It didn't help that I still shook erratically, like a leaf blowing in a strong north wind.

The car slid through the mud as I tried to keep it moving; heaven forbid I should get stuck. Keeping a steady pace on the accelerator kept the vehicle moving. Being off the main highway meant something, but I did not know what. I only understood that this turn of events felt much more frightening than being on the highway. There weren't any other travelers on the desolate, messy, muddy road, and no highway patrol could see me.

Navigating the mushy earth required a stout dose of patience; something in short supply for my captor. Driving in this condition proved stressful for both of us. I wasn't adept at this sort of off-road driving, and he wasn't afraid to bark orders as we made our way down the path.

Clearly, we need to get turned around.

I did my best to drive on the mess and keep my eyes open for a place to get turned around. Eventually, the opportunity presented itself.

"Turn around!" he barked.

Relieved that he felt the same way I did about getting turned around, I tried to get the car pointed back in the direction we came from. All too aware of the knife, I didn't want the car to jostle in such a manner that it stabbed me. I felt thankful I made it this far without getting hurt, but the threat remained.

My efforts to keep the car from getting stuck while I got turned around proved a failure when the wheels turned, and the forward movement of the car came to a halt. The tires dug in. Nervous and scared, I put my left foot on the brake and my right foot on the accelerator to rock the car loose, but it was to no avail. The more I tried, the more the car settled into its place.

"Turn off the car!"

His obvious displeasure made my already-racing heart pick up its pace. The encasement of my ribs probably helped keep it from pounding out of my body. It seemed a miracle my heart could beat any faster, or harder, but physiologically, there must have been a way. I could feel my ribs vibrating with every beat of my pounding heart.

What's going to happen next? What now? There's no place to run, no people to draw attention to. Oh, God, please don't let this savage hurt me! Please let me live!

I wanted to cry but feared for my life, so I willed myself to keep the tears at bay.

Don't cry! If he sees me crying, there's no telling what he'll do to me.

We sat in the stuck car for a few minutes. My mind raced from one scenario to the next, scanning my options to come up with a plan for escape. Given the present situation, the options seemed severely limited. I wanted to run, but we were in the middle of nowhere without an obvious place to run. My skinny little body did its best to manage the stressful condition. My legs were an irrepressible bundle of unpredictable wobbly energy. That and the incapacitating, syrupy mud, made running an unreasonable choice.

How far would I have to run to reach safety? There's no one around, and we're not where anyone can see me. If someone could see me running, who in their right mind would drive onto a road that is clearly impassable? I can't run away. Not now.

Whatever I do, I don't want to make him angry! The last time he got mad, the knife went from my belly to my throat.

I wanted to live, and I knew planning every word I spoke and every action I took was essential to my survival. I didn't want to risk getting stabbed and left for dead.

Every moment felt like an eternity. Sitting in the car without dialog kept my mind whirling chaotically for a plan, while I tried to anticipate his next move. Moments felt like an eternity.

"Kiss me!" He grabbed my face and pulled it toward him. "Kiss me!"

In an instant, I felt mortified. As he pulled my face toward his, I smelled stale alcohol on his breath and his foul body odor. Janice popped into my head again, reminding me to observe every little detail.

Keeping my eyes on the scary, smelly guy demanding a kiss, I noticed his dirty hands, his unkempt beard, and his oily, dirty hair. His empty, harsh blue eyes were more like placeholders instead of windows into a soul. His face was rough and worn-looking.

He could kill me at any moment. Whatever you do, don't move. Don't do anything to encourage him. I have to do what he says. Stay alive.

Frozen in fear, and trembling, my thoughts came out in short abrupt concepts as he leaned toward me to kiss.

Aaaaaaaah! He put his nasty tongue in my mouth. Whatever you do, don't puke!

I turned to stone in fear. I just sat there, not kissing back, and doing everything I could to rein in the energy coursing through every cell of my body. When I felt vomit coming up from my gullet, I swallowed and did everything I could to keep from throwing up all over him.

The sheltered, innocent schoolgirl I was 45 minutes before was erased in that instant. As I stepped into the vast, unknown drama unfolding before me, I turned my thoughts once again to those I knew and loved.

Please hear me! Someone, please hear me. I'm in grave danger and I need your help. Hear me! Please see me here on this dirt road, stuck in the car. My life is in his hands!

~

I thought about my parents, Brenda, Janice, Dude, Allison, and all my friends at church. A roster of the MYF (Methodist Youth Fellowship) leaders, my pastors, and anyone I could think of kept my mind off of his gross kissing. I still directed my thoughts to anyone who might "receive" or "hear" my pleas for help. I distracted myself from being stuck by imagining any place but where I was. Anything to avoid thinking about this horrible person sticking his nasty, smelly, vile tongue into my mouth.

"Take off your clothes. Now!"

I can't undress in front of him. What is he thinking? What does he want from me?

A part of me knew what was about to happen next, but I didn't want to believe or think about it. My protective, ignorant denial was a more survivable place at the moment.

Panic struck like lightning. Between his crystal-clear demands and my thoughts, I saw little recourse to protect myself from the inevitable. Just when I felt I reached my limit of feeling threatened, he dug a deeper well of vulnerability within me. My life at the mercy of this animal, the sharp edge of his knife blade forced me to strip myself of the clothing illusively protecting my body.

My body is mine! I don't even know you! I can't take off my clothes; it's not right!

The thought of exposing my naked body to a rapist made me feel abhorrently sick to my stomach. Fear paralyzed me.

Silence seemed safer than interacting with him. I didn't want him to perceive my nervous chatter as encouragement or a willingness to agree to his demands. However, my silence failed to distract him from his determination.

"Take your clothes off, now!"

I never felt more desperate in my entire life. I knew that, against my will, my future meant obeying this monster's every request, no matter how unthinkable.

Please let me get out of this alive! It's my only choice. I have to take my clothes off. What is he going to do to me? I don't want him to kill me. I have to do what he says.

If removing my clothes meant I was still breathing, then breathing won out. I desperately did not want to believe the fate in front of me. But the intensity of his demands left me clear about my choices for survival. Reluctantly, I mentally instructed my hands and arms to remove my clothes. I wanted to try anything that might keep the inevitable from happening, so I started at the top. Grasping for any opportunity to change his mind, I hoped he would find my small, tiny breasts less than desirable.

I frantically wanted to believe I had fallen asleep and the nightmare would end as soon as I woke up. His demeanor, though, quickly brought me back to reality. I mechanically coordinated the movements necessary to unclasp the buttons and remove my suit jacket, which I wore as a shirt.

Take the button and push it through the buttonhole to unbutton it. Now do the next button. One more button. Now pull your arms out of the sleeves and pull the jacket off.

The surreal slow motion of removing my suit jacket mimicked someone teaching a child how to undress. I sat there, like a statue, in my bra and slacks.

Please let me wake up! It's okay to wake up now! This is a nightmare. Wake up!

"Go on, take your pants off!"

He grew impatient.

I felt like a puppet. The vile monster holding a knife orchestrated every action. With my sights set on survival, I resumed the pedantic process to take my pants off.

Please don't hurt me. Please, please, please don't hurt me!

I stopped, again immobilized with fear, even though my body shook and flailed like someone relentlessly shaking the life out of a rag doll.

If he thinks I'm a freak because I'm shaking, he might kill me!

The harder I tried to control the trembling, the worse it got. There I sat, in the front seat of the car, wearing only my bra and panties. My virgin teen years destined to be left behind for the wild unknown. I felt trapped.

"Take off the rest!"

His raging tone pierced through me like a thrusting sword. The facts drew a clear picture. No matter how frightened I felt, my survival depended on giving in to his demands. I had no choice.

I forced myself to remove my clothes while I thought about my friends and family. It was the only thing I could grasp onto.

Please hear me, I need your help. I'm in trouble, and I need your help. Call my parents, reach out, do something. I need your help!

I begged my friends and family to hear my thoughts so help could find me. If only I could blink my eyes and transport myself from the car into living rooms, bedrooms, and into the hearts and minds of my loved ones.

As soon as all my clothes were off, I sat as still as my juddering body would allow in the driver's seat of the car. I felt cold, scared to death, and completely vulnerable. My physical nakedness removed the tiniest sense of safety I'd had left. Only this life-threatening criminal dictated my bitter chance for survival.

"Get back there." He pointed to the back seat of the car as he barked his next demands.

I believed I had to follow his directions or succumb to death. I hoisted my awkward, shaking, naked body from the driver's seat of the little red Datsun wagon, over the small console, and flopped myself into the back seat. For the first time since trying to get out of the car back at the church parking lot, there was a separation between my body and the knife.

What if someone sees me running naked on this road in the mud? People don't run around outside without their clothes on. Who would take the risk of stopping to help, even if someone were there to see me?

As I settled myself into the back seat of the car, he removed his clothes. My sternum kept my heart from beating out of my chest. As soon as the drape of his smelly clothes vanished from his body, he crawled over the small console and into the back seat with me. He kept the knife close at hand, and the brief reprieve of no weapon on my body disappeared instantly. I could feel the car shaking as my cold, naked body sat trembling as I watched his every move.

When he got into the back seat, he pulled my head to his and kissed me again. I kept my thoughts on Janice and all I learned from my forensic scientist cousin. Realizing there was no way out, I started looking for incriminating evidence to collect. Thinking about evidence distracted me from the intensity of his putrid smell and the repulsive taste of his tongue in my mouth.

While he kissed me, I sat still and stoic, trying to keep myself from shaking. His mouth and tongue disgusted me, and the smell of his body turned my stomach like the smell of rotten eggs.

Don't throw up. Just don't throw up!

After what seemed like an eternity, he moved my body around and sucked on my breasts.

If I let him do what he wants to do, maybe I'll be alive when it's over.

I watched his hands and mentally noted what he touched that might leave a fingerprint.

Maybe it will be over soon. The car seat and console are all plastic. Maybe he'll leave a fingerprint on the ashtray or the cup holder in the back.

I didn't think my body could shake any more violently, but somehow it did. This escalated my fear of angering him. I forced myself to breathe slower and deeper to control the trembling, to no avail.

Please, please don't hurt me. I want to live. You're never going to get away with this. I don't want to die.

My thoughts raced as I imagined someone finding me stabbed, naked, or dead in the car in the middle of nowhere.

After forcefully sucking on my breasts, he pushed me into a prone position in the back seat. The vile predator pried my trembling legs apart and sucked on my vagina. He stuck his tongue in and out, slobbering all over the place. My feet, propped against the car's rear passenger window, pounded the window as I shook and trembled. I tried to keep my feet from bursting through the glass.

He'll never get away with this. I'll collect evidence on him and nail him when I get home (if I ever make it home). I know what to do. Janice said I can't clean myself up. I can't wash my underwear. I can't bathe until I go through an examination at the hospital.

I methodically remembered Janice explaining the best thing to do if you're attacked is to relax. When a body is under that kind of stress, the chance for more serious injury decreases if you're more relaxed. Also, if a person appears less stressed under duress, the offender may experience less sick satisfaction with the attack.

"Give me a blow job!"

"I don't know what that is." Words finally came out of my mouth.

I lay there, trembling and petrified on the seat of the car, and then remembered his lack of patience for my inaction. Not understanding his demand, and realizing I needed to follow through or die, I mustered words to the surface.

"How am I supposed to do it?"

If I don't do it, he'll kill me, and leave me here in the car. What if I'm never found? How would anyone know where I am? What if he kills me and throws me out to rot in this isolated muddy place?

As the scenarios cycled through the projector in my head, he pulled my body up into a sitting position and pushed my head down toward his penis. He held it up with his hand and said, "Suck on it!"

As his forceful hand pushed my head down, I quickly understood his command and stretched my frozen jaw open as far as it would open, and he pushed his penis into my mouth. I didn't want that thing to touch any part of my mouth, if possible. As I took in the awful smell, salty taste, and his filth, he pushed his penis in and out of my mouth. I gagged.

Oh God, don't throw up! He'll kill me if I throw up on him!

It tasted horrible. In my efforts to cling to survival, my thoughts stayed focused on getting out of this alive. I begged for help in my thoughts and continued to collect as much evidence as I could to prove the unfolding events and convict him.

After what seemed like forever, he ejaculated in my mouth.

"Swallow it!"

I gulped a big gulp to get it down as fast as possible. It tasted disgusting, worse than anything I'd ever had. Repulsed, I hoped that, like bitter medicine, it would all go down quickly and be gone.

After he ejaculated, and I swallowed the dreadful goop, he kept pushing his penis in and out of my mouth. A couple of times he pushed it in so far it went into the back of my throat.

No! I can't throw up! He'll kill me if I do that. God, when is this going to be over? Just let me get out of this alive.

It seems like a redundant dialog, but it was the only thing I could hold on to. It distracted me from the horror unfolding before me. While he forced his sexual acts on me, I made myself aware that he had laid the knife on the car floor, still within his reach. It wasn't physically touching my body, but I knew it would only take a matter of seconds for him to reach down and grab it.

What felt like three hours probably only took five minutes. Finally, he pulled his nasty organ out of my mouth. As soon as I thought that the worst was over, he pushed me down on my back on the seat and forced his penis into my vagina. It felt like forcing a roll of sandpaper inside me. I could feel parts of me stretching that had never stretched before.

"Oh, God, it hurts!" I couldn't help the words screaming out of my mouth.

Unconcerned, he kept pushing his penis in and out of my vagina. I'd never felt such pain.

"I have a disease."

I hoped his fear of getting an awful venereal disease or something would keep him from going any farther. But my desperate attempts to get him to stop gave him no pause or sign of remorse. Nothing was going to stop him.

"Help me!"

Petrified, fearful, and in pain, I lay there trying not to encourage anything. I couldn't do anything! The weight of his body on top of mine prevented me from moving.

"I don't know what you want me to do!"

"Act like you're interested!"

My womb and vagina throbbed in pain, but he kept pushing and pushing. I distracted myself by thinking about ways I could condemn him with evidence. The intensity of everything going on shut down all my emotions except fear. This profound horror kept my soul from feeling anything. I wanted to cry. There was no hammer that I could use to beat him over the head. I wanted him gone, even dead— anything so that I was not here in the car being treated like a worthless lump of clay.

I hoped the continuous, painful poking and prodding would end or that he would at least tire of it and stop. In the meantime, I watched everything he touched and every potential thread of evidence created. I hoped with every fiber of my being they would send him to prison and put him away for life. My observations kept me distracted and helped my body withstand the thrashing pain.

Finally. The torture ended. Maybe he wore out or suddenly became freaked out by my tremulous body. All that mattered was that it stopped. There I was, flat on my back, legs up in the air, naked, cold, and vulnerable. At least he'd stopped raping me.

As he lifted himself off of me, he looked around and spotted the homemade wooden box in the hatch behind the back seat of the car. He reached over the seat, pulled the heavy box toward him, and dug around in it. There were all kinds of tools in the box, intelligently placed, should the car break down.

I wonder what he's looking for. What if he's looking for a larger weapon? What's going to happen next? Should I sit up and get dressed?

I watched as he pulled a white cloth from the box and used it to wipe off his penis. When he finished, he threw it on the floor.

When I have a chance, I'll pick that up and put it in my purse. That will surely be some important evidence. They might find sperm on that rag.

My persistent fact-gathering refocused my thoughts. I was relieved to see he had not pulled out a wrench, a hammer, or something else that he might have used for a weapon.

He reached for his clothes and started getting dressed. I took that visual clue to mean it would be safe for me to get my clothes back on, too. My body was still violently shaking. Everything below my waist was sore. It wasn't much, but I looked forward to the safety of having my clothes on as I reached into the front seat to get them.

I cautiously watched his every move to be sure it was okay for me to get dressed. I didn't want to aggravate him! He didn't seem bothered by my actions to retrieve my clothes, so I quickly and carefully started dressing.

Of all the things to think about, a sudden feeling of anger came over me.

He stole my dad's car! How dare he! He took my dad's car! He's a thief! How will Dad ever be able to get another car? I have to watch him; he's bound to touch something and leave a fingerprint. The rag he used to wipe himself off is on the floor of the back seat. He'll never get away with this!

Stuck in the mud, distanced from the highway, away from any sign of civilization, I reeled from enduring the worst hell imaginable. Still, I wondered what was coming next. After he dressed, he got out of the car, leaving his car door wide open.

What's he going to do now? Maybe he'll run away and leave me here. Then, in the morning, I can walk until I get somewhere and get some help.

I looked around to see what he was up to and saw him standing in the same spot. He faced away from where I was sitting. My earnest getaway thoughts stopped when I heard his pee hit the ground.

Oh God! I need to do the same thing! But there's no place for privacy. I just got my clothes back on, and I don't want to invite any more trouble. I need to go! How long will it be before I have another chance to go? I don't want to ask him to stop anywhere. He would surely think I was trying to trick him or something and he'd kill me for sure.

If I get out of the car, it's all muddy and I'll get dirty. Maybe if I just open the car door and hang myself out, I can pee, and he won't think it's an invitation to do what he just did.

I quietly opened the car door and stayed on alert to his location and actions. While he relieved himself, I quickly pulled down my britches and panties and hung my rump out the door so I could pee without getting it in the car, or all over myself.

The warm fluid leaving my body felt like pouring acid on raw, open skin. My bladder felt relieved, but my vagina felt like it was on fire. The moisture coming out burned, but I had to take advantage of the opportunity before me. Sweaty hands and all, hanging on to the car so I wouldn't fall out, I quickly took care of my immediate need and got my clothes pulled back up.

As soon as I settled back into the driver's seat of the car, I reached for the door to close it as quietly as possible. I looked around again to be sure he was still in the same place. As he finished up his task, it was clear he had no intention of walking away as I hoped. My heart sank as my latest plan dissolved. He turned back to get in the car.

"Start the car!"

We're stuck. What good will it do for me to start the car?

I learned from my earlier actions that following his instructions posed the least amount of risk for my innate desire to keep breathing. So, I started the car as he closed his door.

"Put your foot on the brake and give it some gas. Then take your foot off the brake and go!"

My wobbly, muscle-memory legs went to work. I put the car into drive and did the best I could to do exactly as he instructed. I pushed on the accelerator while the other foot was on the brake. When the engine roared, I took my foot off the brake to move forward. I heard the wheels spinning around, but the car didn't move an inch.

"Keep trying. Just rock it back and forth!"

I did the best I could to keep my legs and feet working together and tried it again and again. Once or twice, I thought the car was actually going to take off, but it quickly rocked right back into its place and never moved forward. The wheels spun and spun, and the little red Datsun wagon wouldn't budge.

"Stop!"

It was obvious I did not know what to do to get the car unstuck and he would have to help.

He opened his car door again, stepped out, and left the door open. I watched his every move. As he walked toward the back of the car, I had a glimmer of hope that maybe now he was going to walk off, and my plan to wait until morning might actually work. The picture of my morning escape dimmed quickly as I glanced into the rearview mirror and saw him standing facing the back of the car.

What is he…

"Try it again!"

I followed his instructions, and this time, when I took my foot off the brakè, he pushed to try to help the car into forward motion.

If this works, I'll just drive off. When the car moves forward, I can keep it moving and drive off. I'll just leave him there so I can get away!

We tried this again and again, but the wheels dug deeper and deeper into the mud with every try. The car wouldn't budge. My plan to drive off sank into the earth with the car.

"Okay, stop!"

I heard the frustration in his voice. In the rearview mirror, I watched him try to open the locked latch on the back of the car.

"Open it up!"

There was no automatic latch, so I turned the car off and pulled the keys out of the ignition. I walked through the sloppy mud to the back of the car with the keys and instructed my trembling arms, hands, and fingers to unlock the back of the car.

He reached in and pulled the heavy wooden box back toward him. He rummaged through Dad's box of tools.

Oh God, is he looking for a bigger weapon? What is he doing?

The longer he dug around in the box, the more anger and fear welled up inside me.

He's going through my dad's stuff. What is he looking for? That's private!

The more he rifled through the box and handled things disrespectfully, the angrier I got. I could feel my blood boil. Then my anger turned to shock when I saw him pull out the antique glass doorknobs he found near the bottom of the box.

The more he fumbled around in the box, the more doorknobs he found—three or four of them. After he gathered all the doorknobs he could find, he told me to get back into the car and start it. I noticed the gas gauge hovering ever so close to the E.

Maybe if we can get to a gas station, I can get away!

I sat in the car, awaiting his next command, while he strategically placed the doorknobs under the rear tires to create friction between the car and the mud. When he was ready to try again, he ordered me to move to the passenger seat. I didn't know how to get the car unstuck, so I coordinated my body to shove myself over the gap between the seats and into the other seat.

If he's in the driver's seat, I won't be able to drive off.

My desperate plan was foiled once again. I could only keep my focus on getting to a gas station so I could get help or get away.

It took several tries. Every time he revved the engine, I hoped there would be enough gas for us to get to a station. Finally, the car rocked loose and made some forward progress. With the car unstuck, as he pressed the accelerator, the car jostled violently. I could feel my already widened eyes get bigger with fear.

What the hell? He's going way too fast. What's he going to do, wreck the car? Is he pissed? O geez! What's going to happen next?

I understood a certain amount of speed was necessary so the car wouldn't get stuck again, but this driving seemed awfully reckless.

If we get stuck again, the doorknobs are gone. If we need something for traction, he'll have to use Dad's tools.

Even though the ragged ride had something to do with navigating through the mud, I knew this angry-type driving. At home, my brother drove me to and from school and to violin or piano lessons. He was not without his own temper and teenage "I'm so powerful and you're not" attitudes, especially when he was behind the wheel of a car. I was all too familiar with this angry driving.

My vile captor was now in control of the car. Helpless, I hoped with every fiber of my being that he wouldn't wreck or tip the car over. I could see the highway and couldn't wait to get back onto the paved road.

CHAPTER 5
BACK ON SOLID GROUND

TRIGGER ALERT: This chapter contains potentially triggering material. Skip to Chapter 10 if you need to.

AT LAST. An access road. As the comfortable ribbon of highway settled beneath our wheels, he pulled over, stopped, and fumbled around, gazing for moments at a time away from the road and around where he sat. He was looking for something.

What is he doing?

Feeling around the car surfaces and in potential hiding places, he gazed out at the road before us and then drew his focus back inside the car. Just when I felt some sense of reprieve, he located his misplaced knife and made it available to his heart's desire. My life was still in someone else's hands. Any dribble of safety washed away with my constant awareness of looming danger.

I didn't want to aggravate him by blurting out that the car was nearly out of gas. His obvious frustration about being stuck in the mud and my hyper instinct for survival kept the energy in the car intense.

I watched him closely for any sign that he noticed the gas situation on his own. Given his current agitation level and his recent reclamation of the knife, I didn't want to give him any reason to lash out at me.

Is he going to drive until we sputter and come to a stop? If that happens, he might get angry that I said nothing. But if I say something, he might take it as an insult and get pissed. Do I say anything or not? I'm afraid of what he might do to me if the car comes to a stop and there's no gas. I can't go through what just happened again. Maybe he'll ask me to go find some gas somewhere and I can get away from him. Or, if he goes looking for gas and leaves me in the car, I could wave someone down and get some help. I have to keep things on an even keel.

I took a deep breath and mustered up the courage to forge forward.

"You might want to look for a gas station."

I approached the subject cautiously, with no emotion, and winced for a moment, anticipating a reaction. He glanced at the fuel gauge.

"Yeah, you're probably right."

I heaved a sigh of relief on the inside. It seemed he realized I wasn't trying to pull anything funny and agreed that it was worthy of some attention.

While I was relieved to be back on the highway, I felt filthy on the inside and out. I still smelled remnants of his smelly body, and the awful taste in my mouth lingered. When my hands brushed my face, I could smell his penis. The loitering taste of his appalling ejaculation in my mouth turned my stomach. I wanted to retch.

Despite the offensive reminders, I willed myself to remember I was alive. The horrible, painful poking and prodding was over. Realizing the pause in the wretched nastiness made being on the highway a sweet reprieve. As each car passed, I sent mental messages to the unknown travelers that I was okay, and I prayed for help. I needed help and held on to the hope that someone would get the subliminal messages I sent.

Between passing cars and my deliberate conscious thoughts, my eyes yearned for the first available gas station. As I imagined being in a place where people could see me, brief moments of safety bubbled to the surface. Those sacred moments provided a welcome pause from the living nightmare. But I was keenly aware of the dreadful, recent memories of being raped, and it was pure treachery.

I turned my thoughts again to my cousin Janice. I scraped for any memories that would help me.

If Janice were here, what would she want me to do? What advice would she offer?

My fortitude to survive matched my desire to report this scathing animal to the authorities. He had no business being in mainstream society. He would never walk away from this unmarked. I deliberately ensured my actions and responses discouraged any additional violence toward me.

If I get him to talk, I might get more incriminating information about him. He might give me information that would help the cops locate him. I might even get more information that would help to make this story I'm going to tell them more believable.

If I know what to expect, I can figure out how to get away from him. Maybe there's still a way for me to break out of this living hell if I know a little more about what's going to happen next. There's got to be a way for me to break free.

Stone-cold with fear and not knowing how much to inquire, I rehearsed the dialog in my head as I reached out for more incriminating information.

"Where are we going?"

"I want to take you to California and marry you." He turned his face toward mine briefly as he pronounced his intentions.

The pit in my stomach grew deeper with fear and disgust.

He can't be serious! He's a monster and I can't imagine being married to that! There's no way I will spend the rest of my life with this swine. Though, if that's what it takes to keep me alive, maybe I should be grateful for that response. He could have said he was planning to kill me and throw me out of the car on the roadside somewhere. But no. He wants to marry me. Perhaps there's hope for me to get out of this.

Keeping my mind busy, one of my prior conversations with him replayed in my head.

"What do you think of your God now? What do you think of your God now? What do you think of your God now?"

How can God let this happen to me? What have I done to deserve this? I must be worthless if this is what God has planned for me. Doesn't He care? What God allows such a heinous thing to occur to another human being?

I don't believe God hurts people! God doesn't hurt people. The God I've learned about is a caring God. He doesn't hurt people. People hurt people. God doesn't hurt people.

He wants to take me to California, but he's driving south. Maybe he really wants to take me to Mexico, and he lied. It would be just like him to lie! What is he really planning? Just stay alert and watch road signs.

The only part of my life this guy cannot get his hands on is my thoughts. I have my thoughts. My thoughts are mine and he can't touch them.

After about 20 or 30 minutes of driving, I finally spotted a sign for a gas station. He must have seen it, too.

"Give me all your money!"

His barking orders felt uncomfortable, but it encouraged me he noticed the sign.

I already told him I only had $1 or $2 when all this started. He wasn't listening.

I reached for my purse and mechanically began searching every pocket and scraping the bottom to find any morsel of money. A teenager from a family without a surplus of fiscal wealth had no credit cards to rely on. In this case, having a credit card could help create a paper trail of my whereabouts. A transaction might alert the police or someone.

Not having much money felt like a disadvantage, but perhaps it was an equal advantage. With no credit card, he couldn't abuse it. I also understood that $1 or $2 wouldn't get us much gas or very far. It took $10 to fill up the car.

Oh God, I don't want him to be mad. I haven't given him an answer yet. Dad keeps a pouch of change in the car for parking money. Where does he keep it?

I opened the glove box in the dash to see if I could find Dad's pouch. When I realized it wasn't there, I searched for any obvious or obscure place to find it. I found it tucked away in the small console of the car between the two front seats. When I picked it up, I realized it only had a few coins in it but dumped what was there into my hand to find out what I had to work with. Between my couple of dollars and this newly found change, it still wasn't enough to fill up the tank.

"I have $2.73."

I held out my hand and offered it all to him, but he did not take it as he pulled into a large truck stop.

If he leaves the keys in the car, I can drive off when he fills up the tank. Or maybe a police officer will show up and I can ask for help. Maybe someone will notice that I'm in trouble and offer to help.

He pulled up to the gas pump farthest away from any people, turned off the car, grabbed the knife, and took the keys with him.

"You just sit right here!"

Okay. I guess I'll just have to watch for someone who can help me. I don't want to put anyone else in danger.

He walked around to the back of the car and opened the tailgate. He gathered a fist full of tools he could carry, closed the tailgate, and took them inside the station.

That rat! He's going to sell my dad's tools! As if it's not enough for him to do what he did to me, he's stealing my dad's stuff!

Seething, I wanted to cry.

He has no respect for anyone but himself! Dad is going to be so furious when he finds out his tools are missing!

I sat there with my livid thoughts as I observed my surroundings, waiting for any opportunity to draw attention to myself or to get away.

I could take off running, but he's right there, and he'd catch me before I could get to someone else. It wouldn't be good to make a scene at the gas station. I'm not sure my rickety legs could outrun him! He's watching my every move. If I made it inside the gas station, he's got the knife with him. I don't want him to stab me in front of all those people! He's made it clear he doesn't want me to do anything that would compromise his plan.

I was immobilized with fear, not only for my life but for those around me. Every escape option had too many unpredictable risks. I felt safe inside the car. I could honk the car horn or shout for help, but that felt too perilous. *Please, someone. Please notice I need help. Don't buy the tools! Please! If no one buys the tools, there won't be any gas, and we would be stuck here at the gas station. There are people here. It would draw attention.*

The distance between me and my captor created a reprieve from the incessant turmoil of his presence. Whether or not I could get away, the pressing fear gently subsided. At least my head felt freer to plan and visualize getting away without being at knifepoint.

Soon, I saw him walk out of the gas station empty-handed and step around to the gas tank. He must have sold Dad's tools to pay for the gas. I felt prostituted that he sold Dad's things without even asking.

Someone, please help me!

No one noticed my need for help. All my internal yearning and begging, and no one appeared to perceive the danger I was in. My moments for rescue dwindled as he filled the car with gas. Think about it. When you go to a gas station for fuel, the focus is primarily on the task at hand. Who looks around at other people to see if someone else might need help? This is not a place where people go to observe what's going on with someone else. There was too much distance between the car and the hustle and bustle of normal activities.

I just want to go home! I just want to go home!

The idea of home gave me something to hold on to, while the falling temperature intensified the trembling of my body. I tried to use my thoughts about home to distract myself from the wall of fear. I wanted this guy to drop dead (or something) so I could get away. In a few brief moments, the car was full of gas, and he returned to his position in the driver's seat and started the car.

In the blink of an eye, we were back on the highway, headed south to California from Texas. I made myself stay alert to our present location and the direction we traveled. If I got free, I wanted to identify where I was and the places we'd been.

If we're going to California, wouldn't we drive west instead of south? His actions and words make no sense. I probably shouldn't say anything about it. I don't want him to hurt me. For now, I'll stay observant.

I figured if I kept him talking, I might learn more about him. With that in mind, I deliberately continued to encourage non-threatening conversation.

By now, Dad has figured out his car is missing. Mom and Dad must be worried. It's got to be late enough that I would have gotten back home from my date by now.

Mom and Dad, I'm okay, but I need your help.

I repeatedly said the words in my mind as I pictured my worried parents.

A video of my life projected on the screen in my head. I watched the movie of people, places, and experiences as they replayed in my thoughts. I thought about things I could have done differently. As images of people came into focus, I imagined telling them how much I appreciated who they were and all they had done for me. Then, I deliberately asked each one to hear my plea for help.

I did not know what time it was, but it took a painstaking will for me to keep my eyes open.

No! I can't go to sleep. My contacts are in, and I can't sleep with them in. Besides, I can't trust a thing this guy might do if I allow myself to fall asleep. I have to stay awake as long as he is awake so I can be alert and aware of where we are and what's going on.

Though it seemed like a lifetime ago, the events of the night before crept into my thoughts.

I was at a Billy Joel concert with Brenda just 24 hours ago. Now, look where I am.

I was exhausted, not only from the fearful energies coursing through my body but also from being out late the night before.

Brenda, my parents, the people at the church before being at knifepoint— where did it go? Where are they now?

Just 24 hours ago, I had a life. At this point, it seemed a distant past. What remained portended a horrific mystery.

As I struggled to keep myself awake, I realized blood was soaking my pants. I could feel the warm blood as it cooled and absorbed into my clothes. My clothes felt wet against my skin, especially between my legs. I realized my 'good clothes,' one of my favorite outfits, was being ruined… and it felt gross.

What's wrong with me? I finished my period a couple of days ago. I can't be on my period again! Should I tell him I'm bleeding? What if it makes him mad? Maybe I shouldn't say anything. If I tell him, he might think I'm on my period and get angry. If I don't tell him, what will he do when he finds out?

I hoped my silence prevented behavior worse than what I had already suffered. As the blood dripped, I consciously refrained from saying anything.

I adjusted how I was sitting to prevent the blood from spilling all over the place.

If I can find the right position, maybe I can slow down the blood flow, and maybe it won't make such a big mess.

The feeling repulsed me. Now and then, I'd catch a whiff of blood on top of the other putrid smells. I wanted to throw up. It felt messy and gross, and I wanted the bleeding to stop.

What's happening to me? Why am I bleeding? What's going on?

I yearned for a reason to settle my fear and unknowing. My insides felt like someone reamed me out with a roll of sandpaper. I wondered if I'd bleed to death sitting in the car.

I was embarrassed beyond measure. This crude introduction to intercourse shattered my impressions. It was supposed to be a special practice for two people to share intimately. In my shy and innocent imaginings, I methodically saved intercourse for a special, loving, and precious experience. It was supposed to be a sacred, intimate sharing between two lifetime-committed people.

Is it always supposed to be this painful? Do people bleed when they do that? This means I'm not a virgin anymore! I'm gonna get into so much trouble! I feel dirty! God, why is this happening to me?

While my thoughts wandered tirelessly, my eyes felt like lead weights. The thrashing trembles within my body were exhausting. I wanted to close my eyes.

Maybe I can rest my eyes, but I won't go to sleep. I have to stay awake and aware. My contacts are still in, and I'm not supposed to sleep in them. I'll just close my eyes for a moment.

As I rested my eyes, I consciously mapped out plans, using my thoughts as an incentive to stay awake. To stay awake, I had to keep my mind active. So, I kept going through the address book of my life, remembering people, and spending time with each person who came into focus.

I replayed memories I enjoyed with all my family, immediate and extended. Growing up with my big brother, riding around town on our bicycles. Jane Park—the slide with a tower, the swings, teeter-totters, and all the fun romping around we did as kids. We loved flying kites from the slide tower and invented games as we played together.

As we got older, playing with his little sister became less cool. His interest in me (his childhood playmate) stayed safely within the confines of home and was less out in the neighborhood where others might see us. I looked up to my year-and-a-half older brother. He learned to do things before me, and I was quick on his heels and eager to learn so I could keep up with him. He got to a point, though, where the "tag along little sister" activities only took place at home, or at least in arenas where he was not visible to his other friends.

When my parents were at church for Wednesday night choir practice, there was no nursery to look after my little sister. So, Paul and I watched over our little sister at home for short periods. When she was quietly being a baby or asleep, Paul and I found mischief in our freedom away from Mom and Dad. Often, such an adventure came with the sporty game of "I dare you." Our dares were usually harmless. We'd see who could fill their mouth with the most sugar or how many grapes we could stuff in our mouths and still eat them. Sneaking around our parents' dresser drawers to discover what was different about a grown-up's drawers was always an adventure.

One summer day, while Mom tended to household chores and Dad was at the church working, Paul wanted to see how far I would go to get away with something mischievous. Out on our bikes, Paul corralled me to the slide tower at Jane Park, where he had something he wanted to show me. We were both curious, and I wanted to be like my big brother, so I eagerly followed along.

After climbing the worn metal stairs to the top of the little, red-covered tower at the pinnacle of the slide, Paul reached into his pocket. As he pulled his hand out, I saw a book of matches and a pack of Marlboro cigarettes. My eyes grew bigger than my face, not only at the thought of Paul's possession of cigarettes but at the prospect that he was actually going to light one up. He pulled a cigarette from the soft pack and held it to his lips like a pro. Then he pulled a little cardboard match out of the matchbook, struck it, and held it up to the cigarette like a seasoned expert. Smoke bellowed from his mouth as he drew air through the cigarette to draw the flame and light his smoke.

My heart pounded in my throat, both in disbelief and excitement. He took the cigarette from his mouth in his fingers, like the Marlboro man in the TV commercials. My conflicted thoughts raced—the enticement of the adventure and the obvious demonstration of skill meant he must have smoked before.

"I dare you to smoke," Paul said.

I wanted to be cool with my big brother, so I wasn't about to let my shock stand in the way of being the cool little sister.

"Okay. How do you do it?"

"Put the cigarette in your mouth and suck and then breathe in."

I took the cigarette, put my lips around it, sucked, and then breathed in with a good, big breath. In an instant, the nasty smoke barked out of me as I coughed a big cough or two, three, four, or five, and my eyes watered up.

As I tried to catch my breath, I wondered how he did that without coughing. Paul giggled and encouraged me to try it again. Knowing a little more about what to expect, I inhaled gently and slowly and blew the smoke out without hacking up a lung. I felt cool doing such a big thing that was so forbidden, especially doing it with my big brother.

I smiled on the inside as I remembered smoking with my brother, and then my thoughts turned to my best friend, JoAnne, from Ponca City. We lived a short block from each other, and we enjoyed Wrigley's Doublemint gum and playing in the school orchestra together. I thought about the afternoons at JoAnne's house and walking to and from school. It seemed ridiculous, but I stretched my thoughts from the little red Datsun to my friend, hoping JoAnne might receive my telepathic pleas for help.

I thought about the many other friends from Oklahoma that I hated to leave when we moved to Fort Worth. I remembered how my pride would never let me slip into the Texas twang everyone always talked about. In my mind, I was better than that and certainly more dignified!

I remembered the burn of abandon I felt when Mom and Dad picked up our family and left behind all that was familiar. At 13 years old, I felt betrayed because they took me away from my friends.

I resisted settling into our new place of residence. I didn't want to move, and I didn't want to live in Texas. If my displeasure was obvious enough, I thought they would move us back to Ponca City. As hard as I tried to express my unhappiness, no one ever budged. My parents did not intend to move back. As I remembered my disdain for my parents' decision, being kidnapped at 17 only proved to further fuel my fire about moving to this wretched place.

Keeping my focus and fighting the urge to drift off to sleep, I moved my thoughts to my grandparents. Dad's parents lived simply in rural Fowler, Kansas. Traditionally, all the extended family gathered at Grandma and Grandpa's house. We filled our bellies with a homemade Thanksgiving dinner, complete with second and third servings. Then, the little farmhouse's sofas, chairs, and floors quickly filled with napping bodies.

The souls awoke in time for the football game, with a strong prefer-ence for the Dallas Cowboys. The favored team didn't always come out as the winner, but that never took away from the fellowship of being with family. As the snack attacks set in, there were lots of leftover goodies to dip into for refreshment. Of course, lots of hot tea, iced tea, coffee, or hot chocolate were readily available to wet a whistle.

As the football game came to a close, a rousing game of Yahtzee or Dominoes ensued. I heard echoes of Grandpa's, "Be careful!" It was his way of warding off a Yahtzee. My heart yearned to be in wintery Fowler with my family. Whether gathered for a nourishing meal, engaged in a game, or enjoying a rousing hymn-sing while Grandma, Aunt Kay, and/or I played the piano or organ, I wanted to be surrounded by my family. I wished they would sense or hear my persistent plea for help.

I had to keep my mind active to combat my physical longing for sleep, so I turned to Mom's side of the family. Memorial Day was the holiday of choice for these family gatherings. There were many veterans coloring the landscape of this side of the family. Grandma Birdie's big backyard on 37th Street in Oklahoma City, complete with a more than happy Uncle George from his excess with the juice.

Oklahoma City in late May. The lurking summer heat called for large, cool portions of watermelon to simulate fireside chats in the backyard picnic tradition. Grandma Birdie, equipped with her big old kitchen butcher knife, cut into the juicy melon. Aunts, uncles, and cousins—we all got a slice. With the family all supplied with the sweet melon, Grandma carved a piece for herself and found a shady spot in one of the heavy-iron outdoor chairs. She sculpted an oversized morsel of the crisp melon and used the butcher knife as a fork. For a moment, the leftover foul taste in my mouth disappeared.

Mom, Aunt Betty, and Uncle George talked about their childhood memories. A converted garden room on the side of the house was the perfect spot for hiding out. They talked of their innocent games of hide and seek, to sneaking away for a forbidden puff on a cigarette, or a juvenile beer sampling.

Betty, being older than Mom, would take her little sister to the movies to enjoy Humphrey Bogart, Gary Cooper, and Loretta Young. In keeping with Mom's movie time with Betty, I remembered many fun excursions with my aunt. I replayed unexpected shopping sprees or rare opportunities to go see a movie with her. While we lived comfortably, coming into enough extra funds for a movie proved infrequent. Going to a movie was a special, albeit proper, treat.

I relished every story about my Grandpa George, who I never met. He died long before I was a glimmer in my mother's eye. He enjoyed living large, and family was especially important to him. Memorial Day backyard picnic traditions took root from Grandpa George's urging. He loved to cook and especially loved being surrounded by his five children.

Grandma Birdie's house had a large, attached, enclosed basement where she held lots of Bible studies and prayer groups. Mom and her siblings enjoyed lots of prankster moments during such events. Their mischief kept them on the edge of childhood fun and strict parental discipline.

Janice, Betty's daughter, told us about her job as a forensic chemist at the OSBI and her raccoon hunts in the woods with her hound dogs. She dropped out of high school as a kid. Once she discovered her passion and earned a GED, she got a degree in forensic science. In my current dilemma, remembering Janice manifested like a queer salve soothing an open wound.

My thoughts and mental calls for help gave way to my physical exhaustion. My body, trembling for hours, the natural unwavering adrenaline fighting on my behalf, and my sleep deprivation from the night before took hold. It was in my best interest to capture moments of rest where I could. While my consciousness gave me focus, it clearly provided a calming mantra that allowed me to drift into a half-sleep.

My older sister, Vickie, came to mind as I struggled to keep from drifting off to sleep.

Vickie. Visiting with Vickie.

My sister was severely mentally and physically handicapped from the age of three.

Wait! Vickie might hear me. Perhaps the simplicity of her brain will sense my pleas for help. Sometimes, people who are less encumbered with life complexities are more intuitive. If she hears me, maybe someone who is praying or meditating can perceive my reaching out through her.

A ray of hope momentarily brightened my dismal circumstance. I imagined Vickie in her wheelchair, her buoyant, child-like smile, and her laughter.

Vickie, can you hear me? Tell Mom and Dad that I need help. Think about Mommy, Vickie. Tell her that your sister needs help.

Grandpa and Grandma, if you're praying, open yourself up to hear me. I'm okay. I'm alive. But, Grandpa, please help me. Tell Mom and Dad that you heard me. It's okay.

I forced myself to transform my fear into my memories to claw my way to safety. Periodically, I opened my eyes to catch sight of a landmark or location. I was unsure of our destination, so I made mental notes of my surroundings, as Janice instructed, to ensure I could retrace my steps. I closed my tired, aching, scratchy eyes again and got back to the important mental work of connecting with someone.

CHAPTER 6
HEADED TO AN UNKNOWN LOCATION

TRIGGER ALERT: This chapter contains potentially triggering material. If you prefer, skip to Chapter 10.

ALTHOUGH MY THOUGHTS were busily engaged in a quest for help, nothing audible came out of my mouth while my captor drove in silence. I wondered if he thought I had fallen asleep. When I strayed into sleep, I remained conscious about etching my own dreams of someone capturing my request for help.

"Wake up. I want you to see this!"

I promptly opened my eyes and adjusted myself slightly so he could see a visible sign of my attention. Fear came back into clear focus while I remembered the importance of following his uncaring demands.

What on earth does he want to show me?

When I shifted my position, the sensation of warm blood was a grotesque and concerning reminder. There was no stopping it.

"What is it?"

"You see over there?"

He pointed toward the passenger side car window, toward a large, unfriendly, and cold-looking building.

"That's Huntsville," he said. "I never want to go back there!"

He scolded me as he adamantly pointed out the state penitentiary.

"That's a horrible place, and I'm never going back there. There's no freedom in there! Lights out! Line up! Get to work! I'll kill you if I ever go back there!"

If he's so adamant about not going back there, why is he so proud to call it out to me? Why would he want me to see a place that he hated so perilously?

"I broke into my aunt's house and raped her!"

The tone in his voice bizarrely conveyed a sick sense of pride about his conquest. It was as if he wanted a reward or acknowledgment for his actions.

"I'm never going back to that place! Do you hear me? I'm never going back there!"

The pit in my stomach dropped. It seemed like I was another mark on his scorecard, and he had something to prove by raping me. He seemed confident, albeit determined, to get away with it. My determination to never let him get away with what he did to me intensified.

"You've done what you wanted to do with me. Why don't you let me go?"

"I've kidnapped you! Do you think I can really let you go?"

Hey! He's right! He kidnapped me!

I had not realized what he put into words. He took me away from everything familiar. I felt like he reached into my soul, grabbed it, and tossed it to the wind like a careless candy wrapper. Besides being really pissed off about what he did to Dad, stealing and selling his tools, I panicked. While I yearned to be home and safe, my immediate future, moment by moment, remained a mystery.

Did I say the wrong thing? Oh, God, please! I don't want to die!

His forbidding words were enough for me to understand the seriousness of his threat. The thought of him killing me only heightened my fear. I knew the demon sitting next to me, driving to who knows where, was the only criminal I knew. As if my current experiences with him weren't dangerous enough, a renewed feeling of looming danger crept back into my awareness.

Yeah, right! As soon as I get away from you, I'll have enough evidence to send you right back! He'll never get away with this! If I get out of this alive, I'll nail him to the prison wall!

I imagined retelling his words to the authorities as if etching these conversations into a permanent record. Everything he touched, I recorded in a mental evidence log and imagined reciting my notes to the police. Perhaps the overdose of adrenaline coursing through my body served an important purpose: to keep me alert to details and provide energy to recount facts over and over in my head.

I sat quietly, aware that I continued to bleed. It felt safer to keep my comments to myself. Encouraging conversation about prison felt tenuous. In a bizarre way, I wondered if my unresponsiveness portrayed a mental instability that might scare him into making me get out of the car. Stranded without him seemed safer than being in the confines of his presence at knifepoint. I felt trapped.

"Do you understand me? I never want to go back there! I'll kill you if you tell anyone!"

His adamant command required a response.

"I won't say a word."

In my mind, I affirmed my certainty to recount details to the authorities, and my family, as soon as I felt safe.

Thank you, Janice, for teaching me what to do!

Every cigarette he smokes, I want to locate each cigarette butt when it comes time to tell. Janice told me she could positively identify people from the saliva on the cigarette. Anything he touches might leave a fingerprint. I want to give the police every opportunity to find proof of what is happening.

I looked squarely into his glassy blue eyes and studied his features. He wore a stinky t-shirt and dirty jeans, and I took mental notes about them. I made notes about his reddish hair, unkempt beard, spotty freckles, and the shape of his face and nose. I wanted to identify him beyond the shadow of a doubt.

The conversation about Huntsville woke me up a little, and I wondered what time it was. It had to be close to midnight now. I wanted time references for the police, too. I continued to watch road signs and determined Houston was the next big town.

It was dark, raining off and on, and without conversation, the steady hum of road noise made it difficult to keep my dreary eyes open. My contacts felt scratchy, and I knew I needed to get them out of my eyes. I had a case in my purse but no solution for them. Without my contacts, I couldn't read road signs, but I had to do something.

I had a scratched cornea before. It feels like someone is stabbing your eye with a straight pin. I didn't want that to happen again. Then, I wouldn't be able to use my eyes at all. I moved around a little in search of my purse, and felt myself bleeding again. I smelled the foul stench of blood around me. Between my stink and his, I constantly resisted the urge to vomit.

As much as I watched his every move, he watched mine.

Maybe I should tell him I'm getting my contact case, so I can take out my lenses. If he thinks I'm reaching for a weapon or something, there's no telling what he'll do. Maybe if I tell him what I'm really doing, he won't be so threatened. His responses are irrational. There's no way to tell.

"My contacts are killing me! I've got to take them out."

He didn't say a word in response, so I felt like I dodged a bullet. I fumbled through my purse until I felt the shape of the case and pulled it out slowly and carefully. He watched my every move. I instructed my shaky hands and arms to pop out my lenses and put them in the case. I didn't know what would happen to my contacts with no moisture on them, so I fabricated as much spit as I could from my dry, foul-smelling mouth to keep them wet.

My eyes felt relieved without the hard pieces of plastic in them. I willed myself to stay awake and alert while I rested. My fearful imagination ran away with the consequences of the volume of blood loss, and I tried to distract myself from thinking about my gross, stinky mess. I felt filthy, sitting in my blood. My vagina hurt, and my body continued to tremble.

～

I yearned for a warm shower, a toothbrush, and my comfy bed, but I knew none of that would be possible until I talked with the police. If only I could wake up from the nightmare and be in my room, in my bed, under a warm blanket.

Mom and Dad partitioned my bedroom off the large formal living room near the grand piano. For a while, I shared a bedroom with my little sister, but that was unbearable for everyone because we were always nagging each other. Having the partitioned room gave me space at the opposite end of the house from everyone else.

I remembered my music stand, bed, and desk in my room. I thought about all the stuffed animals filling corners, nooks, and crannies. Being a teenager and a far cry from any socially identifiable in-crowd, I relied heavily on the support I felt having my stuffed animal friends close at hand.

Alfred the Alligator, my tried-and-true friend, absorbed more than his share of growing-up tears. The misfit Fume, a gift from my friend Brenda, always reminded me to smile and was great for snuggling. Chester O' Chimp always looked out for me, and his floppy arms were just right for hugging. Thinking about these friends transported me temporarily from my immediate hell. My room was my haven. I would have given anything to blink and find myself there.

Thank goodness he's driving. My eyes are closed, and it's difficult to stay awake. He's got to be feeling tired, too. There's no telling what time it is.

I heard fumbling sounds on the dashboard, and my eyes popped open with renewed attentiveness and curiosity.

What's he doing? He must be looking for something. It's not like this basic, little red Datsun comes with any special, fancy car features.

"Doesn't this thing have a radio in it?"

The car had no radio, so Dad rigged one. On the driver's side of the car, it was located down close to the floor by the door.

"It's down on your left."

I was glad he wanted to turn it on so I could figure out what time it was.

"It won't turn on!"

"Push the top knob."

The radio came on with nothing but annoying static. We were far out of range for any of the normal pre-set stations to work. He bent down and turned the knob to tune into a station while he drove. Without too much effort, he found a station he could live with.

Hearing voices on the radio felt like a ray of hope. At the very least, having something to listen to distracted me from my intense thoughts about sitting in a disgusting pool of blood. The pace of my thoughts and internal conversation ramped up. I felt like a crazy person.

Music. I can jump into the music, and it will carry my thoughts to someone.

Even with all the radio commotion, my eyes lapsed closed again. As I listened to the radio, I finally heard it was after 1:00 a.m.

I've gone through so much today. I'm wiped out. Perhaps I'll just close my eyes and rest them gently. Stay alert, Alexis. Stay alert!

God, what is happening to me? I'm still bleeding! If I tell him, he might think that I'm just complaining and get angry with me. I can't afford to make him mad. I have to keep things on an even keel.

The car came to a stop.

Wanting to know our exact location, I opened my sleepy eyes and started watching blurry road signs. I squinted and pulled the corner of my eyes to see them.

Maybe the radio will announce a general location. Thank goodness the road signs are large enough to make out a word or two here and there. Galveston this and Galveston that.

"Have you ever been to the ocean before?"

He sounded like he wanted to show me the world. His candor sickened me. I didn't feel like trying to be nice, but I had to respond somehow.

"No."

"Well, you're going to see it now!"

I wondered if this meant seeing the ocean or if he intended to throw me off a bridge into it. He drove across a large bridge, and traffic appeared to be minimal. Every time the car slowed down, I wondered if an end to this nightmare was in sight, but the car continued to move forward along the roadway.

I knew the whole lower half of my body was a disgusting mess. I was still bleeding and secured my brown purse in my lap to hide any visible sign of blood that might appear under the passing street lamps.

He drove through Galveston, and from what I could make out with my blurry vision, it seemed like a very run-down part of town. As each moment passed, a mirage of scenarios flashed back and forth in my worried mind. I did what I could to hope for the very best—my release from this horror.

Still trembling, a part of me hoped I would pass out. But, if that happened, he might find out about the bleeding. I was worried about him getting angry. I kept talking myself through it, trying to keep an all-is-well appearance on the outside.

He seemed to have a specific destination in mind and seemed to know exactly where he was and where he was going. That frightened me. It was scary because he didn't volunteer any information about his intentions. It kept my mind whirring out logical scenarios and how I might respond to his terrorizing comments and orders.

Soon, he turned onto a road that ran right alongside the ocean. The street was fairly well-lit and I could see waves rolling onto the shore. I wanted to jump into one of those waves and hoped it would carry me to safety. Getting out of the car, though, and running, didn't seem like the best plan for a successful getaway plan. I wasn't sure I could outrun him.

What if someone sees me covered in blood? They'd probably get scared and turn away. Who in their right mind wouldn't run away from someone covered in blood?

My thoughts didn't seem rational. I felt ashamed and unsightly.

Not long after turning onto the road running alongside the ocean, he pulled the car over to the side and turned it off. My heart pounded so hard I could hear it in my ears. Boom. Boom. Boom. I thought he could probably hear it, too. I was terrified to think about what might come next.

What's he going to do to me?

"I'm tired. I'm going to get a little shuteye."

He turned off the car, but the radio kept playing.

"Why won't it turn off?"

"My dad has it connected directly to the battery. So, you have to turn it off with the switch on the radio."

"Ah, let's just leave it on."

He settled into the car seat, found the reclining lever, and laid the seat back. He made sure the knife was in his hand so it was convenient for him if he needed it.

While he settled, I thought it would be okay for me to go to sleep after he did. I made myself as comfortable as I could. Every time I moved, I could feel blood pouring out of me, so I kept my movements to a minimum. While I waited for sure signs that he was asleep, the radio announcer said it was 3:00 a.m.

When I felt comfortable enough to do so, I closed my eyes and allowed myself to go to sleep.

I'll sleep lightly. If he moves or awakens, I will be alert, so I'm aware of what is going on.

I felt a brief sense of relief; the car was no longer moving, and he settled into the driver's seat to sleep. The immediate intensity of the situation diminished. That kind of pause was infrequent. I felt like I could breathe.

Remember to sleep with one eye open. With him asleep, maybe I can get a little rest.

I visualized Janice beaming with pride as I recounted every detail of my kidnapping when I told this story to the police. It was comforting to imagine feeling safe and blurting out everything I worked so hard to remember. I rehearsed speaking details about the events up till now. My mind was my strongest ally and my biggest weapon from here forward.

In my dreary in-and-out sleep, the sound of the radio popped into my head. The music stopped, and chatter resumed. I listened intently to find out the time and cracked my eyes open to see what it looked like outside. It was still dark but with hints of daylight.

"It's 6.02 a.m.," the radio announcer said.

Maybe I could open the door quietly to get out of the car. But what if he wakes up? The knife is in his hand. If he gets angry, that would be risky. He might throw the knife at me or burst out of the car and run after me. There's no one around to hear me if I scream. What if I can't outrun him? If I really got away, who would stop and try to help with all this blood? The blood soaked my pants.

What would he do if he discovered that I was bleeding and I didn't tell him about it? If it scared him, he might leave me here to bleed to death. But, if he left, I might get free from the terrorizing, living hell I'm in. Maybe I can find someone who can help me.

CHAPTER 7
RAPED AGAIN

TRIGGER ALERT: This chapter contains potentially triggering material about being raped again. If you want to skip this chapter, it's okay. Start with Chapter 10 to jump into the recovery part of this story.

As the sky continued to lighten, he stirred. I opened my eyes and pulled my head up to appear awake. As soon as he sat up, he started the car and drove off.

"Where are we going?" I asked.

"Let's go to East Beach."

Let's go?! He makes it sound like we're friends or something. What is East Beach? I don't know what it is, but it can't be good! I hate this guy and I just want to go home!

What on earth does he want to do by going to the beach at this hour? I've often imagined myself running freely along the ocean's shore. I imagine it feels liberating and completely peaceful, running with the energy of the sea and feeling the earth beneath my feet. I don't feel that freedom right now, and I don't feel much like running. Maybe he's going to take me somewhere and leave me there. Yes. Leave me stranded, and then I can find help.

I watched for as many landmarks as I could without my contacts. He wasn't making any turns, and the ribbon of road seemed to carry on endlessly along the shoreline.

The sun is cresting where the sea meets the sky, and the natural ocean rhythm is dancing with waves rolling gently into shore.

Never having seen the ocean before, I observed something profoundly beautiful about it even in my captive state. I tried to absorb the beauty of it all while watching the establishments' names, taking mental notes about them. I rehearsed telling someone what I saw so I could remember and describe where we were.

After a few minutes, I noticed a big sign that said East Beach. He turned the car into the beach area and drove a respectful distance from the road. By my observation, it seemed he knew where he was and seemed intent on where he was going.

There's not a soul in sight. That water looks freezing. Please, please. Just leave me here. If he leaves me here, then I can get away.

As he reached his determined destination, he brought the car to a complete stop and turned off the engine. Watching every movement and trying to glean his intent, he sat still for a few minutes, watching the ocean. Then he leaned over, pulled my head toward his, and kissed me.

I tasted the repulsive, days-old alcohol, and his filthy body, like someone who hadn't showered in a while. My instinct was to puke, but I held it back with every ounce of energy I could muster. I sat as still as I could, even though my body continued to tremble uncontrollably. For fear of repercussions, I played along without ever actively kissing him back.

"Isn't the ocean beautiful?"

Not while I'm with you!

"Yes."

For a moment, the sunrise upon the endless oceanic horizon appeared to meet his agenda. He reached over to hold my hand.

Does he think I'm his girlfriend or something?

Holding his hand was far less invasive than what I had endured before, but I felt shocked.

What the hell is he thinking? I don't want to touch him, but if I pull away, it might piss him off. There's nothing nice about holding his hand, but it's better than kissing him!

Terrified, I felt as though holding his hand was a lesser evil than having to taste his awful mouth when he kissed me.

The safety of hand-holding quickly melted away when he leaned over to kiss me again. My stomach turned inside out. Stopping the natural desire to retch felt akin to reining in an unbridled, wild mustang.

If I play along, maybe he won't hurt me, and I can find another way to break away.

As much as I tried to map an escape, my heart knew what was about to happen… from experience.

Oh, God! I don't want to go through that awful poking and prodding again!

I pulled away as if I was timid, but my innocent ploy of body language remained unobserved by his deliberate uncaring. His obvious determination dictated the course of things to come, and a well of terror filled my churning, unsettled core. In the blink of an eye, his demeanor changed from his portrayal of caring and hand-holding to a threatening monster.

"Get back there!"

He waved the knife toward the back seat of the car.

I can't just crawl back there as if I haven't been bleeding. What should I do? Oh, God, what's he going to think? What will he do when he finds out?

As I prioritized my racing thoughts, I understood his severe impatience. I had to act fast. As I instructed my limbs and appendages to turn, lift, crawl, and propel myself into the back seat, I timidly stated the obvious.

"I'm bleeding."

At that moment, I imagined being stabbed to death, getting thrown out of the car, and any number of misfortunes.

Please, God. Let me live!

"What do you mean you're bleeding?"

"My vagina is bleeding."

I felt my entire head flush with embarrassment. His question sounded like a parent scolding a child, and I felt ashamed.

"Are you on your period?"

How am I supposed to talk about this with a dangerous and complete stranger? Those are private things!

"No. I stopped a few days ago."

"Get in the back."

He had one thing on his mind, and nothing else mattered.

Terrified, I slowly, robotically, and reluctantly moved toward the back seat through the separation between the two front seats. My only path to survival lay in following his directions and digging deep to distract my thoughts from my circumstances.

I endured it once. I guess I'll have to endure it again.

My options were bleak, but my desperate, wobbly instinct to survive knew the mandatory nature of his demands.

I plopped into the back seat, and without a moment to pause, his next demand hurled toward me.

"Take off your pants!"

My instructional thoughts helped my body to remove my clothing. As I struggled to remove my bloodied pants, he climbed back into the back seat and took off his pants. I dreaded every thought about what I knew was about to happen.

I can't believe he would want to do this while I'm bleeding. Does he not see that I'm bleeding? That's so gross! Why would he want to do this?

He didn't seem to notice or appear bothered by the sight of my disgusting, bloody mess.

As soon as he got his pants off, he grabbed me, pulled me toward him, and forced me to kiss him. He pushed his nasty-tasting tongue into my mouth.

What if I bite down on his tongue? But then he would bleed, and I'd get that in my mouth.

Please, somebody, hear me! Please! I'm okay, but I need your help. I'm alive, but I need your help to get away.

After an eternity, he stopped kissing me.

Please, God! Let this be the end of it!

He reached down to hold up his penis.

"Blow it!"

I knew he wanted me to suck on that filthy, stinky, nasty thing. I froze, hoping he would think I freaked out, and that would encourage him not to make me do it. The nasty taste in my mouth from the first time still lingered, and the thought of doing that again horrified me.

My efforts to show some kind of mental breakdown were to no avail.

"Do it!"

He grabbed the back of my head and pushed my face toward his penis. I could smell his pungent human smell. With my eyes closed, I ordered my stomach to be strong and grasped to think about something other than how awful it was going to taste. I wanted to vomit, but there was no food or water in my stomach to vomit. If I actually mustered up something to puke and it came out, I feared for my life. I hoped keeping my eyes closed would lessen the horror of seeing his penis go into my mouth.

"Do it!"

I moved my head slowly up and down to appear uninterested. When he realized I had no intention of being deliberate or actionable toward his demands, he thrust his penis in and out of my mouth by force. He pushed it so far down my throat that I gagged. My eyes filled with water and I did everything possible to keep from throwing up. Even with an empty stomach, the gag somehow fabricated something to come up. Not wanting to make a dangerous situation worse, I swallowed my vomit. I could hardly breathe.

If there is oral penetration, you should never drink or brush your teeth. Do nothing that would wash away the evidence.

I heard Janice as I remembered what I learned from her. It was like she was telling me what to do. I listened carefully to my recollections as I remained steadfast about him not getting away with this.

Though it seemed to go on forever, he finally pulled that nasty thing out of my mouth.

Relieved, during a pregnant pause in the torture, the prior sequence of events replayed in my memory, as if to etch every disgusting detail in my mental journal. Like a robot receiving its next instruction, I remembered what happened next. His next actions involved him sucking on my vagina.

Oh my God! He can't possibly want to do that now because I'm bleeding. How gross!

"Lay back!

With his knife still close at hand, I had no option but to comply with his unreasonable demands. I scooted myself into a sort of laying position in the small back seat, closed my eyes, and prayed.

Please, just let this be over as soon as possible. Please let this end! Oh, God, I want this to stop. Please make him stop!

I could barely complete my thoughts before he started pounding me with his penis again. It felt like someone took a fist and rammed it up my insides. My stomach hurt and my vagina hurt; I felt like a raw piece of meat being torn to shreds.

Oh, God! Please make him stop! Please let it be over. Let me live through this!

My thoughts were the only thing I could hang on to. My survival depended on me keeping my mind focused somewhere else, away from the cold, hard reality of another episode of a second horror. The pain from this thrusting remained too great to bear.

Please, God, let it stop! Make him stop!!

The pumping and poking seemed to go on forever, but it did eventually end. When he pulled his penis out of my vagina, I quickly popped my eyes open so I could watch his every move.

Keep anything he touches. Evidence. I have to collect evidence. There might be sperm on it.

I could hear Janice's advice echoing in my thoughts.

After an eternity of pain and disgust, it stopped. Again, he reached into Dad's toolbox and found an old, car oil-stained towel. He used the towel to wipe himself off. In my mental journal of facts, I noted what he did with the towel so I could retrieve that information and the artifact when I needed it.

"Get dressed!"

Of all his unreasonable demands, complicity with this one brought immense relief. My pleas for the intercourse to stop finally came true. I continued to bleed and deliberately instructed my body to move so I could get my clothes back on. Though cold and bloody from before, that didn't matter to me. Having my pants back on felt safer, and as gross as it felt, it brought sweet relief. Even at the mercy of this awful person's wild ideas and with the knife present and visible, I felt relieved.

I navigated back into the front passenger seat of the car. I could smell my blood and felt sick to my stomach. I wanted nothing more than to wash my mouth and bathe. The stench overpowered me, yet I controlled my unwavering desire to throw up.

I did my best to make myself comfortable, moving gently and adjusting to a position that slowed the bleeding. My stomach and vagina both hurt, and I wanted to ease the pain as much as I could.

Good! He's dressed and back in the driver's seat. What a relief! I hurt, I'm uncomfortable, and I'm bleeding, but the harrowing torture is over. I'm scared. We're in an unfamiliar place, and I don't want to take any more directions from him!

He started the car and pulled onto the road again. After a few moments, he turned into a small, run-down-looking gas station.

How much gas do we have? I still have the couple of dollars in my purse, but he's already hocked Dad's tools. How will we pay for gas?

Whew, the gas gauge says we still have half a tank. If we have that much gas, what in the world is he doing? He didn't stop in front of the pumps, so I guess he's not here to get gas.

I watched, looking for any sign of people or a way to draw attention to the car or to myself as he turned and parked in front of the restrooms on the side of the building.

He must need to go to the bathroom. Maybe he'll let me go into the restroom, too. I can just stay in there, and maybe he'll drive off and leave me here. When he's gone, then I can get some help and I'll be safe.

"Go get yourself cleaned up. You're a mess!"

I'm such a horrible disaster! I smell bad! This is disgusting and I feel filthy. Maybe I'll just drop dead. That would be better than where I am right now.

Look at me! If anybody sees me, they'll probably turn and run away screaming. But maybe I can escape by going in. Maybe I'll think of something. How can I get away without somebody seeing me like this? I don't want to frighten everyone away from me.

This was the first time since he kidnapped me that he actually ordered me to leave his sight. He was close to the bathroom door, but he wasn't going into the bathroom with me. Planning an escape was better than focusing on the sheer hopelessness I felt.

I grabbed my purse and looked at my surroundings. I felt vulnerable seeing and feeling all the blood on my pants, but he parked the car out of the direct path for any passing traffic to see me. That helped me feel less intimidated about navigating from the car to the restroom.

I quickly got to the bathroom door, and thankfully, it was unlocked so I could go inside. As soon as the door was safely closed behind me, my shaky hands fumbled to push and twist the button to lock it.

Some 13 hours ago, I sat waiting anxiously for my date to arrive in the church parking lot. That seemed like a lifetime ago. At the moment, with a glimmer of safety, I felt free enough to gather a deep breath.

My God! Look at me! I'm a mess!

I saw my reflection in the mirror above the sink and set my purse down on the sink counter to walk into the toilet stall. I couldn't believe it when I saw the condition of my special-feeling clothes. Carefully, I pulled my sweater and suit jacket back out of the way so I could unbutton my pants.

I'm soaked. This is gross!

I carefully lifted the handle on the zipper between my thumb and forefinger so I wouldn't get blood on my hands. As I sat down on the commode, I thought about what I learned from Janice.

If you're ever raped, never wash your clothing until you've had an exam. Otherwise, the evidence can wash away. But he told me to clean myself up. What can I do? Maybe I could knock on the wall and get someone's attention. I could climb up on the sink counter and yell in the air vent to ask for help. For all I know, he's standing right outside the door. If the lock doesn't work and he hears me, he might get mad, storm in here, and kill me. Maybe he will just drive away, and I will just sit in here forever. I have to think of something.

After I went to the bathroom, what I learned from Janice continued to surface.

If you have to go to the bathroom, never wipe. You'll wipe the evidence away. Never take a bath or wash yourself. Don't eat or drink anything if you've had oral intercourse. Never brush your teeth or wash your mouth out.

If I had any chance of nailing him for this, it was imperative for me to heed these recalled bits of advice. Careful to keep my hands clean, I pulled up my bloodied panties.

He has to see that I cleaned myself up. I guess I'll just wash my outside pants. Don't wash your panties.

I pulled off my shoes so I could pull off my pants. Blood dripped out of me like a leaky faucet, even though my panties were on. The toilet was full of blood.

I guess I better not flush the toilet. They might need that for evidence.

As I carefully pulled my pants off, the blood smell made me sick to my stomach. I tried to keep my mind focused on my task. As I walked over to the sink, blood continued to drip. I walked carefully so it wouldn't get on the inside of my legs, but it dripped all over the floor.

With my pants in hand, I looked around the provisioned little bathroom for a pad or tampon. I didn't have any in my purse because I recently stopped my period. I didn't want to worry about having to conceal the secretive little pad as Mom taught me. All I could do was continue to bleed all over myself.

I turned the water on, stood with my legs spread apart, and started rinsing my pants. They were soaked from the waist and about halfway down to the knee. As I scrubbed and soaked my pants, my bleeding created a puddle on the floor where I stood.

I can't leave this mess on the floor. But the police might use this as evidence. If someone walks in here and sees this, though, they'll freak out. I don't really know what to do.

There had to be a way to leave some sort of explanation.

I think I have a little notepad in my purse.

With my purse opened, I searched through my billfold and every little pocket. There it was—the little pad of paper, and I even found a pen.

My name is Alexis Faere. The blood on the floor is from my vagina. I am okay but I need help. Please call my parents and tell them I'm okay but need their help. Tell them we are in Galveston and that he wants to marry me and go to California.

With that detail, I left my parents' phone number. (It never occurred to me to write a description of the car or the license plate. What teenager in any normal sense of life ever needs that information?)

Today, as I think back on writing, "I'm okay," I simply wanted to convey on the tiny slip of paper that I was alive. As a teenager, if I discovered a piece of paper like this and it said, "I've been kidnapped and raped," I wouldn't know what to do. What if the person who found the clue was a child? It felt scary. In asking for help, I didn't want to frighten a prospective helping hand. The bloodied floor was scary enough.

After finishing the note, I went back to washing my pants. My heart leaped through my throat when I heard a knock on the door.

Someone must need to use the bathroom.

"Hurry it up in there! We need to go!"

The heaven I found being in the bathroom vanished in a flash. The cloud of looming danger came back instantly. My heart sank as I remembered how delicately my life hung in a balance.

If I stay quiet, maybe he'll go away and drive off. If the lock on the door doesn't work and he comes bolting through there, I'm as good as dead. I have to buy myself a little more time!

"I'll be right there."

Fear settled back in like a loyal friend. Worried the door lock didn't work, and fearful of making him too angry, I quickly tried to finish cleaning my pants. I didn't know what might transpire next, so I put my contacts back into my tired eyes.

I looked around to be sure I left the note in plain sight. My blood pooled and dripped all over the bathroom floor. I knew whoever saw it would be frightened.

As I started putting my pants back on, he knocked on the door again.

"Come on! Let's hurry it up in there!"

I noticed, for a short time, I stopped shaking. This crappy gas station bathroom became my refuge; a refuge that would all too soon disappear. The more intense his demands grew, the more my body absorbed my fear and started to tremble again as I reached for the door. It was bitter medicine to swallow as I unlocked the door, stepping back into the relentless unknown. I opened the door slowly and mustered every ounce of strength I had to force myself to return to the car.

He stood sternly just outside the bathroom door. The cold air on my wet pants didn't help the shakes. As I made my way back to the passenger side of the car, he walked to the driver's side with keys in hand. I carefully and disdainfully adjusted myself around the discomfort of cold, wet pants, while the bleeding continued. As I settled back into the car seat, he started the car, and we were off.

He drove around Galveston like he knew where he was going. In a residential area, he parked the car in front of a large, two-story house.

He must know someone who lives here. Perhaps someone will notice my wet, bloodied pants, and I'll finally get some help.

"I want you to meet some of my buddies."

Oh, God, no! Not more like him! Whatever he has planned, I can't go through that again; not with him or anyone else.

"They were in prison with me. Remember! I never want to go back to that place!"

His comments only deepened the terror.

"You want me to go to the door looking like this?"

"You're right. Stay here!"

I watched his every move, hoping he would leave the keys in the car so I could drive away. But no. He took them with him as he got out of the car.

There was a steep embankment with stairs leading up to the front door. I thought seriously about making a run for it, but I knew if he saw me, I'd be in trouble. There was no public place to run to. I imagined running to another house in hopes someone would open the door to help. There was no guarantee that anyone was there.

If these are prison buddies, what kinds of other people are in this neighborhood?

The risk was too large for me to take right now. Bleeding, cold, wet pants, and nothing to eat since lunch yesterday. Weak and shaking, running didn't seem like a good option either. I sat and watched while I tried to sketch out a plan.

He didn't go inside the house, much to my disappointment. He stood on the porch talking to the people inside. I knew he was watching me. He frequently turned to check on the car while he carried on his conversation. He was watching me but not sitting right next to me with his knife in hand. I hoped he would stay and talk for hours.

Too soon, he walked out to the car with some of his buddies. My brief reprieve was erased, once again, with terror.

They're coming out here! Geez! What are they going to do to me?

To avoid a scene and any angry antics, I rolled down my window.

If I draw them to my side of the car, maybe they won't be as apt to get into the car.

It worked! Everyone walked up to my window, all four of them, and my captor started the conversation by introducing me.

"This is my woman. We're getting married and headed to California. These are the guys I told you about. They are my prison buddies."

I plastered a pleasant look on my face.

"It's so nice to meet all of you."

I did what I could to stay out of the conversation, only taking part when the conversation demanded it. It seemed important not to appear encouraging, but I also didn't want to anger anyone. I didn't want any problems. The whole thing was sickening. I wanted the introduction to be over and to get the hell out of there.

They carried on their conversation, catching up with one another after their separation from prison. I paid little attention to what they were saying because my mind was spinning through escape plans. Predicting what was to come seemed futile, but better to be prepared, whatever that meant at the moment.

After a few moments, they moved toward the front of the car where it was harder for me to hear them. When the conversation wound down, my captor made his way to the driver's side of the car and sat back in the driver's seat.

Thank God! No one else is trying to get into the car with him.

What other plans has he made now? Are we going to meet these people somewhere? Or are the formal introductions over? I'm not about to ask any questions.

His buddies walked back to the house as he started the car. I knew that, for now, it was just us, and there were no other people to worry about. My cautious optimism turned to cautious relief. At least I only had one monster to deal with.

"You could have been a little more friendly."

I guess my ploy to stay out of the conversation didn't fool him.

Exhausted, I learned I could not let my guard down. I had to think through every action I took so he wouldn't get any angrier.

Stay on your toes!

He stopped the car outside a little dive café. The parking lot had a few cars, so there had to be people inside.

There's no way he could expect me to go into a café. Not looking like this! My clothes are too bloody to hide.

"Stay here!"

My heart sank as I watched him turn off the car and take the keys with him.

The cars in the parking lot looked more like junk-heap hand-me-downs whose owners probably scrapped, begged, and borrowed to acquire them. I didn't see a name on the café, but its weathered exterior fit the dilapidated part of town in which it was situated. The spiffy, green-painted, weathered exterior looked a far cry from the appealing place it must have been in its earlier days.

When he opened the café door, I saw people rushing around, taking orders, and delivering meals to hungry customers. We were in a public place, however derelict it appeared, and the creepy guy holding me hostage was in there now. I knew I was a bloody spectacle, and the prospect of running inside and asking for help embarrassed me. The shady, run-down surroundings were not inviting to go running around in, especially in my condition.

I visualized myself running on the gravel and hiding in the crevices between trash bins or running away to safety. Without a car, though, I knew I couldn't get very far. I was in no condition to hike back to Fort Worth. Running to draw attention to myself felt more vulnerable than taking my chances in the sacred sanctity of the little red Datsun. Running outside in wet, bloody clothes, with my juddering legs and no dry clothing to keep warm, didn't feel like the wisest choice to my 17-year-old brain.

I could feel blood continuing to ooze out of me as I sat in the car. I felt dirty and I stank.

This is just gross! At least when I'm alone, no one can hurt me. It feels safer, but what is he doing in there? What's going to happen next? Maybe he'll just forget about me and leave me here. Even as shady as this part of town is, if he left me, maybe I could find someone who could help. Maybe I could motion someone to come over to the car and I wouldn't have to get out.

As I waited, thoughts running amuck, I tried again to reach out through my thoughts to my loved ones.

I'm okay, but I really need your help. Hear my thoughts. Feel my energy. Someone, please hear me.

Focusing on people I knew was much better than thinking about how revolting I felt inside and out.

Lost in my thoughts, I suddenly noticed he was back, standing outside the car. He got back into the car but left the door open. One foot in and the other outside of the car. He sat there for a few moments without saying a word.

I watched with intrepid anticipation as he turned his head and looked me square in the eyes.

"If I let you go, you're not going to tell anyone! If you do, I'll kill you!"

Where is this coming from? Is he seriously thinking about letting me go? How will I get home? How is this going to work? What if everyone I see turns away because I'm a bloody mess? I would only frighten people! If he lets me out of the car, there's no safe place to run, but I could walk. Maybe some nice person would reach out to help. Or maybe he'll give me the keys and I can drive away. But to where?

He pulled his other leg into the car but left the door open. He took out his knife and held it to my throat.

"You're not going to tell anyone, are you?"

Is he going to make me get out of the car? Is he going to give me the keys? Please, give me the keys! What about my dad's car? If he takes it, he'll be stealing my dad's car! Which way is this going to go? As long as I'm alive, and he's no longer right at my side, I can make this work. Maybe I'll be safe, at last! But what if someone appears to help me and I'm right back where I started? Please, just let me be safe; let me go.

On the inside, I crossed all my fingers, toes, arms, and legs with hope. Then I fabricated the biggest, most convincing lie I could muster.

"No. I won't tell. I won't tell anyone."

In my heart, I knew I would never let him get away with this, but if it meant I could get away, I'd do anything to convince him of my earnestness in keeping my word.

He reached into his pocket, fidgeted around, and pulled his hand out, revealing nothing. He glanced away to check what was in his hand. Then he reached toward me.

"Here's $15. Kiss me goodbye and promise me you'll tell no one!"

He half-handed me the money but kept it firmly in his grasp.

Not that awful mouth again! Ugh!

I screamed inside with both excitement and horror. Freedom was just a kiss away. I wanted more than anything to be free of him and would do anything to make that a reality. I imagined holding my nose to mask the taste.

This is my ticket out! He's really going to set me free. Just kiss him and it will all be over.

"I promise. I will never tell."

Choking my desire to vomit, I leaned over to kiss him. He held the knife at my throat, so I had to be careful not to cut myself. As I leaned in, he set down the knife, grabbed the back of my head, and pushed my face against his. He stuck his tongue in and out of my mouth.

Aaag! Yuck! Please let this be over! I have to do this so I can get away.

Because he never closed the car door, I had high hopes that if I played my cards right, this would be the end of his wretched captivity. I held onto the money like my life depended on it while he also held on to it.

The kiss lingered for an eternity. Then it stopped. He let go of the money, stepped out, and pulled away from the car.

The keys! What's he going to do, leave me in the car without the keys?

He leaned into the opened door and dangled the keys so I had to reach to get them.

"I don't want to go back to prison! Promise me you'll never tell. I will kill you if you tell!"

His hateful, demanding tone made his position clear.

"I will not tell a soul. I promise."

Like an award-winning actress, I made my convincing promise, with every intention of reporting him to the authorities.

He handed me the keys, closed the door, and walked away. Before doing anything else, I locked all the doors so he couldn't get back in. To ensure my safety, rather than getting out of the car to get into the driver's seat, I moved over the gearshift from the passenger side back to the driver's seat.

Now I felt safe. I had the keys, he was not in the car, and I put the keys into the ignition. My shaking hands started the car, put the car into reverse, and drove away. I didn't know where I was. I only knew I had to get away, as far away as I could get from him.

CHAPTER 8
RETURNING HOME

TRIGGER ALERT: This chapter contains potentially triggering material about my journey home after being raped. It's okay to skip to Chapter 10.

As I DROVE AWAY from the person who held me captive, I retraced the path he drove to get us where we were. Watching every street sign, looking for a way to get back to a highway, I just drove. The farther away I got from him, the more my shaking slowed to a cold tremble. I could hardly believe it—I was free.

Please, God, let me get home. I've lost a lot of blood. I hope I can make it all the way home. Home—all I want is to be home. I'll drive until things look familiar. Surely, I can find my way. If I get lost, I can stop for gas and get some directions.

How much gas do I have left? Do I have enough to at least get out of town? I have to get out of town so he won't find me.

I'll be okay for now. There's just under half a tank of gas. Although I can't make it all the way home, I can still escape.

If I got to Houston, following highway signs would help me get back home.

I can't believe he let me go, but I'm glad he did. What changed his mind? I wonder why he suddenly let me go. Did I piss him off because I didn't chum up to his buddies? Did the blood scare him? Maybe he thought I'd never make it home and I would die. I want to get home. Please, please, let me make it home.

I visualized driving up the driveway on the left side of the house, around to the back where the car usually parked. The long skinny driveway wrapped around the back of the house, where it opened up and there was room for three or four cars. I pictured the light, tan brick of the house and the enormous magnolia tree in the front yard. I saw myself walking into the house through the back patio door. A short walk through the large living and dining rooms with the fireplace. I turned right into the kitchen, and a quick right into my partitioned-off bedroom. My family would be home with my mom and dad.

Now that I made it to Houston, all I need to do is watch for signs to Dallas/Fort Worth. If I drive fast enough, maybe someone will pull me over and I can at least get word to my folks that I'm on my way home.

I remained vigilant about watching the gas gauge. After everything I'd been through, I didn't want to run out of gas. Unsure about my exact location, the road signs felt supportive, especially those showing my desired direction. The longer I moved forward, the closer the gas indicator approached empty.

I'm a bloody mess! There's got to be a way for me to cover myself up before I get out of the car. I'll look like a spectacle, but it might be less frightening than seeing someone covered in blood. Maybe I can find a full-service station, stay in the car and just hide the bloody mess. What can I cover myself up with? All I need is enough gas to get home. I don't want to stand up, because I know the blood will drip if I do that. I'm such a mess.

Finally! A full-service station! I'll pull over there. But, before I get there, I've got to cover myself up so no one will see all this blood.

I pulled over on the access road and stopped prior to approaching the gas station to look for anything that might work.

The carpet on the floorboard... there's an old blue throw rug in the back. That will work.

I stayed in the car and climbed over the back seat so I could reach the piece of carpet. As I got myself resettled in the driver's seat, I felt the oozing blood. I knew I had to move fast so there wouldn't be any puddles in the car seats. I wrapped the carpet around my lap, so nothing was visible, and then I drove up to the full-service pump.

As I waited for help, I thought seriously about telling the attendant to call the police for help. I wanted the safety of home and thought the police could help me.

If I'm not at home, what will the police do? They'd have to get me home. I don't think I'll say anything. I just want to make it home.

Relieved, the only questions asked were about getting the car filled with gas. I felt a sigh of relief. There were no questions about the rug, or anything remotely related to my current condition. As the attendant completed filling up the car with gas, I handed him the money my abductor gave me when he set me free. In a weird sort of way, I felt like it was blood money, but it was all I had to continue my journey home.

With a full tank now, I followed the road signs toward home. I dove as fast as I felt comfortable driving without drawing undue attention. If I got pulled over, I was certain I would still get home. My priority was getting home, rather than having to explain everything to someone that was so far away from home.

Highway and city signs became anchors of support as I replayed visions of home in my thoughts. I thought about riding bikes with my brother on the trails in Tanglewood and Trinity Park. The long and windy roads have big, beautiful houses with cul-de-sacs: lollipop streets ideal for bike riding adventures.

I remembered one of my first bike excursions with Paul after we moved to Fort Worth. We peddled around the neighborhood, getting familiar with all the landmarks, street names, and houses. I remembered passing Pebblebrook Street when I rode in the car through the neighborhood. We rode through the neighborhood with new and adventurous freedom.

As we rode, we came upon the familiar Pebblebrook Street. After riding on a couple more blocks, there was another Pebblebrook Street sign. Had we made a wrong turn? Were we lost? We both stopped, turned around, and rode back the way we came. Sure enough, we ran into another Pebblebrook Street. Puzzled, we turned onto Pebblebrook Street to see where it took us. It was a big semi-circle street with two entrances. I giggled to myself, remembering the adventures and how we learned our way around. When we got back to the familiar Harwood Street, we found our way back home.

Alas, as I drove into Fort Worth, I realized I was coming into the city from an unfamiliar direction. The city name was familiar, but Fort Worth was a big city, compared to the other rural places we lived. The passing street signs were foreign to me. I kept driving through, in what seemed like the right direction, and finally, my uncertain patience paid off. I recognized Berry Street and turned in that direction.

It felt good to be in my home city, as foreign as it still felt. I was close enough to home to taste it! I felt excited and worried at the same time.

Did I turn off the highway too soon? Am I in the right town? I know there's a Berry Street, but none of this looks familiar.

I kept driving on the road with a familiar name in hopes a restaurant or passing neighborhood looked more like home.

Yes! There's Interstate 35. I think I know where I am now!

I'd had my driver's license for less than a year and knew how to get to school, piano lessons, violin lessons, and church. This part of the city was unfamiliar to me and only heightened my anxiety. Once I recognized where I was, my thoughts turned in another direction.

What am I going to do when I get home? Should I run out of the car and into the house as fast as I can? But what about all this blood? What if my little sister sees all this? I don't want to frighten her. I could honk the horn when I drive into the driveway. Maybe Mom and Dad will come to me. I know that would be a little odd to honk the horn at home, but it might be better for my little sister.

Oh my God! Look at me! I'm nearly home and I'm not even crying! What will my parents think? I've just been through hell and my face looks like nothing happened. There's all this blood, but there's no other sign of distress. I have to make myself cry so they will know that I'm not okay with all of this!

I dug deep into the well of my heart to make tears come out of my eyes, but the tears wouldn't come.

What's wrong with me!? Why can't I cry? What are my parents going to think? I've been gone since last night and I'm going to get into so much trouble! Dad didn't have a car to come home from work. What are they going to do to me for this?

While it seems a parent would only relish the thought of their child getting home safely, in my mind, I had disobeyed my parents. I hadn't come home all night from my date. My car privileges were "abused." The plan was for my date to drive so Dad could get home from work. Being "in trouble" and disobeying the "rules" was all I could imagine. The facts told a different story, but my parents didn't know the story, not yet.

Sights for home drew nearer. I knew I couldn't get out of the car in my condition. Without tears, I feared that all my parents could see was that I abused my "permission" to go on a date. I settled on honking the horn to make them come out to the car. That was all fine and dandy, but what sort of wrath awaited my arrival? I had experienced being in trouble with Mom, and behaving was a far better fate than being in trouble.

As I drove into my neighborhood, I felt amazed that I didn't once get pulled over for speeding. I wasn't paying attention to the speedometer, I just drove.

How in the world did that happen? I'm not sure how fast I've been driving, but I know I've been trying to get home as fast as I could.

These fleeting thoughts quickly turned to resolution as I realized I was home. By myself, still breathing, and still alive, I made it home. Before I knew it, I drove into the familiar long, skinny driveway, past the bedroom windows, and around to the back of the house. I brought the car to a stop in Dad's normal parking spot and quickly hid my bloody lap from view. Even wrapped up in the rug, it frightened me that someone could see.

Certain that things were as good as they could be, and still trying to make tears come out, I honked the horn and timidly watched to see how things were going to unfold.

They're probably scared to come outside. They don't know if I'm by myself or if someone's in the car with me.

After a few minutes, I honked the horn again.

Soon thereafter, I saw the back door open, and Dad walked toward me. What a relief to see him! But I still struggled to make myself display some visible signs of distress.

Here I am. Home. After experiencing the vilest hell I've ever experienced, I should be upset! I can't even cry! What's wrong with me? Will they even believe what I'm about to tell them if I'm not crying? Are they going to believe me when I tell this story? I've got to cry! Come on, tears, come out!

As hard as I willed myself to come up with a few tears, nothing came out.

I wanted to get into the house and clean up, but Janice's bestowed knowledge surfaced, and I knew I couldn't clean up until I talked with the police. I took intentional care to preserve as much evidence as possible, and I wasn't about to stop now.

But wait! I promised I would never tell. I never meant to keep that promise. "If you tell anyone, I'll kill you!"

The image of his knife and the deliberate, commanding instructions of my abductor echoed through my thoughts.

Confusion and fear set it. My mind reeled with questions and what-if scenarios. I visualized seeing that monster at school, at church, or even at home, with that dreaded knife. The sight of his steely blue eyes coursed through my insides with a cruel stabbing of believability.

But he's not here right now. It will take him a while to catch up to me, and by then the police will be looking for him.

A flurry of thoughts ranging from my safety to being dead coursed through my brain.

While his threats echoed in my mind, my internal commitment to report this to the police bubbled up to the surface. I was ready to spill every note I mentally recorded.

As Dad walked toward the car, I rolled down the car window.

I'm home, Daddy, I'm home.

As Dad continued what probably felt like a slow-motion journey to the car, I could see he was cautiously relieved. Having his own questions, I was sure he felt relief, concern, and caution all at the same time. Being a spiritual man, I imagined his well-intentioned sense of faith that no matter what he was going to find, he would be a supportive father to his little girl.

I sat still and felt excited and scared all at the same time as Dad approached the car. With the window rolled down a bit I uttered my first words to a friendly face.

"Is Laci here? I don't want her to see me like this." My nine-year-old sister wasn't old enough to understand seeing all this blood. It would be terrifying for her. I wanted my little sis to know I was home and alive, but I didn't want to scare her.

"She's at the Wilson's house. She's not here right now," Dad said.

The reality of actually being home set in.

"I'm a mess, Daddy. I have to tell the police what happened."

Along with my commitment to detail these events to the authorities, I wondered what must be going through Dad's head as he stood outside the car.

He must be wondering why I'm not just stepping outside of the car. What has happened to her? He's got to have his own thoughts and questions, too.

As Dad gently opened the door, I felt tentative about how he would react when he saw the vile mess. The putrid, repulsive stench of my blood filled my nostrils.

"I'm all bloody, Dad. I need to keep this rug around me."

Securely wrapped up in the rug, I eased out of the car. I felt petrified about what kind of trouble I was going to be in. It was not behavior fitting for a responsible teenager to take the car and be out all night without a phone call.

Mom's going to be furious with me!

In his gentle spirit, Dad walked gingerly with me from the car to the house. Acknowledging all the questions and unknowns, I felt relief. I made it home! Numb and out of balance because the immediate future remained a mystery, I took one careful step at a time.

I was completely unaware at this point that the note I left in the bathroom served its purpose. Someone found the note, called my parents, and reported the condition of the restroom. My breadcrumbs worked!

In his wise, professional counseling manner, Dad extended an arm of support and love by giving me the space to allow things to unfold naturally. I wouldn't realize how important this gift was until much later. I was sure he felt relieved to see me in one piece. He must have had his own questions and uncertainties. The absence of harsh words for any perceived "irresponsible behavior" helped me take those brave steps into the house.

When I looked into my mother's eyes, I saw warmth and love. It was obvious she realized something horrible had happened, and that she, too, felt relieved to see her little girl at home: alive, breathing, and walking. Seeing these visible signs of relief about my safe return helped me to understand there was no anger about a missing car or a daughter being out all night. I only saw relief, which allowed me to settle into the reality that I was really home, alive, and in one piece.

Dad gently escorted me, all wrapped up in the tattered, bloodied rug, to a chair in the immediate living room that sat waiting with open arms. I carefully sat down so as not to unwrap myself from the rug's protective cover.

"Where's Laci? She can't see me like this."

"She's safe at the Wilson's house. It's okay."

Mom's voice was reassuring, and I felt relieved that someone safely distanced my little sister from my current condition.

As I settled into the chair, the conversation quickly directed itself to the next logical steps. I methodically told the story of the events of the last 23 hours. The checklist of notes I took helped me articulate the facts as clearly as I could. While I told my story, I made it very clear about my intentions to nail this guy.

I spilled volumes of details about driving, getting stuck in the mud, being told to undress at knifepoint, and the awful things he made me do. I told them about using the glass doorknobs to get unstuck from the mud and how he sold Dad's tools to put gas in the car. His time in jail and driving to Galveston. My mental journal of events didn't fail me. I remembered everything clearly. As I shared details of the events with Mom, Dad stepped away for a few moments.

I was safe but felt reserved about the immediate events taking place. While I shared information that would be disturbing for any parent to hear, I still could not make myself cry. There was no visible sign of me being upset about what had happened. I wanted my story to be believed. And to add on to it, I found myself laughing and nervously giggling, which didn't seem like the right display of emotion regarding the trauma I was sharing.

They will never believe me. Why am I laughing? It's not funny! Why can't I cry? I'm hurt and bleeding, but I can't cry! What's wrong with me?

When Dad returned to the living room, I spoke about seeing the ocean and stopping for a little shuteye. Upon rising at sunrise, he drove me to East Beach and made me undress again; repeating what he had done before, even though I was bleeding. I recounted every detail I could remember, and then the doorbell rang.

Who could that be?

Exhausted and running on pure adrenaline, I stayed seated and let someone else deal with whoever was at the door.

I don't want anyone to see me like this! Not now!

As Dad returned from responding to the ringing doorbell, in walked a couple of police officers and a woman I didn't know. They came into the living room where I sat and introduced themselves. Jenny, with the Rape Crisis Center, quickly put me at ease during introductions.

Oh, my God! He raped me! He raped me!

Like a bolt of lightning striking the center of my core, the reality of rape sank in.

I tried to wrap my frightened little self around that concept as Jenny and the officers gently explained that I needed to tell them what happened. It was a rehearsed conversation. I was ready to recall everything I could to tell the police all the details of the last 23 hours. I felt confident providing all the facts would lead to that monster being captured.

While there was a purpose in my recollection of these details, once again, my heart sank deep into a spiraling abyss. The reality of kidnap and rape, and being raped twice, slammed me like a ton of bricks. Even though I deliberately noted all the events so I could recount them, the sound of the words coming from my mouth sounded like words that should make a person cry. I wanted to cry, but I still couldn't. I recounted the events as factually as I could, but even speaking the horrible facts about each rape, I continued to giggle.

Repulsed and ashamed, I felt nervous about saying the words out loud that communicated the facts. The familiar, uncontrollable shaking resurfaced as I related the pages of mental notes I took over the last day of my life. It was involuntary, but I tried desperately to control the shaking. I felt like I was freezing, but I wasn't cold.

What's wrong with me? I'm home, safe and sound, and I'm a bumbling, giggly, shaking mess! Why am I still shaking?

I tried to make sense of the words coming out of my mouth and the flurry of feelings coursing through me. As I answered the officers' questions with clarity and accuracy, I struggled with a deepening, sinking feeling, with nervous laughter all the way. I went through unexplainable torture, and I was laughing.

What's wrong with me? Get a grip!

I wanted to get the storytelling part over and done with so I could get back to my normal, awkward teenage life. I just wanted it to all be over. As I spilled facts, the officers took copious notes and asked for any appropriate clarifying information.

Let me go back to my room, to the comforts of my stuffed animals, my piano practicing, and my frustrating school existence. Let me get back to what I was doing before I tried to go out on that date!

While I strung the facts together, describing the events that took place out loud, Mom chimed in with a concerning question.

"Don't you think it would be a good idea to get her to a hospital?"

Her words suddenly reminded me I was still bleeding. She was calm with her question, but I could see concern written all over her face.

I'm just a mess! Everywhere I go it gets all messy!

I understood there was more storytelling to complete. I wanted to do everything I could to help the police find and nail this guy. The thought of going to the hospital was unsettling, but I really wanted the bleeding to stop. I felt safe but scared.

My parents drove me to the county hospital, near downtown, while the police officers and Rape Crisis support came along separately. A whir of doubts ran wild in my head as we approached the hospital, and it was time for me to get out of the car. I felt helpless and exposed. I was sure everyone could see r-a-p-e painted all over me, and anyone who saw me instantly judged me as a shameful, inappropriate teenager.

Please, God, just let it all be over!

CHAPTER 9
RAPE EXAM

TRIGGER ALERT: The information in this chapter contains detailed information about the rape exam at the hospital that could be triggering. You can skip to Chapter 10 and still get the gist of the story.

ONCE I TOLD the triage nurse why we were there, she showed me to a room where Jenny and the police asked more questions. At least we were in a room with a door and separated from all the other people who gathered in the emergency room.

I was glad to answer all their questions. It helped me stay focused on my sheer determination to punish that animal. Accompanying my unwavering focus to nail the guy, the idea of rape passed through my thoughts again and again with disbelief.

Their questions and my regurgitation of the cold cruel facts continued for a while. Then they took me back into the treatment area of the hospital's emergency room. Down the long hallway, all the way to the end and to the right, they escorted me protectively into the exam room. I was relieved that the room was private; I didn't have to uncover my bloody mess in front of any other patient who was there.

A nurse instructed me to take off all my clothes and put on the provided "gown" so that it opened in the front. She took my blood pressure and then left the room so that I could change.

I was eager to take off my cold, damp, bloodied pants. They were wet and disgusting. My favorite pair of pants was completely ruined. I realized I'd never be able to wear them again, and a strange emptiness filled my heart. Carefully, I removed all my clothes and piled them on a chair in the corner. Then I put on the light cotton gown they provided me, securing it closed in the front. I hopped back up on the exam table. The room was chilly, so I took the sheet they left in there, opened it up a little, and covered up my legs to get warm.

My body restarted its familiar trembling. No matter how hard I tried to stop it, it was going to be there, so I did my best to relax, breathe, and try to stop the shaking, or at least slow it down to a simmering rumble.

After a few moments, the nurse came back in, took my vitals, and started asking questions. Now, having recalled the events of the ordeal to my parents and to law enforcement, I began sharing the details and events about what happened once again. Another professional required the details of the last 23 hours of my life. Spilling the information out seemed easier each time, but I felt afraid.

I didn't know what sort of "exam" I was about to endure. I could only experience what was coming at me one step at a time. The constant "evidence collector" inside me knew this was all necessary to gather evidence to physically prove the experience I was sharing. If it was going to help catch this guy, I was all in.

The "kiss me and never tell" images were still vivid in my memory, which felt scary now and then. His threat to come back and kill me loomed.

How safe am I, really? What sort of danger am I putting my family into by telling all these people what I've just experienced? I want him caught, but I'm ready for all this commotion to be over and done with!

As the nurses and doctor wrapped up their cursory "vital information gathering," a realization came over me.

Saying that I had to put his penis in my mouth. I never want to say those words again.

My stomach knotted up as I choked back my desire to vomit while I told the story. I remembered the vile taste, and my conscious efforts to keep from gagging. I felt like I wanted to throw up, but perhaps thankfully, nothing bubbled to the surface to come out.

As I restated the facts, I remembered the disgusting smell all over. I smelled like it. My imagination took me to the shower. I wanted to taste the freshness of toothpaste instead of the lingering yuck I still tasted in my mouth.

"And then he put that thing in my vagina. Ewww!"

Listening to the words coming out of my mouth as I re-told the story magnified the horribleness of my experience in my thoughts. My guts felt like they were welling up in my heart. It hurt. It felt gross, every step of the way.

After gathering the details of events related to what I endured physically, the nurses turned to open a pouch full of medical paraphernalia and started explaining what they were about to do. Still sitting up on the end of the exam table, they asked me to open my mouth. They took a rather long-looking Q-tip and swabbed the inside of my mouth, around my cheeks and gums. It was like rinsing out my already dry mouth with a dry cotton ball. All the while, they explained doing these things helped them to gather physical evidence that may help to prove the story I was telling them was true.

Do they think I'm lying about all of this? Do they think I'm making all this up? I can't believe that someone would think I would lie about this.

I knew from talking with Janice that I couldn't eat or drink anything; bathing had to wait until they had all the evidence. I held true to what Janice taught me. It was as though Janice, a guardian angel of sorts, continued to instruct me and guide me along the way.

I was glad to comply because I wanted this guy caught. I followed each direction and answered every question. I grew tired of sitting in my blood and wanted the gushing feeling between my legs to stop.

Good Lord, I've been bleeding since he raped me the first time. How much more blood is in me? I've got to be running out of blood.

As the exam and evidence collecting continued, they scraped under my fingernails and kept what came out. They took a strand or two of my hair. The nurses carefully stored each piece of evidence in labeled, closed containers.

They were kind and helped me lie down on the exam table. They pulled these metal things out from the end of the table. As I laid back, the nurses pulled the skimpy, clean, cotton hospital gown open to continue the exam. It wasn't much, but I felt protected with the gown on. When they opened it up, I lay there naked and started trembling again.

I felt intensely vulnerable while they touched and pressed, examining my naked body.

They have to do this to collect evidence. It will be over soon. It has to be over soon! I have to do this so they can nail this guy. He's never gonna get away with this! It will be over soon. It has to be over soon!

The exposed nakedness felt less intrusive because I pretended I wasn't there. I cooperated, but I felt like a crazy person on the inside as my head screamed with frantic dialog. I didn't realize it, but my numbing, robotic responses carried me through. My committed intentions of nailing that guy kept me willing to do whatever it took to get him caught.

After that part of the exam, they placed the sheet over my legs and asked me to scoot my rear down to the end of the table. I had to scoot down onto the part of the table where I had been sitting, which was all bloody.

Gross! I'm ready for a bath! It can't last too long. They have to do this. I wish Janice were here so she could tell me all of this was going to be okay. This is awful! As if sitting in my blood wasn't enough, now I have to lie in it!

The nurses gently guided my feet into the cold metal stirrups, legs all propped up and my privates exposed for everyone to see. The doctor pulled his sitting stool up to the table and explained what he was about to do and what sort of sensations to expect.

I was glad the nurse talked to me. The sound of her voice reassured me, and even though a stranger to me, the voice and her gentle touch helped me feel less alone.

Before I knew it, the doctor put this cold metal thing inside my vagina. My stomach cramped, like it did when the smelly guy was poking his penis in and out of my vagina.

Oh, God! Please stop poking me! Is that all that place on my body is good for? It doesn't feel good. When is this going to be over?! I'm home! It's over! Please let this stop!

Why do people have to stick things inside there? It's gross, and it doesn't feel good. Yuck! If this is what having sex is all about, I want no part of it! I'm never getting married. I'm never going to do that ever again! It's gross, it smells, and it doesn't feel good. Why would anyone want to do that?

I felt a pinching sensation when the doctor opened up the instrument inside me, and then I felt him scraping around in there. He asked me about my period while he was digging around in there. I didn't know what he was doing, but I knew it had to be done.

"I just finished my period. Why am I still bleeding?"

If having a penis stuck inside me is going to make me bleed every time, I'll have none of that! Gross! Yuck!

The doctor explained that there was no damage, and he didn't see any injury. He explained the bleeding was my body's way of handling stress.

He started pushing around on my belly and I suddenly felt like I was going to hurl.

When is this going to be over? Please let this be over soon!

After he finished pressing and looking around at my vagina, he pulled out the terrible thing he stuck inside, and I felt such relief that, perhaps, that part was over.

After a few seconds, much to my surprise, he stuck something in my anus.

God! What is he doing? When will this be over?!! Aaaaaaaaah!

Thank God, that didn't last very long, and before I knew it, he asked me to sit up. The nurses helped me get my feet off the stirrups and sit up.

"Are you allergic to penicillin?" the doctor asked.

"No. Not that I'm aware of."

Why on earth do they need to know that? I'm not sick!

"We're going to give you a shot of penicillin to protect you from venereal disease. The nurse will be back for that," the doctor said.

Venereal disease! What? Well, I guess I could have contracted it. He did rape me, and Lord only knows… I don't want to think about that. God, I hope he didn't give me any of that stuff.

What if I'm pregnant? What if he gave me herpes or something? What if I can never have children? I just want to go back to school and let everything be back to normal again! What if he comes back to kill me?

Before I knew it, the nurse was back with a big ol' shot, a ginormous horse pill, and some clean clothes.

"I hate to do this, but I need to give this to you in your hip."

The nurse gently helped me down off the table and asked me to bend over.

"Try to relax your muscle as much as possible. I'm going to shoot it slowly, so it won't hurt so bad."

With a swish of a cold alcohol swab, before I knew it, the nurse stabbed me with the shot. I felt like I had to stand there for an eternity while the syringe of penicillin unloaded into my rump. While the nurse pushed the fluid through the syringe, she helped me understand that penicillin would help protect me from venereal disease. If he had something, this should protect me from it because they were catching it so early.

"All done."

The encouraging nurse put a Band-Aid on my tail feathers and rubbed my butt cheek a bit.

"That will help it not to hurt so much later."

The nurse handed me a small cup of water and a little paper cup containing the huge pill.

"Take this. I don't think you can be pregnant because of all the hemorrhaging you've done. But this is called the 'day after pill.' Taking this will help your body not become pregnant."

Down the hatch, the chunk of pill went down. The dribble of water tasted so good. I had not had a drink since I nervously left the comfort of the awkward shenanigans of MYF (Methodist Youth Fellowship) to go on my date. I wasn't excited about swallowing the water because of the unpleasantness left in my mouth for the last several hours. But it helped to get the horse pill down.

The nurse placed my clothes next to me.

"Your mom brought clean clothes for you to wear."

She turned to pick up my soiled clothes and placed each piece of clothing into a separate bag and sealed it.

"We'll take these and give them to the police officer."

What a relief. I won't have to put those yucky clothes back on.

When the nurse finished gathering my clothes, she left the room and encouraged me to get dressed. Those clean clothes looked more than inviting.

"Here's a pad for you."

She handed me a sanitary napkin.

As embarrassed as I felt, the idea of having a pad to bleed into instead of my clean clothes was like a breath of fresh air.

When the nurse left and closed the door behind her, I hastily reached for my clean clothes. I touched the soft fabric, and it smelled fresh. While the idea of clean clothes was soothing, I knew my body was filthy. I imagined how good a warm bath would feel, and the anticipation of that carried me forward.

Without a second thought, I removed the cold, starchy hospital gown and got dressed. My fresh clothes brought relief. My body smell was still offensive, and I could still taste his filthy mouth in mine. I smelled his stale, alcohol-ish smell. I was impatient to get home.

As I got dressed, I looked around the exam room. All the collected evidence sat in neat little packages, and the exam table was a bloody mess, which embarrassed me. Then I heard a knock at the door.

"Are you dressed?"

"Yes."

The door opened gently, revealing Jenny and her familiar supportive voice.

"If you'll come with me, we'll go back to the other room and the officers can finish asking you a few more questions."

Jenny walked with me back to the room and a whoosh of comfort blanketed me when I saw my parents there. The tremors in my body finally simmered to a dull murmur. I survived the exam, and now there were more questions to answer. I finished up the story as best as I could, being sure to give specific descriptive details about where he let me go. It was important to me that the authorities have as much information as they could to increase their chance of finding and arresting him. Not knowing exactly where I was, I could only share the name of the town, Galveston, and the observations I made about my surroundings. With that, and responding to their questions, the officers had all they needed for now.

Jenny gave a spiel about the Rape Crisis Center and the services available there. She was kind and encouraging and gave me phone numbers and ways to get in touch with people should I desire to talk with someone. I listened through the lens of my growing, impatient desire to be home, attend to that warm bath, and the comfort of my bedroom. Even though my clothes were clean, I could still smell my revolting self and wanted to wash all that away. Perhaps then it would all be over.

Mom and Dad escorted me safely and compassionately back to the car. I was glad they drove the other car, so I didn't have to get back into the car where he held me captive for so long. Now, with my pad and clean clothes, I no longer had to worry about messing this up.

As I sat in the car, I could still feel blood coming out of me. I hated that gross feeling, and it turned my stomach upside down. At least my parents were in the car with me, and I felt safe. I knew who was driving the car and our goal was to get home. This was peace a long time coming! I was eager to be home and get the nasty smell off.

Thankfully, there wasn't much chatter. The story told, the facts recounted, it was time to be safe at home and get cleaned up. Exhausted and tired, I pined for my cozy bed. As we drove up into the driveway and parked, I saw the other bloodied car still in the driveway like an unbelievable haunting. We each quietly walked back into the house.

I went into my familiar bedroom, looked around, and headed straight to the dresser to find some pajamas. Mom stepped into the bedroom doorway.

"Is there anything you need? Is there something I can do?"

"I just want to take a bath and go to bed."

"Do you want me to bathe you?"

I'm sure Mom didn't know what to do or what to say. As a mother, she wanted to help me. She wanted to console her wounded child and make me feel safe. The thought of being naked in front of another person, even Mom, repulsed me.

No! I don't want you to bathe me! I've been raped and examined and had to be naked in front of enough people!"

"No, I think I can manage on my own."

I gathered my jammies and walked through the formal living room, where I saw my piano. This is home. I walked through the front door entry hall to the hallway and turned left into the front bathroom. It was clean and meticulously tidy, just like home; not like the dirty gas station restroom I was in before. I closed the door and ran the water to warm it up. While the house felt warm, having to take my clothes off again felt cold, and I wanted the water in the tub to be good and warm before I stepped in.

As the water warmed, I stoppered the tub to fill it with soothing warmth. When I took my underwear off, I saw the now bloodied pad they gave me at the hospital. It was disgusting, but I removed it from my panties and wrapped it up to throw it away. With that taken care of, I stepped my trembling body into the warm water. The clean warmth of the water felt good on my body as I sat down in the tub. I hoped the warm water would help me stop shaking. The water felt as though it was thawing my soul. The longer I sat there, the more my body ceased its incessant trembling.

I could still smell my filth: the smell of blood, the body odor, the way he smelled. My mouth still tasted like him and his penis. My empty stomach wanted to vomit. I had to get rid of that repulsive smell!

When I got the soap in my hands, I gently covered myself with a soapy lather.

If I can get rid of that smell and into my bed, it will all be over.

Once I got started, I couldn't get my bath done fast enough. Before the tub filled with water, I finished spreading the soap all over and was ready to rinse. While the water was still running, I got all the soap off. Now, finally, I smelled clean and like soap.

I could still taste that gagging taste in my mouth, so I didn't want to lie back and relax. I had to get that taste and the smell out of my mouth. As soon as I turned the water off and unplugged the drain, I grabbed a towel. It felt good around my body as I stepped out of the tub. The air was cool after being in the warm water, and I didn't want to shake again. I couldn't get my pajamas on fast enough. The shaking returned like an old friend.

As soon as I finished dressing, I robotically grabbed my toothbrush and piled on the toothpaste. I wanted that awful taste out of my mouth, so I briskly brushed my teeth. It tasted good to have that minty freshness in my mouth, but I was not in the mood for any slow, drawn-out tooth brushing. I spit, rinsed, took a towel to dry my hands and face, and then stood still for a moment and took a breath.

My thoughts were the first sigh of genuine relief. I smelled clean, and my mouth felt fresh. All I wanted to do was savor these soothing moments. They had been a long time coming, and I needed a moment to take it all in.

The pause and cleanliness felt good, but my bedroom called my name. I put my dirty clothes in their rightful place, and my weary legs carried me promptly to my sacred room.

As I walked to my room, Mom was "Johnny on the spot" with an interesting question.

"Are you hungry?"

By now, it was nine o'clock at night, and my last meal was lunch the day before. If I was hungry, I didn't feel it, and the thought of trying to eat food didn't interest me in the least.

"No, I think just a glass of water, and then I'm off to bed."

"Okay. Are you sure you don't want anything to eat?"

"Yes."

As I turned down the covers to crawl in, Mom came in with a glass of water. I guzzled it down as quickly as I could and climbed into bed.

At last. I'm home and it's over! Tomorrow is Tuesday, and I've got school, so I better try to get some sleep.

The thought of sleep was like a soothing salve. I was ready for the comfort of my bed and cushy pillow. My "stadium" of stuffed animal friends nearby, I imagined falling asleep safely, yearning for warmth and rest.

As I nestled into bed and got comfortable, Mom tucked me in and leaned over to kiss her baby's forehead. I savored that feeling: being supported by the bed, warm under the covers, and safe with my stuffed animal friends all around me. Fresh, clean pajamas, the lingering taste of toothpaste in my mouth, I was living the safety I could only dream of a few brief hours before.

"Goodnight."

Mom turned and walked away and turned the light off.

"Good night, Mom. It's good to be home."

My head cradled in my pillow, I closed my eyes, but my thoughts spun relentlessly.

When I go back to school tomorrow, everyone's going to know he raped me. I don't care. I just want my life to get back to normal. This is over and I just want to go back to my awkward, insignificant life.

My mind stepped through the events of the last 30 hours, and with each thought, I consciously remembered I was home, safe and sound. As I relaxed into the bed and snuggled in, my tired mind drifted from being aware of thoughts to safe sleep.

I didn't know what tomorrow would bring, but I was home and protected. It was the top of Thanksgiving week, and our traditional family gathering in Kansas to see grandparents was forthcoming. But these logical thoughts remained unthought as I slept, and earnestly felt things would be back to normal upon awakening.

CHAPTER 10
THANKSGIVING

YESTERDAY and the evening before were all about survival, getting home safely, and getting back to my uneventful life. School, practicing the piano and violin, going to lessons—these were the makings of all things normal in my life. What happened was over and getting back into those routines seemed like the best next plan of action.

The horror was over (so I thought). As relieved as I was to be home and alive, I survived and now it was time to get back to the business of all things familiar and predictable. I returned on Monday and had missed one day of school. Thanksgiving was just a few days away, and that meant a traditional journey through Oklahoma and on to Kansas to spend time with our extended family.

Much to my surprise, when I woke up, it was much too late to get to school. My quest for "normal" would have to wait another day. I slept and slept and slept, and the unanticipated prescription of sleep fell naturally to what my body needed. No more trembling and actual sleep; sleep without having to wonder what might happen next; sleep without having to be aware of everything going on around me. I slept like a long-fallen tree that now rested on a forest floor.

As I rolled out of bed and my feet hit the ground, I felt an alarming, tender sensation. I instantly remembered the violent shaking my body endured yesterday and the day before. When he raped me, my feet pounded on the car window, not because I was pounding them purposefully but as the result of my seizure-like fear and trembling.

The bottoms of my feet are bruised! Ouch! At least I'm stepping out of my bed onto the floor at my house, and I'm safe. I suppose this shall pass.

As I planted my feet firmly on the floor, I winced at their tenderness and then stood up to go about the beginning of a new day.

God! My butt hurts! What did they do to me? I guess that will go away in a day or so, too.

The beginning of this new day seemed surreal. The comfortable rhythm of reasoning out every thought and action stayed with me. I pretended to feel a semblance of routine: getting out of bed, attending to a morning pee, getting dressed… I'm sure you get the idea. As was acceptable for a young teen in the morning, I rustled around for a bowl of cereal. It's what I used to do in the morning before school. Today, though, I didn't feel hungry at all. I wanted my actions to portray normalcy, and eating something seemed like the right thing to do in front of my gently observing parents.

I found my favorite box of Post Oat Flakes, the perfectly convenient bowl of sugar, gathered milk from the fridge, a spoon, and a bowl. Before I knew it, I was constructing what seemed like an obligatory spot of breakfast. It was all for appearance's sake, the motions of all things appropriate and normal.

It was Tuesday before Thanksgiving, and my parents felt an urgency about firming up plans for the holiday. As the customary trip to visit family approached, it was time to decide on a few things. My parents were gracious in this decision and felt it was important to give me as many opportunities as they could so that I could make my own decisions. I didn't realize until much later the importance of this support. Fortunately, they were cognizant of my plight and understood how important it was for me to make my own decisions.

They didn't want to put any undue pressure on me and understood if I wanted to stay home. It was okay for me to make that choice; the decision needed to be mine. As I ate my breakfast, Dad opened up the trip discussion.

"We need to make some decisions about going to Kansas this year for Thanksgiving. We need to let your grandparents know if we're planning to go or not. If you prefer, we are happy to stay home this year. Or, if you still want to go, then we can move forward with our plans. What are your thoughts about it?"

The question caught me a little off guard. I forced the cereal down my gullet and took a few seconds to wade through my thoughts.

Gee, they never ask me if I want to go on family trips. We just go. Why are they asking me that? Why would this trip be any different from any other trip?

"What about school?" I asked.

"If you want to go back to school, you can certainly do that. If you'd rather take a couple of days and go ahead with our trip to Oklahoma and Kansas, we can do that."

With frugal means at their disposal, any type of road trip meant family was involved. A visit to Dad's family in Kansas meant making a stop in Oklahoma to see Mom's family, and we also squeezed in a visit with my sister Vickie.

With Thanksgiving a couple of days away, maybe waiting until next week to return to school might be a better idea. If I don't go to school for a couple of days, I can sleep as much as I want to. That sounds good! I'm more tired than I thought I was. My butt still hurts from that shot, and my feet are killing me.

The prospect of having to be on my tender feet and sitting in those hard chairs at school didn't delight me.

They're leaving the decision to me—do we stay or do we go? I don't want my life to be any different from the way it was before all this happened. I wouldn't skip Thanksgiving just because I got sick or something. Why would this be any different? Besides, he's had all the control over my life he's going to get! If I want to go see my family for Thanksgiving, I'm going to go! Of course, we're going to go! Besides, being around people who love and care for me seems like a good thing to do.

What will I say to everyone? Will they know what happened to me? What will I tell them? Will they think of me differently?

As I talked things through, my parents decided they would call everyone ahead of time to let them know about the events of the last couple of days. I clarified that I wanted life to continue like nothing had happened. It was Thanksgiving, and moving forward with these plans seemed like the best approach to help things feel more routine.

At home, before our trip, I resumed as many run-of-the-mill activities as I could. Piano and violin practice, daydreaming, card games with family, a little television, or whatever. My older brother, Paul, even reached out to assure me of his protection when I returned to school. What little sister doesn't want her big brother to look after her? That felt good and reassuring to me.

Things started feeling normal again. It seemed all that remained was picking up the motions of familiar activities and getting back into the groove of things. Simple as it seemed, these small steps provided a sense of control in my life. I made choices for myself instead of reacting because my life lay traumatically in the hands of a stranger.

I felt hugely grateful for being alive and home, safe and sound. Family was always important to me, but it felt pronounced and deliberate now. I felt thankful for little things; my bed, my belongings, the music I created, the fact I had a family that cared, and my environment felt safe.

I wondered from time to time if anyone had heard the "messages" I sent to family and loved ones while in captivity. I talked with my parents about this and learned that, in fact, Walter, a fellow pastor, inquired about the family. He called to check in with my parents while I was gone to be sure everything was okay. He had a feeling about something and felt it was important to reach out and act upon it.

As creepy as it sounds, I felt he heard my deliberate thoughts. Walter, of all people, heard me and responded to a tugging in his heart that said it would be good to touch base. My not-so-conservative background taught me about telepathic communication. This news about Walter only made me believe more strongly that a common language of thought could exist.

The gas station owner stumbled upon the note I left in the bathroom and called my parents! That phone call precipitated the police looking for me. With all the teenage runaways, when a minor went missing, law enforcement would not start looking for someone until 24 hours passed. I was gone for 23 hours. It shocked me. I made it all the way home; no one stopped me or pulled me over. Perhaps getting home, free from discovery, was best. A certain relief came from realizing that, perhaps, I wasn't entirely alone in my experience.

Tuesday came and went, and Wednesday was a travel day. On the way to Oklahoma City, we stopped in Purcell to see Vickie. Her disability was severe at an early age. My parents placed their oldest daughter in the Pauls Valley State School so she could get the complete care and attention she required. A heart-wrenching decision, for sure. When Vickie was too old to stay in the state school, she moved to a nursing home in Purcell. My parents were adamant about keeping her active as a participant in the family. We always had gifts from her on birthdays and Christmas, and of course, anytime we traveled north, we'd stop by for a visit.

When we got to Purcell, everyone piled out of the car: Mom, Dad, my brother Paul, me, and my little sister, Laci. We went into the nursing home and into Vickie's room. She would either be in there or out and about somewhere in her wheelchair. As fortune would have it, she was under the weather, so she was in her room, in bed.

We gathered around in her little semi-private room to visit with her. Well, visit as best we could. No one really knew if Vickie understood a word that was said, as her mind, in all her years, only matured to about the age of two or three. Her favorite game involved grabbing something in her hand and flailing it around until it broke loose and fell to the floor. When the object hit the floor and made a sound, an abundance of laughter ensued.

Each person stepped up to Vickie's bed and made conversation as though she understood what we were saying. As each person visited, the "throw something on the floor" game ensued, as she mustered up the strength to make it happen, and everyone had a good hard belly laugh. Her laughter was more contagious than the flu!

When our short time together drew to a close, everyone took their turn to say their goodbyes. I carefully laid my purse on her bed, out of reach, so I could lean over and give her a proper hug. Spending this normal time with the family was like a soothing liniment. In some ways, it was as if I picked up right where I left off as if nothing had happened. But it all had a more profound meaning to me. I choked back the tears welling up in my throat so I would look normal and unfazed. I wanted people to see that I was okay.

When we all bid our farewells, we traversed back to the car and piled in to resume our journey to Oklahoma City, where Mom's family awaited our arrival. As Dad pulled out of the parking lot and made his way back to the highway, I realized something was missing.

"I left my purse in Vickie's room. I forgot my purse!"

Guilt sank in as Dad found a place to get turned around and head back. I felt awful that he had to go back, but I was really anxious about not finding my personal item.

Without a wince, a comment, or any sign of the extra burden, he made his way back to the nursing home so I could retrieve my missing purse. When we arrived, I went in by myself and marched deliberately to Vickie's room. As I approached her bed, I explained to Vickie that I left my purse and securely placed it under my arm. When I finished my explanation, I bent down to give Vickie a kiss on her forehead and give her another hug.

With that, I returned to my patiently waiting family, and the journey to Oklahoma City resumed. Settling back into the back seat for the next couple of hours, I reflected on what had just happened.

This was the first time ever that I was in the room with Vickie by myself! We're usually always together, coming and going. I've never been with her by myself before.

A well of gratefulness gushed inside me as I thought about it. My moment of enlightenment filled my body with warmth, and a tear or two gently rolled from my eyes down the length of my face. I was moved by the seemingly insignificant gift, both of my family allowing me to retrieve my purse and the moments I got to share alone with my older sister. I sat in silence and allowed myself to feel love.

Not wanting anyone to see my moment of tenderness, I quickly prompted myself to stop my gentle weeping, so as not to have a sniffle draw any attention. I grabbed a cassette and my Sony Walkman, and turned on some music to distract me from the intensity of the personal moment. It was time to look forward to the next part of the trip— making our way to Oklahoma City.

The plan was to stay with Grandma Birdie overnight and then

make the rest of the trip to Kansas. A visit to Grandma Birdie's house meant some sort of gathering of the rest of Mom's family: aunts, uncles, and cousins. Grandma Birdie was always in favor of gathering family whenever she could, anytime we came to visit, and this was no exception.

I felt solace in having a family that cared about me. As everyone gathered at Grandma's house, we all settled in with our hellos and hugs and chattered about our goings-on since the last time we saw each other. I dared not bring up the events of the last few days, and much to my amazement, no one else said anything about it either. There were only expressions of gratitude for my safe return. Being surrounded by family and those who loved me felt warm and reassuringly comforting.

These were comforting moments, but they also felt different. I knew everyone was being deliberate in not asking pointed questions about my recent past. Awkwardly, I instructed myself to do things to create an appearance of status quo.

You're okay. This is what you do during any other visit. You can do this! Go get yourself something to nibble on. Laugh. It feels good to be with everyone.

I felt like a stranger in a strange land.

Uncle George, perhaps being a little fuller of holiday cheer than he needed to be, displayed his normal rigorous joy. Everyone took their turn dancing with him, even me. I understood George was George, and he got a little carried away sometimes, but it felt uncomfortable. I could smell alcohol on him, which brought instant flashbacks of my recent terror.

This is George, and you are safe.

I called upon my inner strength to keep smiling as if all was right with the world, but on the inside, a struggle ensued. My recent struggle to choke back my vivid repulsion to that smell came back seamlessly as I found myself faced with that same smell. This was different because I felt safe being around my family. In an instant, though, my mind wandered back and forth between my recent past and the joviality of being with family at Thanksgiving.

I must have unwittingly displayed a visible sign of distress. Soon after the uncomfortable feelings surfaced, Mom stepped in to alert everyone about the late hour. Her announcement that it was time for her kids to prepare for bed created enough pause for me to stop dancing with Uncle George. Without dropping a beat, Janice stepped in to relieve me of my "dancing duties" with Uncle George. At that moment, my siblings and I were off to find our jammies and sleeping places for the night.

While it felt good and safe to be around family, it felt different to me. It seemed familiar, but it wasn't. I felt different on the inside, even among these friendly faces. On the outside, I felt branded, as if "damaged goods," "raped," and "dirty" were written all over me and in plain sight. When I looked in the mirror, I looked like the same person. There were no visible marks showing any difference, but my insides felt vastly different.

Dancing with Uncle George reminded me of the putrid smell of the scoundrel that raped me. It was a foul scent I never wanted to smell again. It was over. There was no need to put up with that again. The distance from my captor made no difference. I could still smell it. Because Uncle George drank heavily, he smelled like *him*. My stomach churned with repulsion. Uncle George looked like my uncle. He acted like him, but that smell made it seem like I was right back where I was a few days ago, struggling to survive.

I felt relieved when Janice stepped in to dance with George. In my determination to get life and my brave, bold interior back to normal, I reassured myself that everything was all right. I was safe with my family. These people loved me. There was no danger to be concerned about. The inner struggle and turmoil I felt days before, under very different circumstances, burned inside like a relentless fire.

Why the hell is that smell following me around? He's gone and I'm safe. Why is that smell still here?

I felt vulnerable. My family surrounded me, but they were people I wasn't around every day. I didn't want to cry in front of them—I wanted everyone to see me as okay and that I was the same person I was before the horror. The deeper part of me wanted to display bravery. I didn't want that guy to control any more of my life. In my mind, if someone saw me cry, it would be a sign of weakness and he would still be in control.

No, no, no! No more!

My mind reeled with questions. I was safe, but I realized I broke my spoken promise, however intentional I was about nailing him. It was a promise I never intended to keep, and his threat to come back and kill me loomed. Every other threat he made proved to be serious; he meant what he said. Why would this one be any different? As fear rose within me, I could feel that little tremble creep back into my body —a familiar feeling, but an uncontrollable one. I felt possessed.

When is the shaking going to stop?

I told every little detail I could remember to the police. What prevented him from coming back to kill me?

Is my broken promise going to come back to haunt me? What if they really find him and arrest him? What happens next? If they find him, he will know that I reported him, and my life will be in danger. If this goes to trial, what should I expect? I read somewhere that things rarely work in favor of the victim. God, I'm a victim now! The trial process is not a positive experience. My family could never afford the cost of hiring an attorney. That would not be good!

My thoughts turned from moment-to-moment survival to logically figuring out what the next steps might be.

As I dressed for bed, Mom made sure I got tucked into a safe place. Grandma Birdie's house was full of people, so a nice pallet on the couch in Grandma's office would do nicely. Someone already prepared my couch bed, and it was ready for me to climb into, complete with my trusty stuffed animal alligator friend, Alfred.

I climbed into my makeshift bed and Janice came in to check on me. Seeing Janice was such a relief. In my mind, I felt like she held my hand through the entire experience. Here she was now, in person. Perhaps she could answer some of my questions.

As Janice stepped into my presence, she opened her arms wide to offer me a gentle, reassuring hug. The crying that wouldn't happen before finally broke loose. It was as if the very real safety I felt in Janice's arms had unlocked whatever was caged before. I cried and cried, sobbed and sobbed, deep heaving sobs. Mom and Janice sat with me, holding me gently while I squeezed the living daylights out of Alfred (my alligator friend).

I saturated Alfred with all my tears. I cried and cried and turned into a snotty, embarrassing mess. My face felt flushed. I could hardly breathe from crying so hard. As I caught my breath, the flood of questions rushing through my head came out of my mouth to ask Janice for some consoling assurances.

Janice calmly offered the statistical facts to me. She told me it is a rare few who come back to kill someone after something like this is reported. I learned that if they really found him, I would identify him in a line-up. Janice offered to call law enforcement in Fort Worth to see what she could learn and to do what she could to help. In her sage wisdom, Janice helped me understand I could take all this one day at a time. Glimpsing this mountain of uncertainty in small pieces helped me create an understanding that it was okay not to have all the answers right now. She extended her support to me as time would naturally unfold the things to follow.

While Janice talked, my unstoppable sobs turned to oxygen-gasping whimpers. I had no foundation to believe what Janice was telling me, but her words brought me comfort. As calm wiggled its way back into my presence, the pressing uncertainties whirled through my head. At least now, gasps of air managed their way in, and the uncontrollable wailing subsided. My body was tired from the violent sobbing. I resettled into my couch bed, wet alligator and all. Mom and Janice assured me everything would be all right, and they tucked me in to ensure warmth and safety. The warm, heavy blankets felt like a safe little cocoon, and I could calm myself as my body ached to find sleep.

As they left the room, I wept myself to sleep. I didn't think I would ever stop crying. It seemed record-breaking that a human could cry so many tears.

I slept like a log. As Thursday morning brought with it a new day (Thanksgiving Day), we headed for Kansas. We packed up the car and headed toward Dad's kinfolk to enjoy the other grandma's yummy turkey.

As the car traversed the endless stretch of highway from Oklahoma

City to Fowler, Kansas, I had nothing but time to think about recent events. I desperately wanted things to get back to normal, but "normal" (or whatever that was) proved to be a more challenging state than it seemed. Thinking back on things in Oklahoma City, I decided that all had gone as well as possible. I realized that as awkward as it felt to be around family, it also brought a sense of support. Getting that clarity made it natural to look forward to the Kansas visit as well.

Thanksgiving in Kansas can be mighty cold. This prelude to winter held true to my historical experiences. I'm not one to enjoy the cold, per se. This cold felt sharper and more bitter, perhaps because I felt out of sorts. Arriving at the cozy farmhouse in Fowler and seeing the family brought me comfort.

It had been a good while since I last saw my favorite cousin, Jerry. Stepping into the little farmhouse in the middle of nowhere and seeing him there meant a great deal more to me than I could ever explain. In usual fashion, upon our arrival, everyone arose from their play, rest, or other goings-on to greet the weary travelers with warm, familial hugs.

While it all felt familiar to me, it felt like everything moved in slow motion. Being with family felt safe, but my insides also felt unsettled. It was as if everyone moved in a surreal, slow motion. There were no questions, only greetings of gracious gratitude that our family arrived safely. Nothing out of the ordinary there.

The episodes of violent crying I experienced in Oklahoma City seemed behind me for the moment, but I felt quite tender. Not so much because I was sad or hurt but because I felt an overwhelming, heightened sense of thankfulness for being alive. I felt pointedly fortunate to be a member of this family. In the few sporadic moments of aloneness that naturally occurred over the course of the weekend, tears gently presented and seeped out. I didn't want my family to see me as a bumbling, crying mess. My mission crystallized to create a perception that I was in control of my moments. What happened was over, and I was determined I wouldn't allow him to dictate my experiences beyond that.

While we were in Kansas, Mom and Dad received word from Janice that they arrested the guy who raped me in Galveston, right where I told the police he let me go. When they told me the news, a swelling wave of fear swept over me. Deeply fearful with thoughts about him coming back to kill me, I worried about how events would unfold as soon as we got home. My evil captor made it clear he did not want to go back to jail and spoke adamantly about his threats to come back to kill me. I tried to replay Janice's words about the minimal statistical likelihood of that happening, but they were of little consolation.

The authorities could only hold him for a few days, which meant as soon as I got home, I needed to identify him in a line-up.

Will he be able to see me? Will we be in the same room together? How much is this going to cost my parents?

My imagination ran rampant with scenarios. We lived comfortably, but extra funds were scarce. I knew there would be some expense with the car; no one would want to drive it with my blood all over the seat.

I yearned for everything to be normal. But it seemed like everywhere I turned, life unfolded as a series of automated tasks you did because it seemed like the right thing to do. I had not yet returned to school, and one more missed day was on the horizon—to go identify him. There was nothing normal about that! I desperately wanted the whole thing to be over so I could get back to my humdrum life; just let me have my normal life.

CHAPTER 11
GETTING BACK TO NORMAL

THANKSGIVING WAS OVER, and it was time to get back to school and the normal routines of piano and violin lessons and so on. I yearned to return to these activities. If I got back to these routines, then the whole rape thing would be over. At least that's what I thought. Getting back to school seemed like the right thing for this 17-year-old to get things back on track.

No one is going to know what happened; I've just been out for a few days. But what do I tell them when they ask why I've been out? I never miss school unless I'm sick, and there's no residual cold for anyone to see. Do I tell them there was a death in the family? What am I supposed to say?

I can't just blurt it out—I was raped. Besides, that would be scary for people. Rape is something that happens to other people. Not me. If they don't know, they won't know unless I tell them. I could just tell them I had to travel for Thanksgiving to be with my family. Who would know any different? In fact, we did travel to be with family for Thanksgiving.

We aren't calling everyone to tell them what happened—there are too many people to do that. No one would have any reason to know. I need to get my brave face on, walk into the school grounds, and move around as I did before: life is back to normal, right?

When someone skins their knee, they put a Band-Aid on it, pick up their bootstraps, and just move on. In my mind, why would rape be any different? When it came down to it, I was anxious about returning to school. It's one thing to skin your knee and go back to school, and quite another to be raped and return to school.

Time for school. I comfortably went about my familiar morning preparations: a shower the night before, awakened by the clanking alarm clock, popping up to wash my face, gathering my clothes, brushing my teeth, and grabbing a spot of breakfast. I didn't feel hungry but got something down, anyway.

Paul, my 18-year-old brother, drove us to school. Nothing unusual about that. We both went to the same school, and like any other day, he drove us.

I have a big brother watching out for me. How hard could this be?

As I stepped out of the car with all my stuff, I looked intentionally at everyone to observe the absence of any odd reactions. I looked the same on the outside, but I felt branded with the word 'Raped' for everyone to see. No such brand existed, but I felt like everyone could see right through me.

The hemorrhaging stopped over the weekend, but I wore a pad for security to catch any remnants. In my mind, it felt like a glaring clue that made it easy for someone to observe something was wrong. I hated walking around with it on, even before all this hoopla. At the moment, though, my sensitivity to it metered on high alert. I sat in my blood long enough, and the pad served only as a gross reminder of the treachery. I wasn't bleeding as much, but I impatiently waited for the dirty grossness to end.

At first, no odd looks or comments presented themselves. As I walked around, everything felt like it was in slow motion. I observed finite details while propelling my footsteps from one point to the next. Most of the first people I saw were just people who went to the same high school I did. In my mind, we would only recognize each other as students in the same school. We weren't necessarily friends.

As I approached the orchestra hall to drop off my violin, I saw more familiar faces. I looked for someone familiar enough to jump into a conversation with so that everything would be back to normal. As I saw people I actually knew, I said hi and then continued on my way.

There were some who returned my greeting, and others turned away and continued on with what they were doing. They were probably in a hurry, but to me, being hyper-self-conscious, it felt more like an unusual avoidance. Then there were those who never spoke to me as a general rule and who returned a friendly hello. We were all in a hurry to get to our first-period class on time, so there wasn't much time to just stand around and converse.

Why is she saying anything to me? She never says hello. And Melissa, why didn't she say hi back to me? She always says hi back to me. Do I look different? Do I smell different? Why is everyone acting so weird?

In my frantic attempt to feel normal, my perception of what was going on around me went into overdrive. Perhaps the hurried scuffle provided a necessary focus for me and everyone else to get to class on time.

Maybe once I get into the classroom with a teacher, and everything is the way it normally is, things will not seem so strange.

Truth be told, I probably felt more awkward about these simple tasks than anyone else did. To everyone else, it was just a normal day. To me, though, the events of the last week were such a massive, unpredictable roller coaster. These simple, mundane routines were suddenly more foreign than familiar. With or without a physical brand, "normal" seemed like a relative term.

I got to my first class, and I was still in one piece.

There won't be a great deal of talking. Now it's only a matter of taking notes, doing the exercises, and doing whatever is asked of me as a student. How hard can that be? I'll throw myself into the class. We'll go from there.

Safely in my seat in the classroom, I still felt as if everything happened in slow motion. My excitement wasn't so much about being in school but more about knowing where I was, what I was supposed to do, and knowing how to act. A 17-year-old goes to school—it felt like the "right" thing to do. Being at school meant I was back to my normal, awkward life instead of being in a car fearing for my life at the hands of an unknown stranger. That part felt good and as safe as one can feel in a large-city high school.

If something gets too weird, I can always go find my brother, and he'll protect me. He said he would protect me.

It came and went in a flash—I got through my first class and went through another series of discomfited moments to get to my next class. By all appearances, I navigated through the motions of making it through my first day back to school after being kidnapped and tortured. All I had to do was to get from one class to the other, do what was required in the class, and move on to the next one.

As long as I focused on the class and its agenda, everything seemed fine. Moving around and interacting with people was harder than I thought it would be. As long as the time between classes was minimal, being around other people seemed tolerable. My estranged feelings kicked into high gear, though, as soon as someone who rarely spoke to me engaged in conversation. Or when someone who usually spoke didn't. I wasn't the most popular kid in the school, and this day shouldn't have been any different from any other day. But everything seemed magnified as I over-analyzed every action or conversation.

Soon, the routine of moving from one class to the next felt deliberately comfortable, and then lunchtime rolled around. I only had 30 minutes for lunch, but what to do with all that time felt awkward.

My lunch money came from my weekly allowance. However, being a resourceful teenager, I usually ate much smaller lunches with less money, so I had a little extra cash to throw back for a rainy day or some other treat. Today was no different. I went to the snack part of the cafeteria, got an ice cream sandwich, and went on my way. Light lunches weren't a struggle for me because I didn't feel hungry. Truth be told, the thought of eating anything made me feel more nauseated than hungry.

After going through the line to get my ice cream, I found a wall to lean on while I ate it. When the ice cream was gone, I found a place to throw away my trash. Seems simple enough, but every action was deliberate and mechanical. I took my time, hoping to fill the minutes that seemed to crawl at a snail's pace. Twenty minutes left. I headed to the ladies' room while the moment presented itself.

I felt like an automaton. Once I got to the restroom, I tended to the necessary. The sight of my slightly soiled pad in my underwear repulsed me.

When is it going to stop? This blood running out of me is gross, and I can feel it when I stand up and move around. Am I just going to bleed forever? It's been a week! I hate the way it smells, and I want it to stop. Ugh! Let's just get myself tidied up and get out of here!

As I finished up in the restroom, I washed my hands for a while. The warm water felt good and refreshing. I wanted the mess to be washed away with it. Equipped with bravery, I boned up and realized I was going to have to deal with it and go on. Gross feelings, smells, and all.

I headed toward my next class, orchestra, and saw my friend Abigail.

"Hello, Abigail. How are you?"

"I'm doing okay, how about you?"

"I'm all right."

We engaged in a few moments of normal schoolhouse chatter. For the first time, being at school felt normal, and more comfortable.

I can do this!

"I heard something interesting on the radio coming to school this morning," Abigail said.

"Oh yeah?"

"They were talking about this girl who had been kidnapped and raped, and I'm pretty sure I heard them say your name. Was that you?"

BOOM! Like running full-on into a brick wall, there it was, smack dab in my face! I could feel all the color drain from my face. I hoped my eyes were not popping out of my face, but it felt like they were.

What am I supposed to say? I thought since I was a minor, that any broadcast about it would keep my name out of it. What the hell! If they really said my name, there's no hiding from that or pretending that it didn't happen. What am I supposed to say?

Deep down, I knew there was no escaping the truth.

There's nothing ordinary about the events of last week, but I obviously missed school and there has to be an explainable reason for that.

My rehearsed "Thanksgiving trip" explanation wouldn't work.

"Yes, that was me."

The words fell out of my mouth like a reflex.

"Did they really say my name?"

Now, I had to accept the events of last week as real, and I felt irreparably marred.

"Yes, I'm sure I heard your name. I figured since you were out last week, it had to be you."

While Abigail continued to ask normal questions, I felt like that invisible brand on my forehead was burning brilliantly for everyone to see.

If they really said my name on the radio, who else heard it?

Abigail was not critical, and she didn't appear judgmental about her inquiries. I couldn't run away from the exceptionally raw vulnerability of the words that fell out of my mouth for anyone else to hear. There was nowhere to hide. I couldn't fudge or make anything up at this point. In an instant, I admitted the cruel truth.

"Yes, it was me. I really prefer, though, that you please not say anything to anyone. Okay?"

My vulnerable "keep me safe" instinct kicked in as I tried to protect myself the best I could.

God, if people have heard this on the radio, there's no hiding from it. I don't want anyone going around blabbing anything to anyone. Please, please, please don't tell anyone!

I wanted the events of the past week to remain a secret so I could resume my life as if nothing happened. In my mind, the rapist who held me at knifepoint stole any sense of control from me, and I was determined to take that back. But my normal environment felt far from normal.

"Sure. No problem," Abigail said.

"I'd appreciate it."

The bell rang, and it was time to go to our next class.

Abigail and I turned to gather our things and head into the orchestra room. I felt my legs beneath me, but I wasn't certain they would propel me from one place to the next. It was like I got slammed by a wrecking ball and I had to force myself to act composed.

I got myself into the classroom, got out my violin, and prepared for orchestra, one of my favorite classes. It felt like I was pulling the violin out of its case for the very first time. I instructed my hands with my old friend as if they had never played the violin before.

Once I got my fiddle out and readied, I pilfered through my music folder to look at all the music in it. As the director announced a piece for practice, I rustled around to find the requested piece to get started.

If I focus on the music, I'll be fine. I can do this! I hope Abigail doesn't say anything to anyone. If I focus on Corelli's Christmas Concerto, I can settle back into that which is normal. It will be like the conversation never happened. I can do this!

That's it. Remember, you're the concertmaster, and you need to lead as the music sets into motion. I can play this piece almost with my eyes closed! Thank God we're starting with this one.

Before I knew it, my thoughts sailed into interpreting the marks on the page, into notes and phrases coming out of my violin. The startling hallway conversation came and went. Now, with violin in hand, I was in the middle of what I loved—orchestra.

Parts of me felt relieved, while other parts felt raw, frayed, and completely out of control. As long as I played the violin, I knew I was safe from any unexpected inquiry. I knew how to play the violin, and that familiarity kept me going. Taking part in the music provided a respite from anything else going on, like a protected letter neatly packaged in an envelope. The terraced dynamics and quaint baroque harmonies felt familiar. I savored every tone emitted from my violin and settled into harmonious resonance with the rest of the orchestra. No panic, no anticipation, just me and the music.

Completely swept away for the quickest hour of my day, soon it was time to put the violin away and head toward my next classroom adventure. The orchestral moments were simply heaven. During that hour, nothing reminded me of recent events, and no awkward conversations were required. The tenuous moments with Abigail felt distant and each of us turned our focus toward the next part of our days.

When the closing bell rang, I waited for my brother to get the car to take us home. Day one done. I survived. But not without the shock of hearing about my name being announced on the radio in the same phrase as "kidnapped and raped."

On our way home, my mind stayed focused on the news of the radio announcement. As I walked into the house, Mom's eager and loving eyes met mine. I knew she wanted assurance that her daughter's first day back at school had gone all right. Her kind gaze felt like a relief, but I didn't want her to dote over me or try to be careful. That kind of behavior qualified as being treated differently in my book.

"How was your day?"

"It was all right. Did you know they released my story on the radio?"

Mom's face appeared shocked.

"No. I was not aware of that. I believe, though, that because you're a minor, they should not be releasing any names."

"That's what I thought! Abigail told me she heard it on the radio. I can't believe it!"

"We'll check into it. There's something I need to make you aware of."

"Oh?"

"The police are holding the man they arrested, but need you to go identify him soon."

Great! I'm going to nail him! But will he be able to see me? I don't want him to see me. He said he would kill me if I told anyone. What would keep him from doing that? Oh my God! What have I done? I'm safe as long as he's behind bars. But what happens when he's no longer locked up? I hope Janice is right!

I was happy about the prospect of putting my kidnapper/rapist away. But there was no hiding from the fear echoing in my head because of his threats.

Remember, Janice said the statistics for someone actually following through on their threats are really low. But I'm still afraid. If he sees me, what will he do? He said he would kill me!

"When do we go?"

CHAPTER 12
ARREST AND CHARGES

In QUICK ORDER, it was time to identify the person being held for my reported crime. Nervous energy coursed through my body like a wild electrical storm. I felt elated at the prospect of identifying him to ensure he paid for his crime. But fear settled in about any repercussion that might befall me because I broke my promise about reporting him to the authorities.

I've heard the statistics about how many people actually follow through on their threats. It's not highly likely that anything is going to happen. But he said he would kill me! What if he can see me? The law enforcement folks assured me he couldn't see me, but what if he can? I want him to pay for his crime.

Escorted by my parents, I approached the place where I would identify my perpetrator. My body trembled, much like it did during the kidnapping.

Stop shaking! Someone will see you and think you're a freak! Deep breath! Stop shaking!

As I stood at the one-way glass, I skimmed through the line of people standing on the other side of the window.

That's him. He thought he could shave and I wouldn't recognize him. How stupid is that?

I knew who he was as soon as I saw his piercing blue eyes. No disguise could remove my deeply etched memory of those eyes. He even cut his hair.

The officer handling the line-up gave me clear verbal instructions. On the inside, my teeth rattled with fear. I saw him standing there on the other side of the glass. As each person stepped forward and turned so I could see a side view of each one, I waited impatiently for the demon to step forward. As soon as he stepped forward and turned...

"That's him."

"Are you sure?"

"Yes. That's him."

There he was. That was him. They really caught him. My wildest fears about his threat were still present, but I knew beyond the shadow of a doubt that they had arrested him. They had him. That brought with it some solace because he wasn't out roaming freely anymore. What happened from here, I wasn't so sure, but I knew they had him, and he wasn't where he could do anything to me at that very moment.

In the next immediate moments, the detectives took me into another room with my parents, where the next events unraveled.

Is there going to be a trial? Will I have to be in a room face-to-face with him? Am I going to have to testify in court? How long is this going to take? I just want it to be over! My parents can't afford an attorney. How is this going to work? He's going to be angry with me if he sees me in the courtroom; he said he would kill me if I told anyone.

It's an interesting place to be stuck in the throes of relief and such a broad horizon of unknowns. Relief and anxiety, both at the same time. Safety and complete uncertainty. Words cannot describe the flurry of thoughts and feelings. I felt pulled from one extreme to the other in a fraction of a second—as soon as my thoughts turned one way, they diverted in another. It felt much like the spiraling house in *The Wizard of Oz* or a violent tug of war.

The officer shared they found my blood in the car, but there was no evidence to prove the identified criminal raped me. They found no physical evidence that intercourse occurred—no semen, no sperm— nothing physical remained to prove he actually raped me. The rag I kept after he wiped himself off contained no evidence. They found no evidence at the gas station in Galveston. What remained was my story and a volume of my blood.

Mom and Dad reported their missing daughter. I was, in fact, gone. The cigarette butts I kept in my purse had his DNA, so there was at least proof that he was in the car with me.

Here's a twist: if my parents had reported their car was missing, the authorities would have looked for it immediately. Instead, they reported *me* missing. Because I was a teenager, and the high volume of teenage runaways, law enforcement would not start looking for me until 24 hours passed. A good bit of misfortune can occur in a 24-hour period. I was gone 23 hours, kidnapped, and raped twice. By the letter of the law, no law enforcement authority would have looked for me until after I got home.

Dad chimed in about the note I left at the gas station.

"The owner of the gas station went to clean it about an hour after you left the note. After calling the police, and upon their advice, the station owner called us. That was the first we heard you were alive, and it gave us a clue about where you were, at least at the time you wrote the note. When we got the call from Galveston, we immediately called our local police. After hearing about the note you left, our police also started looking for you."

Nice of them to look for me after I nearly bled to death in the gas station! I made it home. I must have done something right, whether the police went looking for me or not.

Caught with no physical evidence of rape, my captor plead guilty to the more substantiated aggravated kidnap charge. To press charges against him, I would have to file charges against him in the places where he raped me: Corsicana and Galveston. Because he did not rape me in my hometown, I would have to go through that process else-where. With the lack of physical evidence that he actually raped me, it would be my word against his.

This gave us a volume of information to consider. Odds were not in my favor to press any rape charges, at least from a physical evidence standpoint. With his plea to aggravated kidnap, they'd charge him with 12 years in prison. We found out he was on parole when he kidnapped and raped me and still had three years left on that. He'd be looking at 15 years in the clink, with the extra years on top of the 12.

His previous charge and subsequent parole release left him free of any record of rape or sexual abuse. In Texas, a sex offender won't get jailed without the possibility of parole unless they get charged twice with any type of sexual abuse. In my case, the pending charge meant he would, again, have no charge of rape or sexual abuse, unless I pressed charges in a city away from home. Without that, he would be eligible for parole if he behaved well in prison. With the facts on the table, if I didn't press rape charges, he would at least go back to prison.

If he went back to prison and got out, how viable would his threat be that he would come back and kill me? No one really knew, but the statistics leaned in my favor.

If he gets parole, how long will he actually be in jail? He's going to be mad at me for telling. Will that make him more determined to kill me when he gets out? Will I ever be safe if he's not in jail? If I press rape charges, I have to go out of town. How would I keep up with school if I'm not here? How long would it take? What would I tell everyone at school? If I can't go to school, would I have to make up the time?

I discussed the options with my parents, and we pulled Janice in to understand the statistical probabilities of the many options before us. After researching and weighing our options, the most logical choice for me was to let him go with the aggravated kidnap charge. He would go back to prison, and it would put another crime and arrest on his record. For a time, at least, I would be safe from his threats. They charged him with aggravated kidnap, and this part of the drama drew to a close. Or so it would seem.

The car he used when he abducted me belonged to my parents, of course. Being a teenager and old enough for a provisional license meant I drove the family car occasionally. My little sister went to one school, and my brother and I were in another school. Dad needed to go to work every day. There were times it was helpful for me to drive to help make things happen. My brother got his own car through his own savings, bartering, and church acquaintances, but I wasn't quite at a point to buy a vehicle of my own.

When I returned home after my kidnapping, the car was taken to a location for evidence collection. Once that was done, we had to decide about the car. Do we clean it up and continue to use it, or destroy it and replace it with something else? We had to have a car. My parents weren't especially affluent (they were on a pastoral counselor's salary), so getting a replacement vehicle would be a struggle for the family financially.

My parents wanted me to have a say in the decision.

"How do you feel about the car?" Dad asked. "If we keep it, how would you feel about driving it or being in the car?"

He's taken all the control from me I'm willing to give! I just want my life to get back to normal. If I tell my parents to get rid of the car, how will they afford a new one? It doesn't seem fair to put our family through that. If I say it's okay to keep the car, it's just a car. It's a means to get from one place to the next. What's the big deal with that?

"It's just a car. What's the big deal? Why get rid of a perfectly good, operating vehicle? I don't see any reason to get rid of the car."

It was important to me to prove I remained unaffected by what happened to me. I didn't understand why they would leave such a decision in my hands. Unwittingly, though, the act of them allowing me to take part in the decision proved to be a gift.

Letting me be a part of the decision put power back into my hands, allowing me to experience control in my life. From the time I got home, until this day, something in me remained determined to retake the reins of my life. My kidnap and rape were all he was going to get! My life was no longer in his hands, and he no longer had control of me or my choices. Little did I know this self-made mantra would be words for me to live by. I latched on to these ideas and made them my missive.

In my mind, the car was simply a car—a vehicle for providing transportation. That's all. From that perspective, a justification to get rid of the car seemed absurd. All cleaned up, it was a perfectly functional means of transportation. The car was not an experience; it was simply a car. That's all.

That.part was over. He was going back to prison. All that remained was my quest for all things familiar. For me, normal was school, music, and being a teenager. I threw myself into school. Without my intentional awareness, my grades improved. My grades were never bad, they just got better because that's where I threw my focus. My anchor was focusing on school instead of thinking about anything that had to do with being raped or kidnapped.

With the piano and violin, many musical activities kept me engaged. I was involved with the youth group at church, which involved different choirs. I played in our local Youth Orchestra outside of school. At school, I always involved myself with anything having to do with music. Music, music, music! That suited me just fine. I loved music, and these engagements kept me occupied and focused on things I excelled in and enjoyed.

As a teenager, being a music geek was my identity. Being driven by this passion kept me focused, and these undertakings didn't require any special social skills. Dating was for other people, not me! I had friends, and some of them dated, which was fine with me. I was comfortable in my circle of friends and didn't have to be part of any "in" crowd.

A NOTE ABOUT THE REMAINING CHAPTERS

Up until now, this story has been chronological. From this point forward, the chapters are more topical in nature. They are reflective of some of the larger points of impact this experience introduced in my life and how I navigated my way through them.

Recovery isn't always linear.

CHAPTER 13
MARKED FOR LIFE

AFTER THE KIDNAP AND RAPE, and certainly after the terror with Phillip in Robert's van at church (more on this in Chapter Nineteen), I had zero interest in dating. The idea of dating only stirred anxiety within me. I lived comfortably without the stress of having to deal with sexual consequences. Better to leave the door closed than create an opportunity for such loathsome episodes to surface.

I kept my life busy with practicing. School, orchestra, and church gave me a sense of security and normalcy. It was simpler for me, emotionally, to not be in a dating relationship with anyone. The piano and violin never tried to kiss me with their tongue, didn't smell bad, and never tried to have sex with me. I was okay with that, and we got along nicely!

When I focused on music, past events remained in the past. Those thoughts found a cupboard to rest in, hidden from view or awareness. It was easy, at first, to pretend the kidnapping and rape didn't happen. It worked as long as I kept busy. When unoccupied moments bubbled up to the surface, I scrounged for the next "right thing to do" to fill my downtime.

In some respects, living became robotic. I slept (or pretended to sleep) at night, got up the next morning, and filled my moments with my routine. It worked as long as I didn't give myself any free time to think or feel.

When my busyness fell into a pause, my mind wandered, and the not-so-savory memories flashed into my awareness. I hated those times! When they occurred, I twisted my thoughts to something completely unrelated. Television allowed me to get involved in entertainment personae. I could always pick up the violin or sit at the piano and practice—that was always a pleasant escape. As long as I focused on something other than the horror of kidnap and rape, I got by (or so it seemed).

I temporarily hid from the spewing dragon by throwing myself into other things. The ugly truth about my experience wanted out. It behaved like a caged animal, looking for a way out. My laser focus on staying busy got my familiar life back on track, but I didn't realize how much my determination created a festering wound that eventually demanded attention.

This duality fought with itself. My screaming insides and my pretended strength stirred. It took a massive amount of energy to hide the hurricane. The more I tried to pretend it wasn't there, the intensity of the war within me strengthened. The loud, raging, screaming parts were winning and demanded attention.

I painfully learned, on more than one occasion, that asking for help proved futile and only complicated relationships. This left me feeling damaged, marked for life.

Trying to find the right person to talk with, especially early on, proved to be a fruitless waste of effort. I brimmed with unanswered questions and worries. On a roller coaster of struggle to feel normal, I found myself in a cycle of shame and constant fear. I wanted to understand the vulnerable, insecure ideas that provided a steady undercurrent in my private thoughts. These thoughts occupied every unfilled moment.

My desperate need to spill the hoard of internal turmoil led me to an unsuspecting notebook. I picked up a pen, and a flood of thoughts stained the paper before me. The notebook was always close by, so I could blurt my thoughts and feelings on paper. If I didn't have my notebook in my possession, I kept it as securely hidden as possible. It would be a disaster if someone found these pages and read them.

I threw myself and my energy into my music. Piano, violin, orchestra, school, church; I tried to keep myself invisible but focused on the task at hand. When I was alone and inconspicuous, I wrote about my thoughts. It was the only safe place for me to say unsavory things about people who disappointed me—a place for me to let the crazy rattling in my head out into words on a page. It was my sacred venting place.

My inner dialog screamed to make sense of everything. I knew that one day, it might be helpful to have the details of what happened to me. So, I wrote as much as I could remember, as fast and as furiously as I could. This proved to be the birth of my personal journal.

Writing became my refuge. My thoughts boiled over from mind to paper. I used writing to bleed the festering, crazy-feeling thoughts from my insides to some external source. The only ears that could apparently hear me were the lines on the paper. When I wrote the words, the page didn't throw them back at me. It didn't refute any fact or idea I created through words. I found a certain sanctuary in writing, screaming, cursing, or jotting down whatever idea or thought passed through my mind.

As a teenager, I had my share of disdain for having to get my chores done to meet expectations at home. I was not always compliant in my efforts to meet those expectations, which created a breeding ground for familial drama. This was often a topic of discussion in my journal.

Three to four months after the rape, on a typical day returning home from school, a particular familial war commenced, which would forever impact the sacred coping space that was my journal.

"Alexis! Get in here right now! We don't ask that much of you, but as long as you live here, you are going to complete the chores you've agreed to and do them right!"

Put out and exasperated by Mom's demand, I went into the kitchen, where Mom opened the silverware drawer and other cabinets where pots and pans lived.

"How am I supposed to prepare a meal if there's nothing for me to cook with?"

A sinking feeling consumed my gut as I realized the dishes from the night before sat patiently in the draining rack, waiting to be dried.

"You can use these dishes here." I motioned toward the patiently waiting dishes.

"Your responsibility this week is to wash and dry the dishes. Why are these dishes still here in the dish rack?"

"Can't you just use these? They are clean. What's the big deal?"

"You're missing the point! We don't leave dishes out overnight for someone to pilfer through the next day. We wash and dry the dishes and put them away so that they are ready to use when someone needs them."

Mom sounded like she was teaching me how to do the dishes for the first time. Angrily, I grabbed a handful of silverware and started slapping them into the drawer Mom had so conveniently opened. Tossing the knives in their rightful place, demonstratively getting the spoons in their cubbyhole in the drawer, until my words came flying back at me through Mom's sarcastic voice (along with some additional dish guidance).

"'My Mother is such a bitch and doesn't understand anything about me!' And you can handle our things with respect and place things in the drawer without throwing them."

I mechanically grabbed the next bunch of silverware and robotically placed each fork, one at a time, in its rightful place. I treated them with the care of a fragile piece of antique glass. Mom stood there and watched my enraged antics as I handled each small piece of silverware and escorted it to its rightful place. *"My Mother is such a bitch and doesn't understand anything about me!"* The very words I'd written in my sacred journal echoed in my head from our angry conversation.

Devastated, while I attended to my chores under Mom's supervision, I desperately clung to the head of the pin I was balancing upon.

Is nothing about me sacred? My journal is my private space! I can't believe she read my journal! She had to have read that in my journal! Those are my words! Nothing is safe! I can't talk to people; I can't write my thoughts down — nothing is sacred. What is wrong with me? Why can't I have any privacy? I can't believe this!

My thoughts unraveled in my head while I seethed with rage at my new awareness. That which I thought was sacredly and safely private was neither private nor sacred. The ensuing personal betrayal left me feeling all alone, misunderstood, and isolated. I felt like a freak! My own mother betrayed me and revealed the one thing that was helping me keep my sanity and it was forever out of my hands.

Journaling provided some relief (until someone discovered my turmoil and quoted it to me out of context). My angry parts came out on paper in a flood of unadulterated fury. It felt safe to spill my irrational thoughts. Words on paper didn't react like other people did.

I wanted to keep my closest relationships with friends on stable ground. My true thoughts and feelings with friends had to be doled out in small quantities, and even then, some ideas were better left unsaid. The sacred paper and the safety of my journal were my refuge. With pen in hand, I wrote with abandon about my inner turmoil — without any filters.

My frustration with Mom boiled. I felt free to write the hateful expressions any teenage daughter has in the confines of my notebook. I wrote about my curiosity about experimenting with marijuana or other drugs that might take away the intensity of my raging insides. In fits of anger and frustration, I could contemplate getting off the carousel of life and ending it all. The paper didn't react. I could say anything about anyone and write about topics that might otherwise prove to be uncomfortable conversations with peers. That all came to a screeching halt when Mom quoted my written rantings.

In short order, after the experience, the emotional wounds from my experience crept into my sleep. In my mechanical modus operandi, I felt unsafe to sleep. When my head found a pillow and sleep ensued, my dreams took me to places of danger and fear. I didn't want to see those things in my sleep. I didn't want to feel them. If sleep felt unsafe, the logical step seemed to dictate only sleeping when it was absolutely necessary.

At bedtime, I lay in my bed and closed my eyes. *I'm going to lie here with my eyes closed and pretend to sleep. I'll think about music, hanging out with friends, school shenanigans, church, or orchestra.* My mountain of good intentions eventually met a relaxed enough state that I drifted off and slept. As soon as I realized my dreams were violent or scary, I aroused myself and tried the process over again.

Sometimes, I read or picked up a coloring book. It seemed foolish, but it was relaxing for me to color, and I enjoyed doing it. I'd color while everyone else in the house remained in slumber. It was important to me not to disturb anyone. I was a "big girl." What happened to me was in the past, and it was over.

I can do this. Even now, I refuse to give him or that horrible experience any more time. I've given it enough. There's no need to dwell on things.

Fortunately, my bedroom was away from everyone else's. I could color, and no one was the wiser. It got me through the night hours, but I still felt lonely. I wished for hours to hurry forward toward morning. Then, when morning arrived, I quickly prepared for another day, and my agenda consumed my attention.

As other family members stirred and awakened to begin their days, they were completely unaware of my long nights of avoiding sleep. By all appearances, everything seemed to hum along in its usual fashion.

I drove myself wherever I needed to go (school, church, or whatever). Familiar activities brought me comfort. With other people around, my energy turned toward bravery and pretending everything was okay. In those moments, my mind occupied itself with something other than horrible thoughts or memories.

Along with the sleep drama, those dreaded, awful days when I had my period crashed my well-intentioned avoidance. I hated it when I bled. The oozy feeling of the blood dripping out of my body only reminded me of the hemorrhaging I experienced during the rape. I hated the way it made me smell. My belly ached with cramps, and I wanted to rip what was causing all the fuss out of my body. It felt messy and gross and reminded me of the terror I diligently worked to forget. It reminded me of the hours I sat in my blood, unable to do anything about it. All I could do was sit there and bleed. My normal menstrual cycle made me want to vomit.

I tried to trick my mind into believing I wasn't really bleeding. When I went to the bathroom and saw it, though, it ruined my fairy tale. I did what I had to do to take care of myself and promptly returned to other distracting topics. When memories forced themselves to the surface, I did what I felt I had to do to survive. I abhorred those recollections and flashes of ugliness that came into my consciousness. Denial 101! If I pretended my period wasn't really happening, I could keep my mind on other, more pleasant things. That denial, though, only goes so far. I yearned for the days when my cycle stopped. It paused those reminders until the next cycle came around, and then I was faced with it yet again.

This all seemed like a manageable approach until one time a few days of bleeding turned into a week, and then beyond a week, and then it was two weeks. Something had to be wrong.

What did he do to me? Why won't the bleeding stop? This is ghastly! Dammit! What is wrong with me? Oh, God, I'm going to have to tell Mom so I can get to the doctor. This isn't normal; something is obviously wrong.

The thought of telling my mom terrified me. The horror of having to admit something was wrong and knowing I needed help made me feel weak and exposed. How long was I going to keep bleeding? I'd rather drink castor oil than tell my mom about my embarrassing plight. I felt like a failure because I needed help—the worst viable solution.

I didn't like the way Mom tried to "baby" me when I asked for help. I was hell-bent on pretending that nothing was wrong, no matter how much I needed or wanted help.

In my frantic state, I worked up the courage to tell Mom, and soon enough, we had an appointment with the doctor. I didn't want to admit defeat by seeking help elsewhere. The defeat compounded when the nurse asked me to take off my clothes and put on a little gown so that it opened in the front.

Is my only lot in life to make myself naked in front of others? Do I always have to take my clothes off? It's the doctor's office; I guess I better do what they ask me to do.

My vulnerable heart pounded. The situation repulsed me.

If I take all my clothes off, I'm going to bleed on the table I have to sit on. Aaaaaaaah! I hate this so much!

Soon after I got situated on the exam table, I felt blood dripping out of me onto the protective paper covering. I wanted to throw up. This was torture!

I hope I don't have to wait very long. It's cold in here, and I'm a mess. Please hurry, please hurry, please hurry!

It seemed like it took forever for the doctor to come into the room. Eventually, I heard the familiar knock on the door and the rustling of paper, and the door opened. With my file in hand, the doctor stepped in with his familiar little grin on his face, and the pleasantries of "hellos" and "how are yous" started. I put on my best award-winning performance, pretending to be all right and being nice, just like I was supposed to.

Before long, the conversation turned to what brought me to the doctor's office, and now I had to tell him about my vagina bleeding abnormally. He asked me to lie back on the table, put my feet in the stirrups, and expose the most personal and defenseless part of me for all to see. I felt vulnerable and out of control. My body betrayed me. I wanted to run and hide. I anxiously wanted to cover up, get dressed, and leave.

Here we go again. He's going to stick things into me, and I know I'm a bloody mess. Is my only purpose on this earth to make my vagina available so people can put stuff into me? This sucks! If this is what I have to look forward to, what is so great about being alive?

My thoughts spiraled in despair. I wanted everything to make sense, and most of all, I wanted the torture to be over. No more!

For whatever reason, it seemed I was on a perpetual period, and the next steps were to stop it. My doctor prescribed birth control pills to help regulate my periods so I wouldn't bleed for weeks at a time. Rationalizing the steps in this process felt gross and horrible. I felt like a freak! It seemed everything came back to my vagina and someone getting into it or trying to control the messy bleeding.

I was miserable, but again, I rallied up some courage to make an appearance of having it all together so I could carry on with my life as if nothing had happened. In short order, after taking the birth control pills, the bleeding stopped, and over the months, things seemed to regulate a little better.

With my wretched period under control, having to deal with my periods became more manageable. However, nightmares plagued me. When they were regular, I stayed up as much as possible, not letting myself drift off too deep. Awake and actively involved in doing things, I purposefully managed through the moments of each day. Memories, thoughts, and feelings were all kept at bay, and I seemed to function with the appearance of a common routine.

The birth control pills made sure I was in sync, but they did nothing for the disgusting feelings I got every time the "blanks" came up in the pill pack. I came up with a process to manage the period process, and the rest of the time, I engaged my big imagination and did what I could to pretend it wasn't happening.

Just when I found the right rhythm, and everything seemed doable, tired as I was from time to time, something was still wrong with my vagina. It was itchy and burned, with really gross, clumpy white stuff coming out. My personals smelled horrible! I hated the way I smelled but continued to pretend everything was all right. I told myself I was a freak and over-reacting.

My desire to eat was nonexistent. At school, it was easy to pretend to have lunch but not really eat anything. When I was at home, though, in order to pretend everything was okay when the family sat down for dinner, I had to eat. I ate when I had to and wasn't so concerned with eating when there were no appearances that had to be kept. I didn't feel hungry, so I didn't eat. If I felt hungry, I'd eat a little, but the whole eating thing became less and less of a priority.

I didn't mind drinking water, cokes, or whatever as long as I wasn't on my period. During my period, though, I cut back on my fluid intake in order to limit the need to go to the bathroom any extra during that time of the month. Going to the bathroom and seeing my blood, feeling it trickle out, was gross. On the one hand, I knew I had to go to the bathroom to change my pad periodically, but there was no point in dealing with that any more than necessary.

I used pads for my period a long time after I was raped. That's how

Mom trained me to deal with the mess growing up. However, as high school teens will be teens, and young ladies will be young ladies, the conversation of tampons arose from time to time. The topic made my insides turn inside out, but on one occasion, I bravely took part as if nothing about it revolted me.

In my conversation with the other girls, I learned that with a tampon, there was no bloody mess to sit in. The prospect of not feeling blood dripping out of me was inviting! One less reminder to deal with!

In one of my braver moments, I struck up a conversation with Mom about tampons, and she agreed to let me try them. The idea of stuffing something up my vagina grossed me out, but the idea of not having to sit in my blood appealed to me more. Tampons revolutionized the whole monthly torture and made things much more bearable.

The bleeding part was under some control, but the itchy, red, burning part did not go away on its own. When I wasn't on my period, my underwear had a nasty discharge that smelled horrid. When I wiped myself, white, chunky, yucky stuff came out. At one point, it was a little runny and looked slightly greenish.

As much as I tried to ignore it, I knew something wasn't right. I had to get to the doctor, yet again, to figure out what was going on. Like taking bitter medicine, I stuffed my bravery and "I can do this by myself" attitude aside. Backed into a corner, and not knowing what was going on, I asked Mom to get me a doctor's appointment so I could find out what was going on.

Again, I found myself in the doctor's office, being asked to take off my clothes and place the funny little gown on so that it opened in the front. I felt violated. It seemed every time I went to the doctor, I had to take my clothes off and make the most personal part of me accessible for examination. Nothing about that felt normal. I hated it! I felt like these exposures were my destiny in life—to make my vagina accessible, and it was just a thing for poking and prodding.

Yuck! Why did I have to have a vagina?!

I assumed the position in the stirrups, and the whole mashing and prodding in my vagina started once again. While I lay there, I told myself it wouldn't last forever and that it would be over soon.

As I sat back up on the exam table, I covered myself up with the extra sheet. I must have visibly become rather thin, as when I got upright, Doc asked me if I was becoming anorexic. I didn't know what anorexic was, but to be brave and portray a powerful image of ordinary, I assured him I didn't think so.

"I'm concerned about your weight. You need to be careful about becoming too thin."

Then, the real bombshell fell.

"You have a yeast infection. I'm going to prescribe some cream for you. You will need to dispense the cream into your vagina for the next couple of weeks."

The thought of having to stick something creamy into my vagina revolted me beyond measure. But, if I had to do it to get things back to normal (whatever that was), then I resolved to accept what I had to do. I was getting well-rehearsed at pretending, and this was no exception.

I got through dispensing my first dose of the stuff, but I didn't understand that as the creamy medicine melted, it would ooze out of me. It was just like it felt when I was bleeding.

God! I'm such a freak! Am I going to have to mess with my vagina forever?! How can I put all this behind me if I always have to mess with this stuff?"

My relationship with my body resembled opposing magnets arguing for the strongest repulsion. I resorted to doing what I had to do to get by, tending to the ugly mess between my legs and keeping myself otherwise occupied in the meantime.

This can't last forever. This is only temporary.

Like a person running from a swarm of bees, I felt chaotically crazy on the inside. Once again, I absorbed myself in school and in my musical affairs. Being engrossed in those things made the world seem as livable a place as possible, and I could do that one day at a time.

At every sunset, when it was time for sleep, I asked for peaceful sleep without nightmares. At every sunrise and the dawn of a new day, I instructed myself with the agenda of events of the current day: school, practicing, lessons, church, rehearsals, and so on. There were, of course, those times when I hung out with a friend and got out of the house for something other than my routine activities. As a teenager, I tried to be away from home as much as possible. While it all seemed manageable on the outside, wild chaos stirred on the inside.

Months passed, and I existed as I needed to. I had a few close friends who treated me like nothing happened. That made the chaos inside bearable, but it didn't obliterate it. At least with this handful of friends, I felt comfortable. Even in that comfort, though, I remained aware of my fervent pretense that everything was normal. I figured if I pretended long enough, it would seem natural. The embarrassing, dirty, gross feelings would go away, and the false sense of being okay, connected, and put together would eventually feel real.

In those rare moments when I allowed myself to feel my authentic feelings and not pretend, the chaos inside raged like a typhoon. It didn't take long, in those moments of awareness, for me to feel overwhelmed and scared. It was too big for me to conquer on my own. I spiraled, raged, and screamed on the inside while I tried to portray an exterior of "all is well with the world" and "I'm okay—nothing can hurt me."

Once they arrested him, and I knew he was behind bars, I looked over my shoulder less. The looking I did after that was more geared toward being sure I didn't exhibit any signs of distress. The wild stirrings I felt on the inside would be scary for anyone who didn't understand them or where they were coming from. I felt like everyone could see rape written all over me. It was my scarlet letter. I didn't want anyone to know, and I went to extremes to be sure there were no obvious signs for people to observe.

At a moment's notice, if I smelled something that reminded me of the experience, it was like I was right back in the car fighting for my life. My appetite shrank immensely. I never felt hungry. I just had no interest in food or eating. People might not see it on the outside, but I felt like it marked me for life.

CHAPTER 14
ASKING FOR HELP

My involvement in music activities at school made my participation in church music a simple decision. I played the piano well enough to accompany the youth choir at our family church—a large Methodist institution in the heart of downtown Fort Worth.

After completing the litigious line-up activities, the MYF teens had a talent show brewing. Playing the piano was my identity, and I loved doing that. Because I played well, and people enjoyed my playing, I signed up to take part in the show—an event right up my alley.

I selected an appropriate piece to play (one of my own compositions), and after weeks of practice and preparation, the time for the performance was upon me. The talent show was my first solo performance since the rape and kidnap.

I always had natural performance jitters, especially in a solo capacity. But this time felt different. These nerves came filled with angst and a large dose of panic about being on a stage, alone with an audience with nothing to do but purvey performers.

For months after the ordeal, I felt secretly branded: raped, damaged goods, shameful, and dirty. With this pending performance, all these self-perceptions felt exaggerated. I felt exposed and trapped—a freaky raped teenager who could play the piano a little.

The location of the talent show was also the scene of my abduction. It stood to reason that a good number of the folks watching also knew about my sordid recent past. I struggled to put that in perspective. How do I pretend the wart isn't there and just go on as if nothing happened? I felt transparent, and what seemed second nature to me was now my enemy: playing the piano.

I felt like I needed to be strong and handle things on my own. I wanted the outside world to see me as strong as if nothing ever happened. The rapist took 23 grueling and horrific hours of my life; that's all I wanted him to have. It seemed like the best use of energy to press forward and try to put all the pieces back in place to get back to normal.

The prospect of putting myself in front of people crumbled my strong will like a house of cards. I didn't have any instructions about how to put the house back together again. How was I supposed to step up to the piano and play like I knew I could while everyone watched me? I felt overwhelmed and exposed!

In this hour of internal drama, I turned to a place for help that seemed the safest, my youth minister. He always made sure to let us know we could go to him for anything.

If I go to Marvin, perhaps we can pray together, and I can find the strength to do what I'm about to do. They always talk about how we should come to them for "anything." We're always encouraged to ask for support and guidance. I don't think I can do this by myself. I don't know how! Maybe Marvin can help me.

As I traversed the cold, gothic church hallways, trying to locate someone to talk to, I tried to pull together a dialog that made sense. I wanted to ask for help, but I also wanted to appear okay, together, and unshaken. I didn't want anyone to see the chaotic horror stirring inside the core of my being. The rape was over. This was just another day and another opportunity to play the piano—something I loved more than anything in the world. Deep in thought, I saw Marvin walking toward me.

"Hello Alexis. How's it going?"

"Hi. Do you have a minute?"

Asking for help was out of my wheelhouse, so I felt unsure about the looming conversation. My raging discomfort about the talent show was every bit as intense as sitting in a car at knifepoint. Different, but just as intense.

"Sure. What's up?"

"Perhaps we could go into the parlor for a moment."

I opened the heavy wooden door near the talent show backstage area and ushered Marvin into a room where we could speak privately. I didn't want anyone else to overhear our conversation in passing.

My ribs rattled with every beating pulse of my heart. As we found a comfortable chair to sit in, the foreign reality of speaking words and asking for help slammed into my consciousness.

"I'm so freaked out! I'm always a little nervous about performing, but it seems out of control. Would you pray with me?"

"Why do you need me to pray?"

"I play the piano all the time. I know I can do this, but I'm frightened. Would you please pray with me?"

"Just pray for yourself. You don't need me. You can pray by yourself."

Marvin grasped my trembling hands as if to support me, stood up, and left the room.

I sat there for a moment in complete shock. I reached out to a person I was told would help. He ignored my desperate plea for help, and he made it seem like taking a moment to pray with me was some gargantuan imposition.

Why wouldn't he pray with me? When I told him about my nerves, he couldn't have cared less. He wasn't even willing to say a prayer? He's a preacher! What am I supposed to do? I must be such a freak. Even the youth minister doesn't want to have anything to do with me.

Like a natural reflex, a recent conversation with my captor resurfaced.

"What do you think about your God now?"

His question echoed in my memory over and over.

I guess now, after being raped, there is no "God" to rely on. How dare He abandon me like this. I thought He was supposed to be a loving and caring God. My youth minister won't even sit with me to pray for a moment. Is there something wrong with me? Why did he run away so quickly? I just wanted a little support!

Deep in my heart, I quickly figured out how negative it was to ask for help. And when people say they are there to help, they don't really mean it. I learned that when I'm scared out of my wits, all I can do is buck up and muster up some courage on my own. I needed to calm my nerves enough to step out on stage and play the piano.

Suck it up!

I closed my eyes, tried to still my shaking body, and took a deep breath. I had to find the courage on my own and just do it! Asking for help seemed an obviously shameful notion, and I swallowed my feelings, pretending they didn't exist. I forced myself to think about something completely silly: ice cream dripping from someone's nose or popping balloons with pins.

I told myself to breathe, to quiet myself, and to forget my fear. Before I knew it, I sat in the large fellowship hall at the grand piano on the wooden stage floor. I was front and center, and the rich burgundy curtain drew open, and I started playing. At first, it was a familiar feeling I could immerse myself in. As I played, though, my awareness crystallized that I was on stage and people were watching me. In the pit of my stomach, the raging anxiety I fought so hard to swallow welled up like a fountain of untamed water.

While I played my composition, I told myself that fear was not useful. The best tool I had at this moment was to stuff the fear away on a shelf somewhere, turn, and walk away—all while keeping the performance going. The process proved more than my body could process all at once, and my body visibly shook. I played the piano for people while my body felt like an uncontrollable bundle of energy writhing back and forth like a cut electrical line.

I made it through the piano piece. The performance finished, people clapped, and I graciously took a bow. By all perceptions, it was a successful performance. Unknowingly, I taught myself how to swallow my feelings, which turned into a destructive pattern. It worked in the short term, but I had no idea how that fed a festering wound.

~

Rehearsals came and went. Days of school happened, weekends, and months. I never spoke about anything that happened. Figuring out all the feelings and questions that raced through my heart and mind was an impossible puzzle. I kept an eye open for any safe opportunity to tell someone and vent my madness. All I wanted was some reassurance about the torrent of thoughts cycling feverishly in unoccupied moments. I wanted someone outside of me to understand the relentless fury of self-flogging and crazy ramblings. My journal was no longer a safe option.

As my innards boiled, a faint yet promising memory re-surfaced. I remembered being in the room with my family at the hospital while I regurgitated the details of my experience. As the police wound down all their questions, Jenny handed me her personal card. A card for the Rape Crisis Center. She told me to call if I ever needed anything.

I didn't understand the purpose of the offer, but I stashed the information in a safe place for future use. The card was like a holding hand to me. It was there for me to see and remember. My pride and strength were much too impenetrable to have to call someone else to talk, but there was comfort in knowing there was an offer there, should I ever need it.

I remembered Jenny explaining that Rape Crisis was a place that came complete with an available person to talk to. I remembered her saying something about providing services to people who have experienced rape. There were groups and people to talk to, and there was a number I could call.

The idea of having to admit the inferno raging inside to someone else humiliated me. I was strong. I lived through it and was back at school, back at church, and back with my friends. What else could be wrong? Shame settled in as I realized I couldn't handle everything on my own, especially now that my private notebook was no longer private.

I felt like a failure. If the God they taught me about wasn't real, there was no use in seeking comfort. What kind of solace was that? A loving God who was willing for "one of His own" to be raped. What generous and kind love is that? Really?

Now, 18 years old and nearly a year after being kidnapped and raped, I seriously considered calling the number on that card.

If I call this place and decide to take part in one of their groups, I'd have to tell my parents about that. I'd be admitting that I wasn't strong, that I couldn't handle it, and that I needed help. If I actually told someone about what happened to me, what kind of support would I get? When I reached out to someone at church, he threw it back into my face, "Handle it yourself." What is so incredibly wrong with me? I can't seem to calm the storm raging inside. Something must really be wrong with me. Besides that, if I actually sign up for a group, either someone will have to take me there, or I'll have to beg to get my parents to let me drive myself. Will Mom and Dad have to go with me? I can't say all of this stuff in front of them!

My dad, being a pastoral counselor, imparted bits of life knowledge to me. Asking for help was part of that. This wisdom seemed logical as far as conceptual thought goes. At this point in my process, those were only conceptual thoughts. I didn't understand what it meant to own this wisdom deep down inside my soul. At least conceptually, I had an idea that help was available somewhere. Finding the right help, though, was not as easy as just asking people I thought I could rely upon.

I battled my internal demons for months (unsuccessfully). Finally, in desperation, I appealed to Dad and his counselor persona to hedge a conversation about the Rape Crisis Center.

I won't just come right out and say it. But maybe I can tell him I've been thinking about it and just get a feel for how he's going to respond to that. It's probably better for me not to reveal the actual truth of what's going on inside me. I don't want to scare Dad off! If he shows me some kind of support, though, maybe I can be brave and at least make a phone call.

The perfect opportunity presented itself.

"Hey, Dad. Do you remember when we were talking to the police, Jenny told me about the Rape Crisis program?"

"Yes."

"I've been thinking about that. I was wondering what you thought about it. Do you know anything about it?"

"No, but I think it is probably a good place for people to talk about things."

"I've been thinking about calling them."

"If it's something you want to do, call them. It doesn't hurt to get some more information about it."

A wave of relief enveloped me. Dad didn't pry with nosy questions or express in any way that he was overly concerned. I was safe. I felt relieved that I didn't have to justify why I was interested in calling. He simply answered my question and replied to my curiosity. That's all. That was it. I didn't have to uncover any of the ugliness going on inside of me. Much to my surprise, I simply asked a question and got a response that didn't make me want to run and hide.

I had the encouragement I needed to make that call. Finding as private a place as I could, without siblings or parents around, I found my sweaty, nervous hands dialing the number on the card I hung on to like a good friend. My heart pounded with anxious anticipation as I waited for someone on the other end of the phone to answer.

What am I going to say? How should I start this conversation with a complete stranger?

"Rape Crisis Center."

I gulped a big gulp and quietly, so no one else in the house could hear me, started the brave albeit awkward conversation.

"I'm interested in speaking with someone about the groups that are available."

There it was. I was actually getting information about something someone offered to me. I didn't know what to expect, and I didn't know what to ask or what to say, but the words found their way from my head to my mouth, and there I was, asking for information.

Without judgment or scorn, I found it as comfortable as it could be to gather information about the availability of groups at the center. I got information about what to expect: how large the groups are, how they take place, what the cost for the groups would be, and the day and time for the groups. They gave me the name of the group facilitator, Sherry, and a phone number to contact her.

Armed with information but not yet ready to commit to anything, I had a new volume of details to mull over and think about. The group varied in size because the people attending were free to come and go as they liked. There was no commitment to go for a specified number of weeks. They took place on Monday nights at 7 p.m., and they usually ran about an hour and a half. There was no cost for attending the group, so there was no concern about that if I took part in them. Monday was a good day, as it did not conflict with any piano or violin lessons, and there were no conflicts with the church or Youth Orchestra. I also found out it was something I could take part in myself. No parents required! Everything would work.

Now I had to decide if this was something I was going to do. If I took the plunge, I'd have to get my parents' permission. I knew Dad wouldn't have a problem with it, but I wasn't so sure about Mom, especially after she went nosing around in my journal. After thinking about it for several days, I called Sherry to get more information.

I wanted to make that call privately (without my parents around), so I made the call during my lunch period at school. Sherry let me know the group was freeform in nature and confirmed all the info I got from the center. When people showed up, they introduced themselves so that everyone had a name to use. She helped me understand I could say as much or as little as I felt comfortable with. There were no requirements to say anything. There was no agenda or prescription for anything I was required to share. Sherry eased my fears about having to tell people what happened to me. I could say as little or as much as I wanted to about that.

With my mind at ease about the whole idea, I thought I'd give it a go. Now came the hard part—asking my parents' permission to attend. Armed with information and Dad's support on the topic, I checked with him first to get his reaction before broaching the topic with Mom. With all the manner of any trained counselor, Dad responded favorably and supportively.

Half of the parental unit was on board. Now, I had to muster up the courage to have the conversation with Mom.

"I talked with Dad about attending a support group at the Rape Crisis Center, and he's okay with me going. They meet on Monday evenings, there's no cost, and there's no commitment for me to attend a specified length of time. They meet downtown on Lake Street. Would it be okay for me to go try it out?"

"Would we need to take you? Or is it something you can do by yourself?"

"I can just go by myself. It's really not intended to be something other family members take part in."

I was relieved that my parents didn't have to be there. I didn't want them to hear all the wild thoughts that were really going on in my heart.

Much to my surprise, and without interference, Mom agreed to allow me to take part in it. While I was glad for the support, a part of me took it with a grain of salt, almost in disbelief, after the betrayal I felt when my journal words came back at me unsolicited.

I had my parents' permission. Now I had to let Sherry know I was interested in coming. The other phone calls seemed easy compared to this one. I didn't have to share anything about myself; I was only gathering information. This phone call, though, would be quite another thing.

Mom and Dad left my brother and me in charge of looking after my little sister from time to time when they attended church functions that didn't involve us kids. This seemed like the best time to make the call. When the planets aligned, I went to my parents' bedroom to use the phone where no one else would bother me.

Wrestling the wad of nerves in the pit of my stomach, I called Sherry once again to get signed up. The phone rang, and Sherry's inviting, non-threatening voice answered. Now, I had to plan a coherent string of words and hope that I could carry on from there.

"My name is Alexis. I was raped, and…"

Oh my God! This is real. The hole in the pit of my stomach has no bottom. I can't believe I just said those words out loud to someone else. A complete stranger!

An uncontrollable well of tears boiled up from an abyss somewhere, and I thought I would never stop crying. How is it that a human being can cry so many tears? Where did it all come from? Once I gathered my snotty, crying self, I was ready to find out what my options were.

Sherry gently and supportively helped me discover there were, in fact, other people in this world who had similar experiences. The group provided a time and place for those to gather, to share, and to learn. The idea of being in a room filled with other women who also experienced rape or some other form of sexual abuse felt amazingly supportive, even though I felt wretchedly nervous about being there in person.

The person on the other end of the phone helped me feel I was not alone and that there was a place to go for help. At that moment, I didn't know what "help" really meant, or where that would take me. The idea of being in a room with someone who might have an inkling of an idea about the drama going on inside proved to be an anchor of immediate relief.

My second quest for help began. The adventure of actually going to the group was at hand. I didn't know what to expect. I knew I didn't want to be labeled as "crazy," so I didn't dare mention anything about this to my friends. For a long time, only my parents knew about it.

While I drove myself there, that familiar, uncontrollable shaking I felt during the rape settled in. Nervously, I drove to the small building on Lake Street downtown. It was evening, I was by myself, and I drove to a place I had never been before. I had no reference for what I was about to experience. I felt timid, vulnerable, and afraid.

In all my trepidation, I dug deep to find my pretend courage. Keeping a certain exterior finish visible to the outside world remained my goal. I made it there, parked the car, and walked into the little building on Lake Street. Upon entering the building, I walked up the stairs, the only place to go. When I reached the top of the stairs, I looked around for some guidance for where to go next. No one was visible, but I could hear voices. I walked toward the voices. Easily, I found the room where people were gathering and stepped inside.

"I'm here for the support group."

Those were mighty big words to muster up and communicate in an unknown place, to an unknown person, and with other unknown people in the room.

"Are you Alexis? I'm Sherry. We talked on the phone. You're in the right place."

Sherry reached out her hand to shake mine.

"Welcome here. Before we get started, I need you to fill out some paperwork."

Sherry walked with me to a desk at the end of the hall, where she picked up a clipboard with all the papers.

"You can sit here and fill these out. I'll be back in a moment."

I settled into a chair by the desk where the clipboard sat waiting and filled in the blanks. All the vital statistics—my name, address, phone, and contact information. The form asked for some general information about my purpose for coming to take part in the group. The thought of having to write the words that I so shockingly spoke just days before felt intimidating. Knowing I was making a paper record felt vulnerable, but I found writing it much easier than having to say the words out loud.

After a few moments, Sherry returned and gathered the completed forms I was finishing up.

"Come with me. We'll go join the others."

Sherry ushered me back into the room where I was before.

"You can take a seat anywhere. We'll get started in a few minutes."

Sherry made me feel at ease, even though I felt like a stranger in a strange land, timid and unsure. I had no idea what to expect.

I walked into the circle of chairs where other women were gathering. I didn't recognize anyone, but I knew they were all there for a similar purpose: to talk about an evil experience that was big, scary, and ugly to talk about. As unfamiliar as it all felt, there was a foreign relief that went along with being in a room with other people who understood what it felt like to say, "I—was—raped."

I picked a chair where no one sat on either side of me and clung to the chair as if it would somehow keep me safe. That safety quickly fell away as other people arrived. Bubbles of anxiety effervesced on the surface.

These people are all here for the same reason. I don't have to talk. Sherry told me I would not have to talk. I'll be okay. I can just watch and see how things work. There's no need for me to talk.

As the group got started, Sherry introduced me by my first name, and everyone else introduced themselves without saying the "r" word.

Even then, the choice to speak remained mine. Sitting and listening worked well for me at this point. That slight gesture, that choice to speak or not speak, provided immense relief to my anxiety about being there. I got a sense of what this was all about before I had to make words come out of my mouth.

There I was, in a room full of other people. The thoughts and ideas coming out of their mouths were snippets of my own exact experiences and feelings. Each story was different, but the people sharing seemed to have the same stirrings. Their self-talk and doubt, fears, chaos, and anger sounded completely familiar to me. I wasn't alone. For the first time, I felt understood, and I didn't feel like I had to pretend. I wasn't ready to talk, but it seemed like this was a safe place for me to feel the things I felt. People were actually talking about it and living to tell about it.

I didn't say a word, but I felt like someone might truly understand the annoying buzz going on in my head. The group ended and Sherry gave us a phone number to call anytime we wanted. I tucked the phone number in my purse and walked away, feeling ever so slightly that I was not alone. Driving home, I felt uneasy, but replayed the dialog of the few people that were brave enough to share the chaos rambling in their heads.

As I listened and observed, I heard others actually speak about the wild thoughts spinning around in their heads. They actually said this stuff out loud. Their spoken thoughts and ideas met without criticism or belittlement. Some women cried, some yelled, and some giggled. Every emotion, thought, or idea came out without recourse. No one felt pressure, inept, or incapable. I viewed these speaking women as amazingly brave.

In a few weeks, I saw supportive sharing along with helpful, constructive dialog. I finally felt like it was okay to share what happened to me. I was unsure and untrusting, given my prior attempts to share my insides with friends or those I thought I could go to. It seemed, though, that I could speak without being made to feel like I was a freak. I still felt like I had to present an exterior of bravery and strength, but what came out of my mouth felt received with care.

In a matter of moments, words spilled out. I heard myself speaking about the horrific details of my experience. It didn't yet feel as though I was the person the story was about, but the facts came spilling out.

Astonishingly, the other women in the group listened and seemed to understand the wicked chaos I described. What came back from the rest of the group felt supportive, and no one made any indicative gesture or comment that led me to think anyone thought I was crazy. As I slowly shared, I learned that feeling damaged, ashamed, and broken were all common feelings for the other women in the group. They expressed similar feelings on their own journey. For the first time, I shared a thought or idea, no matter how fearful I felt or how crazy it seemed, and in this forum, I felt supported and understood.

This was a good start. I didn't know at the time how big of a start it was. It was nice to have somewhere to go, to be understood, and to say what I was feeling without criticism or judgment.

Between the nightmares and the rapist's release from jail, two and a half years after being raped, I still had a mountain of inner turmoil. I wasn't getting good sleep because every time I fell asleep, violent dramas played on the canvas of my dreams. I wanted more than anything for all that to be over! The more I pretended everything was okay, the more my fears and anxieties surfaced. It felt like trying to keep water from coming out of a firehose.

Music was my refuge, but when a public audience was involved, my nerves got the best of me. When I played the piano, my legs shook so much that it was hard to keep my foot on the pedal. My hands trembled so much that it was hard to keep them on the right notes, and my memory sometimes failed me. I always pushed through as if nothing was going on, but it was getting to be more than I could control. The last thing I wanted was to make a fool of myself in front of a listening and observant audience.

It was more troublesome than I wanted to admit, and something had to be done.

Why am I so afraid of performing? I know this music inside and out, like the back of my hand. When I'm in the practice room, I can sail through like a pro. Why should playing in front of someone else be any different? I don't get why these nerves are getting the best of me! I try pretending I'm in the practice room, but that doesn't seem to help. Maybe I'll talk to Dad to see if he has some suggestions.

Dad was a counselor through and through. When we talked about my captor getting out of jail, his approach came across as very counselor-like. I could always count on Dad to handle these kinds of queries with his counselor hat on.

Not long after I made this decision to talk to him, the right opportunity presented itself.

"Dad, can I talk with you a minute?"

"Sure, Alexis. What's up?"

"I've been having trouble handling my nerves when I'm performing. My hands get shaky, my leg trembles, and sometimes, it's hard for me to remember the music I've memorized. It's stupid! When I'm in the practice room, everything is fine, but when I get in front of people, I get nervous. I've tried pretending I'm in the practice room, and that helps a little, but my nerves are still distracting. I can't seem to control it! Do you have any suggestions, or do you know of someone I could talk to about it?"

"What about Margo? You know her, and I'm sure she can help you."

"That's a good idea. I hadn't thought about her."

The idea of talking with someone I knew and who knew me was comforting. I took care of Margo's kids every day after school when I was in high school. That gig helped me pay for my first year of college. I hadn't had daily contact with her for about a year or a year and a half, but I babysat her kids for a good three years before that. She knew about me being kidnapped and raped, and she was a counselor. Duh! It never dawned on me to think about her.

At my scheduled time, I updated Margo on my life since high school, and then the conversation proceeded.

"What can I help you with? You mentioned something about dealing with performance nerves. What's going on with that?"

"Yes. When I'm playing in front of people, I can't seem to keep my nerves under control. My hands shake, my legs shake, and I sometimes find it hard to remember the music I've memorized. I can sail through it just fine when I'm by myself, but put an audience out there, and I turn into a shaking mess."

"How have you been with all the rape stuff lately?"

"Okay, I guess. We found out the guy who raped me got out of jail recently, and I've been having lots of nightmares. I'm still attending the Rape Crisis support group, and I talked with them about it. We also talked about some challenges I've been having when I go on dates. I recently went out with a guy named Drew. It felt gross to kiss him, and we talked about that. But I'm staying busy with school and work, and it doesn't really bother me otherwise. The support group encouraged me to remember dating was a different circumstance from that rape. When I go on a date and physical exchanges of affection surface, they encouraged me to remember this is different. It's not rape."

I also shared this was not the first time this happened with kissing, recounting my dates with Dennis and Ian in high school. I spoke about my frustration with nightmares and how I tried to limit the amount of sleep I got so I didn't have to deal with them. Why, after two and a half years, does this stuff keep popping up? I felt like it should all be over by now.

Margo listened to my ramblings and then replied.

"There are many people who get nervous when they get in front of people. It's natural. When you're in front of an audience, you're in a position of vulnerability. It has nothing to do with rape, but being in front of people can amplify what's going on."

"I never thought about that before."

"Are you holding your breath when you play?"

"Yes, I am." When I replayed the video of my last performance in my head, I could see myself holding my breath.

"When you are in a stressful situation, and you stop breathing, your body does what it can to accommodate what's going on. If your body needs oxygen, it's going to tremble, nerves aside."

"That makes sense. Perhaps what I need to do is remember to breathe, and that will help. I think I can do that."

"Try it and see how that works. Now, about that kiss with Drew. Were you in the car with him when he kissed you?"

"Yes."

"I think all you need to do is have sex with someone in a place other than a car. Because your rape happened in the car, your mind conjures up a relationship between that and what's going on when you go on a date. Is it possible for you to be intimate with your date and be someplace other than a car?"

Did she really say that? Have sex with someone somewhere? But kissing isn't having sex!

"People think having sex is only having intercourse," Margo said. "Being intimate, kissing, holding hands, hugging, it's all part of sex or being sexual with another person."

I tried to hide my embarrassment and talk about this like an adult.

"Yes, I think so. Drew lives at home, but he has his own space. His parents aren't always around like mine are."

Margo planted a startling seed. If Drew asked me out again, I'd figure out a way to go into his house and see what happened. My mind came up with a plan, like it always does. I imagined going inside to listen to some music.

"Now, about those nightmares," Margo said. "When you sleep, and you dream at night, it's your body's way of dealing with stress. You stay pretty busy, and if you're trying to sleep as little as possible, you've probably got some exhaustion setting in. When you sleep, your mind processes everything that's going on in your life without interruption or distraction. Your nightmares are probably your brain's way of processing all the stress in your life, with school, work, someone getting out of jail, and all."

"I'd like for you to sleep a little more and see if easing your exhaustion will help with your nightmares. For a while, while your body gets caught up on its rest, you'll probably still have some nightmares. But over time, perhaps they will lessen in intensity or even go away. Give it some time. It won't happen overnight, but with some better sleep, perhaps things will relax a bit and be less intense for you."

I hated the idea of having to sleep more. It was like forcing myself to be in a place I really didn't want to be.

It makes sense that if I'm tired, things might be more intense. But is she crazy telling me to go there? I just want them to stop. But Margo's the counselor and she probably knows what she's talking about.

"What have I got to lose? It can't get any worse."

"Give these things a try, Alexis, and let's get together again in a couple of weeks and see where we are with things."

As I left Margo's office, I set another appointment for a couple of weeks out and went on my merry way. She gave me lots to think about. Breathe when I perform, sleep more, and be intimate with someone in a place other than a car.

I'm not a hussy! After all this time knowing Margo, how could she suggest something like that? I guess she has a point that sex is not just about intercourse, but kissing is kissing. Not sex! She's trying to help me, and her advice must be good for something. I guess I just need to try it out and see if things get any better.

As my first semester of college wound down, the concept of final exams and juries became crystal clear. Finals were easy enough—a test to see how well I learned the curriculum. Juries meant performing two or three pieces in front of a panel of professors, like a mini recital. I was required to do this for my piano and violin studies, but also for the 20-plus voice lessons I played for. This gave me ample opportunity to test out my new breathing suggestion, to see if it helped to keep my nerves under control.

I tested it out in the practice room first.

Breathe. Give yourself a few moments to breathe in and out before you begin. Remember to breathe while you're playing something.

I got a natural rhythm for that established in the practice room, and then I put it to the test during formal lessons. That gave me a framework to use when juries came around.

The first few juries were unnerving. But I persisted in telling myself to remember to breathe, physically taking a deep breath here and there, and it seemed to help a little. The nerves weren't totally gone, but things seemed to be more manageable. An audience of three professors differs from a larger audience, but these were performances for a grade. No pressure there!

~

This story would not be complete without a mention of one other helpful person who catapulted my recovery.

My coping strategy of getting back to my normal life as soon as possible became a habit, a way of life. Without realizing it, I turned into a robot. I got up, went to school, and threw myself into all things musical. My busyness was my refuge for a while until being busy made me feel empty and robotic.

I got to a point where I could no longer put off what ached to be acknowledged. When I stepped into the dangerous woods of feeling the intense hurt that results from rape, I wanted out. I was doing everything I thought I was supposed to be doing to function in life, but it was empty. Suicide was prominent in my thoughts. Reasons to stay alive eluded me. I wanted help or I wanted out.

Once again, I turned to Dad for guidance. He referred me to an Episcopal priest who was also a pastoral counselor. The priest wasn't the least bit churchy in his approach to talking with people. Without his collar, you'd never know he was a priest.

When I met him for the first time, I was nervous. After Margo's help, I had serious reservations about what I was walking into. He was extremely welcoming and down to earth. There were no pretenses or pressures. I shared with him the story about my kidnap and rape, and the challenges I faced. Nightmares, not sleeping, the crazy advice I got from Margo (more about that in Chapter 19), and I told him I either wanted some relief from the pain or I wanted out. I was ready to step off the planet and walk away from this life.

He listened to my stories without judgment or criticism. When he interjected comments or asked questions, he always came from a place of calm and genuine interest. We made an agreement that I would not off myself without checking with him first. I thought that was odd. Why would he care?

I only spoke with him a few times, but he said something to me that still echoes in the framework of who I am.

"Look how well you've taken care of yourself. You are sitting here, and we are talking with each other. It looks to me like you've made choices that have kept you alive. That's amazing! You've shared some horrible things with me, yes, but I'm glad you're here so we can visit with each other. Looks to me like you're doing a pretty good job."

He gave me total credit for my choices. I was alive (well, sort of), and I survived a wretched horror. It never dawned on me to observe how I was taking care of myself. I was just trying to survive from one day to the next. His observation adjusted my perspective, and I started seeing life in things that were just motions to me to this point. Sure, they provided a predictable rhythm, but I was doing things in my busyness that mattered to me. I saw that, and my desperate desire to escape (to kill myself) shifted to seeing the value of what I was doing. This was a big corner to turn for me.

Music was my art, my way of expressing myself. I was going to school to complete a degree but also to learn a skill I could use to support myself. Getting up out of bed in the morning was more than routine. It was a vehicle for me to get closer to the "finish lines" I set out to achieve. It wasn't an overnight accomplishment, but it was leading to that.

PART TWO

SURVIVOR

CHAPTER 15
A NEXT STEP

RECOVERY IS A SCARY TOPIC. If you've never gone through a process like that before, it can feel intimidating, even overwhelming. But don't let it! It's a scary proposition, but it's something that you will thank yourself for, one hundredfold!

In my recovery journey, I was hell-bent and determined to be strong enough to do it all on my own. To pick myself up and get back on the bicycle, so to speak. That's a great attitude to have, and it helped me navigate through the weeds. But only to a certain point. What I learned is asking for help, and accepting it, makes the process so much easier.

With help, I discovered new personal strengths. I found great comfort in realizing I was not alone. Getting help opened new ideas for me and new things to try, and I learned about healthier ways to cope. As I learned these new things, the rough stuff was easier to see and learn from. It also helped me understand I didn't have to feel yucky all the time. Yucky feelings are an important part of the healing process (acknowledging these genuine feelings), and I learned I didn't have to stay there. It's okay to feel better, to feel okay, to feel loved and accepted.

Some resources I went to for help were more helpful than others.

Rape Crisis was a good first step for me to get used to talking about what happened to me. It was liberating to say those hard words in a group. When I spoke out loud about my difficult thoughts, it helped me see things from different perspectives. As I got more comfortable about that, then I learned how to talk more about the scary emotions that go along with this recovery.

Oh, my goodness. I did everything I could to avoid talking about feelings. Once they started coming out of my mouth, though, I learned how to feel more comfortable with them and talk about them. Believe it or not, talking about them helps them to feel less overwhelming.

I learned how to chat with my feelings, much like I converse with a friend. Feelings like to be acknowledged and heard. When they know I hear them, then I give them a sort of identity so that I can speak with them. Here's an example. Sometimes, my vulnerability looks like a cowering, gargoyle-like creature hiding in the darkness. I can see its beady eyes glowing, just daring me to take a peek. It seems scary and unapproachable at first. But when I talk with it a little, I see it's really a teddy bear trying to keep me safe. I can talk to teddy bears!

Upon further conversations with this teddy bear, I learned that my vulnerability is really something that wants me to feel safe. So, I ask it how it can protect me without turning into a scary gargoyle. When the teddy bear feels safe, I know I can feel safe. When we stay in touch with each other that way, that teddy bear's paw is always there for me to hold when I'm looking for safety (well, in my mind, it is).

I know it all sounds a bit off the wall, but with the help of others, I learned how to do this. Emotions really are full of sage advice when we give them a chance to be heard.

On the flip side, there were some people I reached out to for help that turned into a disaster. Reaching out to Marvin to pray with me and heeding Margo's advice to have sex with someone in a place other than a car were two instances where I asked for help, and it was debilitating.

So, how do you go about getting help without having to go through something like that? There's no magic wand or formula I can offer. However, listen to your intuition and ask as many questions as you need to in order to feel comfortable that you're in the right place. Some people are better equipped to help with different traumas than others are. In hindsight, I think where I ran into trouble was not asking questions. I was so fearful about my big uglies, I didn't know what to ask (or was afraid to ask). In both cases, I think neither of those people had a clue about how to help someone with rape trauma.

Kidnap and rape (as well as other traumas) are rugged experiences. They are intensely horrific. There isn't anything about these experiences that is easy. If you've ever broken a bone, you know that's something you can fix on your own, to a certain point. Turning to someone with knowledge about how to navigate the healing required to repair a broken bone is something you'd do in a heartbeat. What is it about being human that when we suffer from a broken soul or a broken heart, we shy away from reaching out for help?

Physical hurts are one thing. With physical hurts, it's much easier to step away and look at what needs to be done to encourage repair. We easily seek help with that. Physical hurts are easy to put words around. I broke my arm. My stomach hurts. My knee is killing me. Can I have a Band-Aid for my finger? There's a bone sticking out of my leg. You get the idea. These are things we put into words with ease. Physical hurts may be internal or external, but talking about it or seeking help for them seems easier.

Emotional hurts are quite another thing. These hurts are harder to describe (not impossible, but harder) because we don't hear people talking about them as much.

My son died, and I feel empty.

My daughter is missing, and I don't know if she's dead or alive. Who would do such a thing?

I lost my job, and I don't know how I'll ever be able to take care of my family. There is a pit in the bottom of my stomach, and I don't think I'll ever find the bottom.

When I cut myself, the physical pain is easier to deal with than the pain in my soul. If I cry, I don't know if I'll ever stop. It's intimidating!

Now. Saying these things out loud feels more vulnerable than announcing a cut finger. As humans, I think we naturally shy away from anything that makes us feel vulnerable. It's harder to admit to them or to acknowledge them. Asking for help with these things feels harder because we want to appear capable and strong. These hurts, though, are extremely real (just like a broken bone), and we all feel them because of different circumstances.

Someone raped me—the physical part of this is easy to define (hard to say, but easy to put a definition around). Aside from the hemorrhaging I experienced (due to shock), there was no physical trauma. (Truth be told, I think all the blood scared my captor, and that's probably why he let me go. It probably saved my life!) Other than that, there were no outward, visible signs to show to anyone that such a thing happened. Same with being kidnapped. If you saw me and knew nothing about me, you'd never know he took me at knifepoint from all that was familiar. The trauma, in both experiences, is completely internal.

Asking for help or consulting with a professional in both instances is harder. When you break a bone, it's easy to consult with a doctor to get help. When you're raped, consulting a counselor is intimidating and feels harder (if you've never done that before).

These big-ugly traumas are overwhelming. Doing what you do to take care of yourself and start your healing is all good and necessary. Getting help with it frees you from having to endure it all, all by yourself. It helps you learn how to create perspectives to transition from being a victim to being a survivor.

Some people have an insatiable desire to exercise and make their bodies strong. They work out and sculpt their muscles into what they dream themselves to be. This recovery process led me to have an insatiable desire to grow my soul. I approach disturbing nightmares and uncomfortable feelings with curiosity. When I experience these things, I've learned there's more to learn from it. Sometimes I can figure it out on my own, and sometimes I want help. It's a dance that requires experimenting with new moves.

CHAPTER 16
TRUSTING

Trust is a thing we are all born with. As infants, we don't understand conceptually what it means to trust. There is an innate trust that someone will feed you, protect you, clothe you, love you, and take care of you with your best interest at heart.

Fast forward to when we learn how to walk, put food in our mouths, use the toilet, and put a shirt on. If you're fortunate enough to live in a loving environment, you still have an innate ability to trust. You trust an adult will continue to ensure your safety and best interests. There is a place for you to call home. You relate to other people in new ways. At this point in our lives, we learn more about what trust is. We learn about boundaries and trust. Along the way, you learn the word trust and what it means.

As we continue to mature, even into our teens, we have experiences that teach us when to trust and when not to trust. This is a natural progression of things. Trust has a little more depth and meaning at this point in life, but we can discern when it is okay to trust and when it isn't. If we've grown up in an environment where we can learn about our intuition, we can learn to trust that it will guide us through life. We learn to trust our gut. We also learn how to second guess that wisdom with sometimes undesirable results.

When I adventured into the spectacle of a blind date, my nerves overrode my intuition about the person who approached the car. My instinct told me that was not my date, and it was right. The guy who approached Dad's car was, in fact, not my date. When I didn't listen to my inner wisdom, my gut, I learned how to question it. This led me down an interesting path that I'll share more about later.

Kidnap and rape forever changed my innate ability to trust. How do I learn to trust again after such an experience? I don't know how to trust anymore, not like I did before this experience. It is something I am still learning about.

Immediately following the rape, I always looked over my shoulder. I still do, but not like I used to. After the rape, I learned anything can happen. I learned the world was not a safe place. The only way I knew how to protect myself was to always keep a watchful eye on everything and everyone. If something seemed dangerous, I just didn't go there.

Needless to say, blind dates were OUT!

When someone says they're going to do something and they don't, what happens to trust? Here's an example. When your friend says they will meet you at the library to study and they don't, what happens? Maybe something happened along the way, and they couldn't make it. Maybe they got in trouble and couldn't use the car. As often happens with teens, if someone got into trouble and lost phone and/or car privileges, there was no way for them to make it to the library at the arranged time. There are many circumstances that could impact a person's ability to show up at the library. If someone says they're going to do something and they don't, they are simply not trustworthy (unless reason explains otherwise).

Let's look at journaling for a moment. When I turned to my journal to vent all the chaos in my life, I had an innate trust that my notebook would be private. Aren't journals supposed to be private? When my mom quoted my journal writings to me in the heat of a moment, I lost my trust in that relationship. If I can't trust within my home, where is it safe to trust? I didn't know. I felt disrespected and felt I could not trust my mom after that. Nothing felt safe or sacred.

If your husband tells you he's going to take out the trash and doesn't, where's trust? In the larger picture of things, taking out the trash is not a life-or-death thing. Journals are not life-or-death, either. Nor is meeting someone at the library. If I can't trust my husband to take out the trash, can I really trust him?

I embarked on a journey of trusting at arm's length. People had to earn my trust. For me to trust people, they have to pass all the tests to prove their trustworthiness. And even then, I only trust them for as far as we've come to this point in time. I don't know how to trust tomorrow. If there's a track record of trust, there is an indicator present, but it isn't certain.

I have learned to weigh in when things don't go as I trust them to. When things don't go as planned, I may experience a broad range of emotions about that, depending on the situation. Take the trash scenario as an example. The trash didn't make it to the curb. But he said he would do it. Can I trust him?

Trusting rubbish removal is one thing. Trusting your life companion to respect and honor you (and all your ability to manage your growth through life events) is quite another. Which one is more impactful? I lean toward the respect and honor choice. Sometimes, blanket observations can lead to destruction.

If I am self-talking that he is not trustworthy, aren't I creating the very thing I fear? When I self-talk, "I can trust him; he just didn't get the trash out today," I'm creating a picture that aligns more closely with what my soul wants.

Then, there's a flip side to this conundrum. How patient is he going to be with me when I cannot trust him? Doesn't he deserve the same trust from me that I want for myself? Of course, he does. It is a learning process. Examining my observations and their sources gives me a chance to grow. I've learned to adapt and give myself room to wiggle and grow. Just like recovery, it is a process that is fluid, and there are always opportunities to continue my growth.

What about work relationships and trust? The work culture is unpredictable. The relationships I need to keep the workplace chill and running don't always match up with what I want. Some people in my work environment were clearly untrustworthy, but I still had to work with them. It messed up my entire plan with trust. I allowed them to be who they were and made sure I didn't compromise my personal integrity.

I started relearning trust by taking baby steps first. This brings me back to my intuition. I've had to re-learn how to trust my gut. It is so easy for questioning thoughts to worm their way into what I think my gut is telling me. My thoughts usually go wild, so the first indications often get derailed. My what-ifs, along with playing different scenarios through my head, redirect that first instinct. When that happens, I can easily overrule what my gut says first.

Understanding this about me, I know to be aware of it. When this happens, I step away from it and then come back to it, and I make myself alert to whatever instinct comes to the surface first. I make a choice based on what I glean from that first response. What I experience beyond that decision validates or invalidates my choices. It seems arduous, but it works, and it teaches me how to trust the voice inside me that knows.

The more I practice, the better I get at it. I'm still wrong sometimes, which means I'm still learning how to do this. This is where being gentle with myself comes into play. I give myself grace and patience to try, try, and try again. I've improved, but I wouldn't say I have it all figured out. Trusting School is still in session.

My nature, now, after this experience, is to trust but verify and rely on my instincts to guide me. If someone breaks that trust, they're over, they're done, they're voted off the island. They are not trustworthy, period. The way life works, there are always going to be people present that I'd rather walk away from. Walking away, though, is not always an option. Sure, I still have some growing to do here, but this is how it works for me right now. Who knows where I'll be two or three years from now?

Think for a moment about you and me. You are a reader I may or may not know. Can I really trust how you're interpreting what I'm saying? Are you receiving what I'm offering in the spirit in which I give it? This is an interesting experiment! A brave experiment.

The process of writing about this experience is both frightening and enlightening. Telling the story and the details of the experience feels raw. It is akin to pouring alcohol on an open wound. Who in their right mind would even expose a wound like that? I have experience talking about this life event in my volunteering with both victims/survivors and criminals. I'm not telling this story for the very first time, but it might be the first time for some of you to hear/read about it.

Talking about the recovery process feels more like shining a flashlight into a dark place so I can see. It feels safer than sharing the gory details. I feel vulnerable talking about all this with people I may or may never know. My experience tells me that exercising this vulnerability is where all the good, juicy life is. I do this to open doors for others on their own journey. I've learned, over time, that talking about it and putting it into words helps to create different perspectives about it. Being a person who strives to grow my soul makes this fit for me.

Now, let's talk about trust.

The recovery journey I share with you on these pages is just that: my journey. There are several ways to go about this recovery. One person's journey is not better than another; it is simply different. Perhaps my sharing helps you relate to things on your own journey. Maybe my words give you words to express what you feel. Maybe sharing my journey gives you hope. I'm trusting you, kind reader, to grasp this.

CHAPTER 17
THERE'S MORE TO LIFE THAN ONE DAY AT A TIME, AND YET...

SEXUAL ABUSE TRAUMA is something that sometimes requires a one-day-at-a-time approach. It is big and overwhelming. Breaking it into smaller chunks makes it more manageable, and I highly recommend it. I may spend more time on things that don't settle within me as quickly. That's okay. It's a process. Sometimes, it requires stepping away and looking at my progress to a point and looking forward to what the future holds. That requires looking at things from a larger perspective, from larger periods of time. It's good to step out of the weeds and get a fresh perspective, especially when things seem cyclical.

I've learned that this trauma is big, and the ensuing recovery is a process that happens over a lifetime. As I evolve, what recovery means evolves. How many times have I achieved a milestone with it and thought, *It's all over now. I'm cured!*? Writing that makes me laugh on the inside. It feels tiresome sometimes to think that this is a lifetime process, but it truly is, and it does not have to be laborious.

As I got out of the nitty-gritty stuff, I came to realize things got easier. I felt like I was coasting, and all was right with the world. Then BOOM! Something new (or old) surfaced, and I felt like I was taking two steps backward. Time to tie my shoes and start walking again.

I've already done this. It's over! Why does this keep coming back? I've already looked at this! I'm over it! Enough already!

I got sick of having to struggle with the memories that came up when a smell or someone's careless barking order made me feel like I was still fighting for survival. It is amazing to me how quickly I can find myself right back in that car—in the middle of the ugliness. When that happens, I remind myself how far I've come and that these memories are part of the life experience that makes me who I am today. The intensity of the memories is not as raw as it once was, but the twinge of "I just don't want to remember that anymore" still bubbles to the surface.

When it was intense and overwhelming, one day at a time worked better for me. When these little things broke my serene interior, then it was good for me to remember larger blocks of progress. Now, when a harsh memory comes to the surface, I realize that this is a part of who I am. Is there more to process? Yes. Do I still tire of "having to deal with it?" Sometimes. It's all a part of the ebb and flow of recovery, though. The ocean doesn't always wash up on the shore; it also washes out. And thank goodness for that.

For many years, when Thanksgiving rolled around, I would fall into an unexplained depression. Once I realized it was an unconscious response to the time of year he raped me, I could then give myself different messages about it. I acknowledge my discomfort, and I remember I can choose to feel differently.

Yes, this is the time of year that this happened to me. It is a part of who I am, and I can enjoy a different Thanksgiving now. The circumstances are different, and I'm grateful that I can be who I am today. It's okay to feel happy and look forward to new Thanksgiving adventures.

I held on to old feelings because they were familiar. Sometimes, the familiar feels more comfortable than the unknown. If I was surviving, I knew I was making progress. But what if I didn't have to feel like I was surviving? I felt lost and awkward with that. When Thanksgiving rolled around, I felt obligated to feel bad, to feel sad, and ashamed. The time of year and feeling depressed were married to my existence.

When I started intentionally creating a unique script for myself, the depression lost its thunder and was no longer useful to me. It became less intense. I learned, through time, that it was okay for me to experience Thanksgiving without feeling obligated to feel depressed. And it was okay to let that go. Thanksgiving no longer equaled rape. Thanksgiving was family time, and I felt grateful for all things in life. Rape no longer had to be the focus.

If I'm surviving my trauma, isn't the trauma still in control? I wondered if there was more to it than just surviving. I think there is. What if I was just a whole person instead of a person who survived rape? That was a picture I knew very little about, but I explored that. What if I'm just me, regardless of my experiences? Sure, my experiences color my perspective of the world, but rape doesn't have to be at the forefront of that picture anymore.

When you skin your knee, you bleed, there's a scab, and when the scab falls off, there might be a scar. With rape, my soul bled, a scab formed, and sure, there's still scar tissue from those events. Back to that skinned knee—when you dress, you might see the scar, but the event that caused the scar is of little consequence. The scar is now a part of you. It's just there. For me, with rape, when I see the scar, I accept it as part of who I am. I am not my scar. I'm a person who has a scar.

I'd like to know what my life would be like today if I didn't have that scar. But here are the facts. I fell off my bicycle, and I have a scar now. I experienced rape, and I have a scar now. The journey of healing has let me become a deeper, more vibrant me. I'm still on that journey, but I'm loving it. The scar tissue is softening and becoming a part of who I am.

I enjoy growing myself. When the Alexis seed was planted, I never knew that I'd get hit with the weed whacker. I got hit by the weed whacker, but I'm now part of a beautiful plant that produces roses. That's pretty exciting!

CHAPTER 18
FRIENDSHIPS

IMMEDIATELY FOLLOWING THE RAPE, I was extremely cautious about who I talked to about it. I didn't want anyone to know about my big secret for fear of what it might do to the relationship. I discovered when you tell someone about being raped, the whole dynamic of some relationships change. People rarely know what to say or how to handle that kind of information. Sometimes, the after-effects of that information change the entire landscape of a friendship. At first, my friendships were more important to me than them knowing this horrible thing about me.

When I felt safe enough to tell my close, personal friends, there was always an element of shock. Rape is something that happens to other people, not someone in your close circle of friends, let alone me. The reality of that was always shocking. My closest friends, though, responded supportively, and we picked up right where we left off. That brought me so much comfort when that happened.

There was an element of trust present when I shared the information. I didn't want them blabbing my business to anyone else. So, I shared small pieces of it with them and took a wait-and-see approach. If the experience revealed I could trust them with the information, then

I'd share a little more. I repeated this cycle over and over. This is another way I dabbled in understanding how to trust.

I lightened the burden by sharing what happened with "safe people." Friends who knew about it without impacting the relationship helped me feel less wild on the inside. We didn't talk about it all that often; just knowing they knew (and still loved me) brought comfort.

There came a point in time, though, when that wasn't enough. The more I struggled with nightmares, loss of appetite, and trying to keep myself busy, the more I realized I wanted a tribe who understood me. My friends knew little about the language of rape and its after-effects. It was good they knew this happened to me, but that only carried me so far. (That's when asking for help came into play.)

Then, there were some friends I thought I could share with that went all haywire. There were those who were so frightened by it that our friendship ended. Imagine my shock! That added complexity to the process that I wasn't expecting. I tested the waters with less threatening or less intense conversations. This gave me indicators about what was safe to talk about and what wasn't. I wasn't friendless, but my circle of friends was pretty small, and I didn't want to lose any of them because of the rape.

My determination to resume my life helped me learn. When I tested the waters and got an uncomfortable response, I dropped it and never spoke about it again. Friendship was more important to me than our ability to talk about what happened to me. Again, this only carried me so far. At some point, I realized those friendships were simply not as close, but it was okay to have them. There wasn't any viable support for what I was going through with those friendships. The connection was decent, but it wasn't as meaningful or intimate as the friendships I had where I could reveal my true self.

Some people are simply more equipped to be supportive and understanding than others. The significance of understanding this helped me weigh the value of different friendships. I have some amazing intimate friendships with people, and we never talk about rape. I have other amazing intimate friendships with people and it's okay to talk about it. One is not necessarily more valuable than another; they are just different.

Again, though, the recovery process was one that could only happen when I was free to voice my true feelings and the true after-effects. This is where getting some professional help came into play. The Rape Crisis Support group was one forum where I could talk about just about anything and still feel supported. The people in the group didn't drop off the face of the earth when the word rape came out of my mouth. In the support group, I could talk about the nightmares, my wins and losses with dates, the way I felt my body betrayed me, and everything in between.

As I transitioned from being a victim to a survivor, and as I got a little older, I learned how to be more discerning about the friendships I created. There were still people who were more suited to know about my experience than others, but I learned where the boundaries were.

People who have experienced traumatic events in their lives are more open to talking with me about my experience than those who have not. I think this is just part of human nature. The more I learned about myself, the more I understood how people work. This helped me shape my circles of friends.

Not everyone I have a friendship with knows about my experience. That is okay. We can still be friends, and it is okay that they may never know this "truth" about me. There's no requirement that says all my friends have to know this about me. If they ask me about it, or conversation weaves its way around to sharing that, I'm comfortable talking about it. With a little life experience under my belt, I've learned how to talk about it, so it deepens our friendship when that happens.

Goodness happens when a friendship opens up so that we can talk about it. It doesn't negate or lessen the value of the other friendships I have, but it is sweet when the planets align, and it's something that is okay to share. There is a connection with people that happens when I can share this deeply personal experience with someone. It's good to have friendships where people see me without judgment, and it is okay to share our personal experiences with one another.

CHAPTER 19
DATES

TRIGGER ALERT: Some of the details in this chapter could be triggering. I've noted where that may be within the chapter. These relate to interactions with guys that exacerbated my rape trauma. Feel free to skip those parts if you'd like. Listen to your heart. You're in a safe place. It's okay to be where you are right now.

YOUTH CHOIR at church was one of my favorite activities. We had a hip director, Robert, who put together a group of kids to build an instrumental ensemble to support the youth choir. Robert was a student at North Texas State University, and he had a knack for creating jazzy arrangements for our repertoire. He was relatable and got along well with our age group.

With my piano skills, I played as the choir's accompanist. The musical ensemble had brass, winds, and drums, all made up of kids from the youth group. On Sunday afternoons, before choir practice, the instrumentalists got together to rehearse.

The people in the group were fun to be with—my older brother included. Paul played his silver alto sax in the high school band, so it was fitting for him to take part in the ensemble as well. Everyone went to different high schools in the area, but we gathered at the same church. We all enjoyed getting together to play. Robert had a robust collection of sound equipment he brought with him to help us out. Everyone from the church group chipped in to load and unload Robert's gear so he didn't have to do it alone.

Phillip, my brother's good friend, played the flute. He played in the high school band with Paul. Over time, Phillip and I began getting to know each other a little better, and we got along rather nicely. He was tall, literally dark, and handsome. Not having a sound "social dating" experience, I didn't really want such things. I enjoyed having friends, but my interest in acquiring any type of boyfriend was about as far away from my thoughts as Egypt is from Fort Worth, Texas.

This Sunday afternoon, like any other, Phillip, Paul, and I helped Robert unload his old, slightly rusting white VW van. We hauled amplifiers, an electric piano, and a bunch of other gear up to the third-floor choir room for our ensemble rehearsal. As unloading came down to just a couple more items, my brother took a seat on the short wall around the main front parking lot. He exchanged a few words with Phillip, and we went out to lock up the van. As I approached, Phillip joined me as we gathered the small remaining items to carry up to the rehearsal room and then lock the van.

"Come here."

Phillip invited me to sit with him inside the open back part of the van. I had no reason to distrust him, so I stepped into the van and sat down across from him, slightly.

"What's up?"

"Are you dating anybody right now?"

"Not really. I have a good friend at school, and we hang out, but we're not dating."

"Well, would it be okay for me to kiss you?"

His question took me by surprise! We were friends and played in this little ensemble together. I saw him at school, but as a general rule, we didn't hang out together much. Phillip was older than me, and I never thought of him as a boyfriend, just a friend. I was a lily-white preacher's kid, and Phillip was tall, Black, and handsome.

My mind took off with ideas about dating a Black guy and how my parents might react to that. I didn't have guys knocking down the door or ringing the phone off the hook, waiting for a chance to go out with me. It was flattering that an older guy was asking for a kiss; I felt special about this interesting turn of events.

I leaned forward toward Phillip, and his large hand gently caressed the back of my head as he pulled me gently toward him. A whoosh of excitement swept through me. Shockingly, he appeared to really want to kiss me! Caring and loving like, I melted a bit at the thought that someone would even be interested in being romantic with me, let alone this beautiful Black guy.

I resettled myself a little closer to him, and he began with a gentle little kiss or two. Before I knew it, Phillip was pushing his tongue inside my mouth, and that special, swept-away moment turned instantly to horror.

(*Trigger alert!* Sensitive information ahead. Skip to the part where I've indicated "Trigger alert end.")

I remembered the rapist's vile tongue. Once again, I found myself in a car, being held by someone larger and certainly stronger than me, being kissed, and his tongue coming into my mouth. I froze with fear. The helpless trembling that I felt months ago came rushing back in an instant. I pushed back on him as if to say, "Stop it," but he pulled me closer and held me tighter.

The side van door was closed, and we were inside. As I scanned the van for an easy getaway, I realized the challenge before me. I would have to break away from Phillip, open the side door, get outside, and get away from him. I felt trapped and my mind furiously arranged escape scenarios. I just wanted out and back in the safety of being around other people.

He has the keys to the van. There's no way for me to lock him in here. My brother is sitting out there and knows I'm in here. He's not doing anything! I thought he said he would protect me! He knows Phillip. Why is he just sitting there and not doing anything?

I wanted to scream for help, but nothing came out of my mouth.

I continued to push back, but Phillip just kept pulling me closer and closer. In my struggle, Phillip stuck his hand into my shirt and touched my breasts.

Oh, God! This can't be good. I'm at church! My brother is outside! When I asked Marvin for help, he refused! Is my only purpose in life to be someone's sex toy? I hate this! Please, God, make him stop!

In the next moment, I noticed Phillip's pants were open, and he aggressively started taking my pants off. I knew all too well what came next. Rehearsal time would begin soon, and I didn't want to be late. I rationalized that whatever his actions, it would not last long. I kept my eyes on him, watched his actions, and everything he touched, and tried to anticipate his next actions. A flood of recent memories ran through my mind as I forced myself to remain aware of the events unfolding before me.

He rubbed his penis on my vagina. I urgently wanted to get out of the van and back into the church around other people. That image felt safer than being in the van with Phillip. He wasn't responsive to it, but I continued to push him back to show him I wasn't interested in his offer. I wanted out! I wanted this to be over and be out of the van.

He finally got the message that I didn't want to pursue anything further. After a few moments, he pulled away from me and zipped his pants. As soon as he pulled away, my shaky hands pulled my pants back up, and I quickly prepared myself to step outside of the van. I told myself to be strong and to be sure my face didn't give away the horror I had just experienced.

I felt ashamed as my thoughts rattled on.

Is this all my life is about? Really? I want to be in the choir room, sitting at the piano, ready to start rehearsal.

(Trigger alert end.)

I stepped out of the van and headed toward the church building. Paul still sat outside. I looked at him and reconsidered his empty promises to protect me. I looked away from him and focused my vision on the quickest path to get into the building, up three flights of stairs, and into the choir room.

Disappointed in my brother, I felt tears well up in my eyes and choked them down so no one would see me crying. I wanted to tell my brother about Phillip's actions, but that seemed futile. After all, he just sat there and watched!

Why didn't he come after me when he saw the van door close with me inside? I can't trust anyone! Not even my big brother!

I'll just go up there, get out my music, and start playing. As Marvin said, no one needs to pray for me. I can just do this on my own. I don't want anyone to know what happened. They'll think I'm some kind of slut or something. If I'm playing the piano, nothing can happen to me. I have to put my "happy face" on and just move forward.

My inner dialog kept my brain busy while I walked up the stairs and into the choir room. The sight of other people already in the room brought relief. Having other people around felt safer than being by myself, especially in Phillip's company.

"What are we going to work on today?" I asked Robert to distract me from my immediate horrifying past.

As soon as the instrumental rehearsal finished, choir rehearsal began, and the rest of the evening unfolded like any other Sunday. Well, it seemed normal to everyone else, but in my heart and mind, I was determined to make myself seem normal. I conversed with others and mechanically and methodically focused on the immediate details to distract my thoughts from the events in the van.

Phillip never approached me again, which was fine in my book. Neither of us said another word about it. I felt resolute about accepting it as an evil of the world that I had to put up with.

In the spring of my junior year of high school (about three months after being kidnapped and raped), I played the piano for every choir I could. The show choir was a smaller group of a dozen students who had more exceptional talent. Being a smaller group, we had more opportunities to do extra events such as musicals, fund-raisers, and talent shows.

I often spent my lunch periods in the choir room, working on extra music with these folks as we prepared for different programs. It was not uncommon for me to stay after school for a couple of hours to rehearse. It helped Ms. A, as we affectionately referred to our choir teacher. I often helped her review new pieces of music to see which new material best fit her budding musicians and stretched their capabilities.

One such afternoon, I was helping a couple of kids with some popular musical selections. As we plowed through different music, the choir room thinned out to just one or two people. Ian sang in the choir but was equally skilled at the piano. I often brought piano duets to school and enjoyed sticking around with Ian to play through some of those.

Ian had the longest ol' fingers—every piano player's dream. I almost had hand envy with my average yet small hands. He enjoyed the extra piano time as much as I did. His popular yet gentle persona made him quite likable. His thin, nearly balding head of hair was just enough to accent his clear, grayish-blue eyes against his perfect olive complexion. He always dressed in the latest styles, and his equally charming accents of cologne made him easy on the eyes and the nose. He was dreamy!

Ian drove a sporty little VW bug with a Rolls Royce front end. By all exterior appearances, he was not the most likely person to be the same sort of music geek I was. He did, however, enjoy music just as much as I did.

As the extra after-school time raced away, Ian and I enjoyed each other's company. He often invited me to his house after school to work on homework. We studied and found moments to sing or play the piano in between. Moments became hours, and a string of after-school hours turned into weeks and months. Ian and I enjoyed each other's company as friends.

I felt safe with him. He never displayed any outward sign of wanting anything sexual from me. He genuinely enjoyed my company, as I did his. Dreaming of being a world-renowned conductor while we listened to awesome, majestic, romantic orchestral works, Ian took a baton and pretended to be that world-class conductor. He was sure to become the next Leonard Bernstein or André Previn.

I was never happier! I found someone I connected with and he connected with me. No threats, just two people enjoying one another's company. Ian was understanding and fun to be with. I almost felt like I was part of an "in" crowd when I was with him.

I was still attending the support group on Monday evenings, but now, rape was the farthest thing from my mind. I finally found myself in a routine that felt more exciting to be in, rather than a whirlwind of struggle and pretending. Between my musical commitments and spending time with Ian, my world settled into more of what common teenaged life was supposed to look like. I felt normal, however fake it was at the time.

One spring afternoon, in the choir room, Ian and I rehearsed some show tunes from different musicals: *Oklahoma, Lil' Abner, Carousel*, and *South Pacific*. When we finished up, I stood up from the familiar piano bench to gather my things and make my way home.

"Alexis, when you have all your stuff ready, come over here. I want to show you something," Ian said.

What in the world? What does he need to show me?

My tummy got butterflies, but the excited kind you get when something fun and exciting is about to happen.

When I had everything ready to go, I picked up my books, threw my purse over my shoulder, and walked toward the piano where Ian was sitting. He rifled through his show tunes music book and pulled up a particular song from Rodgers and Hammerstein's *Carousel*. As he sat the music up on the rack, he motioned me to sit next to him at the piano. Nothing extraordinary about that. It seemed like Ian just wanted to share a song or something.

He started playing and singing the chorus for *June's Busting Out All Over*.

I thought Ian was just having fun, so I joined in, playing the melody in the octave above where Ian continued to boom-chuck in rhythm with the song.

He turned toward me and said, "So, what do you think?"

"It's a great song! It's such a cheerful song."

Ian continued to sing the chorus and then asked,

"So, what do you think?"

I failed to understand exactly what he was saying.

He continued to boom-chuck away at the tune and then threw in his own lyrics.

"Isn't June bustin' out all over? I'm so happy with you and we make such a pair. You make my June go bustin' out all over."

Oh. I get it now! He's singing to me!

I was shocked and embarrassed that I didn't catch on to what he was trying to say! Having a boyfriend was the farthest thing from my thoughts. I enjoyed being with Ian, and we were friends.

I innocently replied, "What are you saying?"

"Alexis," Ian stopped playing, "we have so much fun together. Don't you think we should make this official? Do you want to be my girlfriend?"

I choked back my desire to squee out a squeal of joy while I tried not to let my eyes pop out of my head. I struggled to remain upright and not pass out right there.

"Well, that seems like a logical thing for us to do."

I made the words come out with eager pleasantness. Being inexperienced with this sort of thing made me feel awkward and ill-equipped to respond. I didn't want to turn him down, but I didn't want to seem overly eager, either. Ian was so likable, and I felt comfortable with him. I was perfectly happy being his friend and enjoyed that, but this came at me out of the blue! In my wildest dreams, I never imagined someone like Ian would ever want to be my beau.

My thoughts raced around like fireworks while I consciously tried not to appear too eager about the whole thing. Ian leaned toward me and kissed me on the cheek—a sweet, innocent, young-love peck. I smiled, and I'm sure my eyes lit up like a kid at Christmas time.

"We don't have to make any big deal of it," Ian said. "We just seem to fit, and we might as well make it 'official.'"

His words comforted me, and I only felt relief. I set my books on my lap and turned toward Ian to give him a hug. As we embraced, I remembered I needed to get home for a violin lesson.

"I've got to get home. I've got a violin lesson."

We said our goodbyes and see-you-tomorrows. I could hardly contain my excitement. I was embarking on a new chapter. We had no pretenses or pressures; we were just two people who enjoyed spending time together, and things were falling into a logical progression.

As I made my way to my violin lesson, my heart and mind reeled with excitement. I had my violin lessons at Ed Landreth Hall on the TCU (Texas Christian University) campus. It wasn't far from the high school, but it was a drive.

The woman we rented our house from had TCU ties, and she introduced me to many of the professional musicians at the university and in Fort Worth. Kenneth Schenewerk, my teacher, was one of the violin professors at the school and was the concertmaster of the Fort Worth Symphony Orchestra.

As I entered the building, I navigated up the stairs to the second floor. Mr. Schenewerk's studio was in the corner at the end of a long hallway lined with practice rooms. Coming out of the stairwell, the hallway echoed with a fury of tonal sounds oozing out through cracks and crevices. I heard pianos, violins, flutes, voices, and saxophones. Sounds from the practice room occupants reverberated through the hallway. The sounds helped me remember I was there for a lesson and helped turn my focus to the activity at hand.

I knocked on Mr. Schenewerk's door to announce my presence, as was customary. The door opened and I stepped inside. He piled his studio with different scores of music, both solo and orchestral, for the violin. The upright studio piano took up most of the space. There were a couple of wooden chairs and music stands, and a small desk. They were all littered with printed paper filled with dots, scores, sharps, and flats—the language of musicians.

Making space on the piano bench, I sat my instrument and music down and opened the case to prepare my violin for play. This was old hat for me. I tightened and rosined my bow while my stomach turned somersaults. Ian's words, "Do you want to be my girlfriend?" echoed in my head. I grabbed my rosined bow and pulled out my red-stained violin from its cozy burgundy velvet-lined case.

I have to focus on the violin now. Let's get this puppy tuned up.

Ian popped a loaded question, and I accepted. The time between question and violin lesson brimmed with kid-like excitement and the peace that came with any pending musical activity. I pulled my violin to my chin and told myself to concentrate as I tuned my instrument.

At the end of my half-hour lesson, I packed up my fiddle and headed home. Being raped and distracting my thoughts from that were not even whispers in my mind or heart. June was busting out all over! I was excited! My friend Ian, who was not bad-looking either, actually asked me to be his girlfriend. It was more than I could contain. My thoughts bounced from "Keep it together" to "Oh my God, he actually likes me!"

For once, my sleeplessness came from giddy, girlie, swirls of adolescent love. I felt special! Ian's sudden question sent my attempt to look okay and my need to hide my fear flying away like nothing ever happened. All I could think about were musical moments at school, fun times with Ian, the loaded question, and my violin lesson. I drifted off to sleep with a unique energy.

Getting in bed to sleep was part of the routine, but for once, it was pleasant. Instead of the robotic routine of painting my life to make it seem normal, this sleep came at the conclusion of a full and fun day. A starry, googly warmth in knowing someone in the world thought enough about me to commit to being a full-fledged boyfriend.

Life seemed more normal. Not because I pedantically forced my thoughts to be so, but because the dangling excitement about Ian created fresh adrenaline. As I drifted off to sleep, I fell into a much more restful sleep than I had in months. The torrid nightmares about rape, abhorrent smells, and fear for my life turned into an easy, more peaceful sleep. The morning after brought with it a fresh outlook. For the first time in months, I transformed from my robotic survival to eager anticipation.

As our budding romance evolved, I shared my new lease on life with the support group at Rape Crisis. Finally, I had something positive to share. I felt the events of my past fade away as though the wounds of my savage trauma healed, or so it seemed.

As winter turned to spring, my relationship with Ian grew. Sweet hand-holding and endearing, gentle, affectionate kisses escalated to more involved touching and kissing. Hands roamed from gentle embraces to delicate explorations of touching those parts of the human body that define a person sexually. From "June is bustin' out all over" to now, Ian treated me with honorable respect. Even in his subtle yet largely more adventurous touches, his affections were sincere and endearing.

Even with his respectful, gentle touches and my carefree "I'm over it" sense of freedom, though, memories of my captor turned to fear and questioning.

Why does he have to touch me there? I love Ian. He's a good guy. Why do guys have to touch my breasts and vagina? Those are mine! I suppose this is part of being in a relationship with a guy. But why do they have to touch me there?

My torment quickly took over. His personal, physical touching only aggravated what I was trying to walk away from. My respect for Ian and his otherwise completely trustworthy actions and friendship suddenly turned to shaky ground.

Everything about him was a perfect fit until his hands roamed ever so gently to those forbidden places. The concept of intimacy, where touching goes, confused me. At this point in my life, it seemed only to serve as a terrifying reminder that had nothing to do with the dreamy feelings of being loved by someone.

I like Ian, and he certainly seems to love me. Why, though, does he have to touch my private places? When I went out with Mark before being kidnapped, he touched my boobs, and it was exciting. It seemed like the right steps to move things forward to the next level (whatever that means). But now, it seems like everyone just has to get their hands on me and my private parts: doctors, Phillip, and now Ian.

I rolled with the flow as much as I could without letting on to the banter going on inside of me. As Ian's wandering touches continued, it felt good. It was confusing to feel horrified and frightened. His romantic touches felt loving and luscious, like melting chocolate. I let things unfold, but my thoughts planted a seed for me to explore outside of the fiery moment of passion.

Ian and I enjoyed our humming romance through the spring. As summer approached, though, Ian's senior year of high school drew to a close, and so did our relationship. I knew once he graduated and went to college, his time for me and being with me would change. It was sad having to say goodbye because I got along so well with him, but I knew things would change.

~

I was never part of the "in crowd," so I didn't get wrapped up in many of the activities that catered more to that population of people. I wasn't into football, other than to attend a game as an outing with friends. It was something to do on the weekend to get out from underneath my parents at home. Without a boyfriend, homecoming didn't interest me. The dance, getting wrapped up in the frou-frou hubbub of mums, and other indiscriminate social lore surrounding the event, was not my thing. I sailed through that part of the year with minimal notice or recourse. That was fine with me!

Through the course of my senior year of high school, I became good friends with a freshman, Dennis. Being friends suited me fine. I had zero desire to be in any kind of relationship, however exciting. That only proved to be stressful in the areas of my life I preferred to keep compartmentalized and hidden. To this point, aside from Ian, dating always led to things I wanted to hide from—sexual things in particular.

As spring rolled around, talk of prom and the senior girls' backward dance was all the rage. I had twinges of wanting to take part in something—to celebrate this milestone at the end of my senior year. It was another step I could take to prove to the outside world that I was okay.

Prom was out of the question. It was a senior ritual best suited for love birds. In my chatter with Dennis, we entertained the idea of going to the Senior Girls Backwards Dance. We weren't dating, per se, but we were great friends. Even with the age separation, we rocked along like two peas in a pod.

I found the right moment in one of our after-school extra rehearsal shenanigans. While we shared the piano bench, me boom-chucking at the piano, I turned to Dennis.

"Wanna go to the Senior Girls Backward Dance with me? I know neither one of us dance, but it might be fun to hang out."

"Really?"

"Sure! Why not?"

"Sounds like a fun thing to do. You know, Alexis, I know we're good friends, but I wonder if you would be interested in going to the dance like it was a date. We can just see how it works out. No pressure one way or the other; we can just see what it's like for us."

I was completely comfortable with Dennis and our friendship. I especially liked that it existed with no pressures of being boyfriend/girlfriend. Romantic relationships always led to touching each other in places I felt more comfortable keeping hidden. I liked that my friendship with Dennis had no innuendos or pretenses in that way. It felt safe and mutual. Dennis's proposal sent my mind whirring.

I enjoyed my companionship with Ian last year. And even though there was touching and experimenting, it was palatable; required, but palatable. The same would probably be true for Dennis. We are such good friends. We have a good thing going and I don't want to do anything to change it. It's easy and innocuous; no fuss, no muss, no strain, no tension.

My thoughts created a pause in the conversation. Dennis, feeling the hesitation, calmly offered a suggestion.

"If it doesn't work, it doesn't. If it does, it does. However it works out, we can still be friends."

These additional remarks set my mind at ease. It seemed what he was suggesting could be approached more like an experiment, with no danger of harming the friendship I savored.

"Sure, Dennis. We can give it a whirl."

As I prepared for the dance, I kept my conversation with Dennis on replay.

If it doesn't work, it doesn't. If it does, it does. However it works out, we can still be friends.

The mantra of his words echoed at every turn: getting my makeup on, getting all dressed up. Imagining myself at dinner and then the dance. As any fabrications related to any more intimate events raced through my mind, I resorted to repeating the words in my mind. "*...we can still be friends.*"

Dennis was pretty laid back. While this whole dance thing was as new for him as it was tentative for me, I did my best to keep "laid back" woven into my fantasy about the events soon to unfold.

Being a backward dance, the rules of engagement were reversed. I would drive and pay for dinner (instead of the traditional rules of dates initiated by a guy). When I got myself ready, and it was time to pick up Dennis, I stepped into the same little red Datsun wagon in which my captor held me hostage some 16 months before.

Once the car got cleaned up and returned, there was some discussion about selling it. It was a cost my parents weren't prepared to absorb. They would have gotten rid of it, though, if I wanted. I was firm, though, in my determination to get on with my normal life, and I would not let a silly thing like a car bother me. It was just a car—a vehicle to get from one place to another—that's all.

When I stepped into the car, if I had a flashback of memory about what happened there, I told myself it was just a car and went on about my business. Tonight, though, with the added pressures of this experiment with Dennis, the rush of recurrent memory seemed a little more pronounced—a nuisance I didn't want to deal with.

It's just a car. It's just a car, that's all. I'm just going to keep my thoughts focused on Dennis and our experimental date.

My heart pounded with excitement, boutonniere in hand, as I walked to the front door, rang the doorbell, and awaited a reception. Dennis's mom opened the door and graciously invited me in. I noticed the acknowledging sparkle in her eye as she called out to Dennis that his date had arrived. After standing uncomfortably in the living room for a few moments, he appeared in his lime-green tuxedo. I saw his always warm smile as the nervous chatter started.

We each did our floral pinning and nervously discussed our whims about the night's event. Dennis gently took my hand, and we made our way to dinner at the Burgundy Tree. They sat us in the corner booth, and we chose our cuisine for the evening. There were moments of pause, but the conversation carried on comfortably.

I noticed him admiring his dressed-up self in the mirrors blanketing the deep red wooden walls. He wasn't stuck up about it, simply noticing and studying himself in this strange new setting, all dressed up in a tux. The warm restaurant atmosphere complemented our chummy, familiar exchanges. Now and then, we held hands without pretense or pressure.

I felt relaxed as the successful dinner wound down, and we stepped into the ballroom, decorated with our purple and white school colors. Familiar 70's tunes filled the room. Punch bowls glistened as lights swept across the dance floor. There were plenty of tables set up to host dance attendees. We spotted some choir friends and joined them at a table set back slightly from the dance floor's front and center. Perfect for us non-dancers. It was fun to see each other in our formal attire, but the conversation carried on like any other common gathering of friends.

We shared light-hearted laughter and even bravely shared a dance or two. There was a steady stream of iced tea and a cup of punch here and there; all the makings of merry memory-making. I was glad we took the plunge.

As the dance came to a close, attendees made their tired exits to their cars. As I drove into Dennis's driveway, I left the car running and put it into park. We chatted about our evaluations of our successful evening, and it was time to say good night. This was the first time in the whole evening that things got awkward.

Dennis held my hand and gently leaned in for a threat-less kiss goodnight. My heart pounded heavily and nervously as we shared a gentle peck on the lips and then held one another in an embrace for a deeper, romantic kiss.

Dennis bravely gave it a go with a gently affectionate French kiss. I found myself bewildered by immediate memories of not-so-friendly tongue kisses in my recent past. Choking back my desire to pull away, I gave it a whole-hearted try. This was the experiment part in action. I smelled something repulsive as I dealt with his slobbery, wet kiss. I endured the brief experiment but found nothing about it, or him, attractive.

As the kiss quickly concluded, Dennis amicably released his embrace, found the car door handle, and turned toward me.

"That was a fun evening. Thanks for going with me. I'll see you on Monday. I'm looking forward to working some more on that chorus!"

"Great, Dennis! I had an enjoyable time. Yup. We'll get it worked out, that's for sure."

Nothing was intimidating or forceful about what took place. His unpleasant smell was not something I cared to endure. Nor that sloppy kiss. From my perspective, the girlfriend/boyfriend trial and error racked up on the error side. What remained to be seen was how well we could settle back into just being friends.

When Monday rolled around with school and classes, it seemed like any other day. When Dennis and I ran into each other, the intonation of the conversation showed no sign of interruption. In my mind, Dennis stuck to his end of the bargain, as did I. We mutually picked up right where we left off without dropping a beat.

I felt a deep sense of relief and also felt secure in my friendship with Dennis. We tried something new, and per our agreement, we went right back to being friends. This was huge for me! Finally, someone proved himself trustworthy, at least as far as things transpired so far.

After Margo's advice, Drew asked me if I wanted to go to a concert. I met him in college. He played the flute. He found a small venue for someone who played the alto and bass flutes—not very common, but an earthy sound from an instrument and some out-of-the-mainstream music. I was completely on board with it. We set a date for dinner and a concert.

I navigated dinner and conversation smoothly. We talked about school stuff and some mutual acquaintances, and we both looked forward to the concert.

"Have you ever heard of Claude Bolling?" Drew asked.

"I don't think so."

"I discovered him not too long ago. He's a classical/jazz musician. I have some of his flute stuff. If you've never heard him before, I need to share one of his tapes with you."

"Sounds interesting! I like jazz and classical, but I'm not sure I've ever really heard anything like that outside of Gershwin. I'd like to hear it!"

We got through dinner without the awkwardness we experienced at the end of our last date when Drew kissed me. There were no pretenses, just pleasant conversation. While Drew was driving, he told me all the places to look in his car for a Bolling recording.

"If it's not in the car, I guess it's in my room at home."

A light went off in my head.

Margo told me to have sex with someone somewhere other than a car. Maybe after the concert, if it's not too late, we might go inside his house. He'll probably try to kiss me again. Guys always do.

My thoughts were purely mechanical. I wasn't looking to encourage anything sexual.

"No problem," I said. I dared not let on to any of the ideas rolling around in my head.

As we settled into the small venue for the concert, I noticed everything was pretty even-keeled. The conversation trickled along as easily as it could between two introverts. Fortunately, we were both interested in what we were about to hear. We read our programs and commented as points of interest spawned dialog.

The program included different music: folk, tribal, and even some classical—all for the alto and bass flute. I liked the bass flute the best. It has a soft whisper-type tone to it, unlike anything I'd ever heard before.

When the concert ended and we made our way back to the car, we had lots to talk about. We commented on our likes and dislikes of what we just heard. The conversation stayed lively while Drew drove toward my parents' house. The conversation paused after we exhausted the concert topic. My mind reverted to the private observations and the potential "opportunity" before me.

My hands grew moist with nervous sweat. I observed our surroundings as he drove while my mind reeled with uncomfortable thoughts. My mind whirred with ideas about how to get together with Drew in his house without inviting myself in. And I didn't want to do anything to encourage anything inappropriate or risqué. I imagined ways to ask Drew about listening to his Claude Bolling stuff.

"My folks are at a party," Drew restarted the conversation. "If you'd like, we could drop by my house and listen to a little Bolling."

"I'd love to hear some of it."

The words fell out of my mouth as easily as tea pours from a pitcher. My body trembled ever so slightly. I was excited to hear the new music, but my mind focused on Margo's recommended assignment. That didn't help the nervous energy stirring.

How could he have known what I was thinking? This is perfect, and I didn't even have to say anything. What a relief!

Drew adjusted his course to head to his house. I could feel my nerves kick into high alert. I wanted to be completely aware of what was going on, and I didn't want to be raped again.

When we arrived at Drew's house, like a perfect gentleman, he opened my door, and we walked to the front door. My heart pounded as he unlocked the door, and we stepped inside. His house wasn't too far from my parent's house, which brought some comfort. It somehow felt safer being closer to home.

There wasn't anything pretentious about the home. The daily paper strewn over the sofa where someone indulged in catching up on current events. The kitchen was tidy, but not nearly as tidy as Mom kept her kitchen. It was a small house, so it didn't take long to get to Drew's bedroom, where his stuff was.

I felt a little creepy about being in a strange house with a guy, no parents, and heading into a bedroom. The red flags exploded in my head. Drew was as introverted as me and didn't make any inappropriate gestures. He invited me to sit on the end of the bed (the only place to sit) while he pilfered through his stuff to find a Bolling recording.

His room seemed ordinary enough. No evidence of embarrassing articles of clothing. He had a small desk, a single bed, and one wall filled with bookshelves and his stereo. I recognized some of the book titles from college classes. My eyes scanned the music books to see if anything looked familiar. It was a great way for me to gather more information about him and calm the scarab beetles in my belly.

"Ah. There it is! Let me play some of this for you and see what you think."

I watched his every move and felt relieved when I heard the first phrase of music coming out of the stereo.

He sat on the side of the bed near me as we listened. There was nothing obnoxiously loud about it. The unfamiliar melodies were classical-like, with a gentle jazz influence. It wasn't like anything I'd heard before.

"I like it!"

"It's really a unique style. Not classical, and easy jazz."

Drew handed me the tape jacket so I could read it. We listened as I read the list of songs and examined the cover.

"I like that 'Baroque and Blue.' Very clever! It doesn't get any better than Jean Pierre Rampal, eh?"

"Yeah, I like his stuff," Drew said.

He re-situated himself next to me on the bed and reached over to hold my hand.

Here it comes!

As he situated himself, I kept my focus on Claude Bolling's innovative magic so my uneasiness could hide. My conversation with Margo echoed in my brain while I imagined the next sequence of touching and kissing might reveal itself.

As he stroked my hand and forearm, I tried to reassure myself.

This is different. I'm not in a car. This is not rape. I'm in Drew's bedroom. I have to remember this is different. My life is not being threatened. It feels nice that he wants to hold my hand, but what else is he going to want?

I didn't show any obvious sign of dismay or drawback, so Drew wrapped one of his arms around my back while he continued to caress the top of my hand. We listened to a couple more tracks on the tape. Because I didn't want to seem uneasy, Drew thought everything was fine by all appearances. He released my hand, gently turned my face toward his, and leaned in to kiss me.

(Trigger alert! Sensitive information ahead. Skip to the part where I've indicated "Trigger alert end.")

I went with the flow, and before I knew it, his hands were on my breasts. Bravely, I embraced him and caressed his arms and back. As I fought my fears, I turned my focus back to the music playing in the background. Drew encouraged me to lie on my back and unfastened his belt. My brain boiled with reassurances, questions, and cautions as I followed his lead and unfastened my blue jeans.

I need to have sex with someone in a place other than the car. I guess every guy I go out with is going to want to have sex with me. I hate this! My life is not being threatened, and I'm playing along, but I just want this to stop! Keep listening to the music. Don't let him see how scared you are. Be brave and man up! This is totally different. How does it feel when he touches me? Sherry told me to notice how my body feels. There's nothing about this that feels good to me. Is something wrong with me? I'm just going through the motions, but I'm not feeling anything. I just want it to stop!

I endured the episode just like I did when I was being raped.

It won't last forever. It will be over, and then he can take me home. I could walk home; it's only a couple of blocks away from where I live.

As we undressed, Drew pulled something small out of his pocket, unwrapped it, and put it on his penis.

What the hell is that? Oh, yeah. It's a condom.

Any innocence I had left suddenly turned to experience. Scared, Mom's sex education talks replayed in my head. At least he took precautions. That differed from the rape experience.

I felt his penis uncomfortably pumping in and out of my vagina. It hurt. Nothing felt good about it. I tried to stay focused on the music in hopes the incessant thrusting would stop. My body trembled, and I did what I could to keep from being awkwardly freakish on the outside. It was all a matter of survival.

If this is what dating is all about, I want nothing to do with it! I enjoyed being with Drew at the concert and listening to this music.

When things turned to kissing, touching, and intercourse, none of it seemed worth it. I never wanted to experience that again!

Drew stood up, removed his condom, and got dressed. Relieved, I followed suit. My vagina burned like a raw rash, but I didn't see any bleeding. By now, the music stopped, and getting home was the only thing on my mind.

As he got his shirt tucked in and belt fastened, his polite inquiry was none too soon.

"Are you ready to get home?"

"Yes, I'm good to go."

(<u>Trigger alert end.</u>)

I took Margo's advice and had sex with someone in a place other than a car. I felt horrible. Fear and agitation coursed through my veins. The only thing pleasant about that experience was the music I heard. I walked away feeling like being with a guy one-on-one always resulted in having to be sexual in a way I abhorred.

The ride back to my house was short. I tried to keep the conversation light by talking about the concert and listening to the music at Drew's house. I felt like a freak inside and didn't want to have to explain anything about it to him (should he notice or inquire). When we arrived at my house, I opened the car door, exchanged polite gratitude for the evening, and made my way into the safety of my parent's house.

When I got into my room, I replayed the events of the evening.

I wish I could write about all this in my journal, but it isn't safe. I don't want Mom reading about all this. There's no escape. I guess I can't go out with guys without sharing my body. They have to touch me where I don't want to be touched, and having sex hurts! I'm never going back to see Margo. I feel like someone raped me again, even though he didn't have a weapon. This sucks! I'm so much happier when I focus on my work and school. I'd much rather be in the practice room. When I play the piano or violin, I don't have to worry about any of this stuff!

After another night of sleep terror, I was relieved to be absorbed in the mad rush of my first semester at college ending.

CHAPTER 20
MY BODY BETRAYS ME

AFTER IAN GRADUATED, I stepped into my senior year of high school. I continued to attend the Rape Crisis support group and felt more comfortable sharing what was going on in my life. I talked through all the emotions and sorted out coping processes related to being raped and kidnapped. What a relief to have a safe place to talk about all this stuff.

It was nearly a year now after the trauma I desperately tried to pretend did not exist. The course of time and my fierce determination to get on with my life naturally took me from being a victim to becoming a survivor. Rape was no longer something I felt like I had to cope with daily. Instead, it turned into a piece of luggage I could stuff with feelings and emotions as long as I kept the lid fastened shut.

Survival changed from a moment-to-moment coping strategy to something that just popped up from time to time. Having that luggage to stuff came in handy to keep me on track toward normalcy. The support group, along with my journal (before Mom quoted from it), gave me a place to vent my frustrations and learn new ways to cope. It was a suitable venue for talking about things and sorting them out. The people in the group understood the language of rape and how it changes a person's life in a matter of moments.

I figured out where it was safe to talk about my rape experience and where it wasn't. When I shared the chaos in my head with friends, sometimes I found support, and other times, I sacrificed seemingly wonderful friendships. For every friend I lost, I learned more about when it was okay to talk about it and when it was better left alone.

I had a new focus on the horizon: college. My busyness kept rape off my mind, but it also kept the deeper feelings I had about it sufficiently brushed under the carpet. It worked, for now.

The hardest part was still having my monthly period. My monthly cycle served only to remind me about how gross I felt. I hated the bleeding and the way it smelled. Cramps triggered memories of being raped and how it hurt. I understood this was a normal part of being a woman, but there was nothing pleasant about it. I felt disgusted with myself and my body. It was something I tolerated, but deep down, I hated myself and my body. I felt embarrassed, and it was inconvenient. It's hard to keep the "mask" in place when this was popping up every month.

The more stuffed my luggage became, the raging beast inside found other ways to get my attention. When I experienced the dire fear of not knowing if I would live from one moment to the next, my body took on that stress by shaking and hemorrhaging. I think stuffing my feelings and pretending the rape didn't happen manifested in other ways. For me, that was having irregular and painful periods, not to mention yeast infections.

When I was in college, one of my violin comrades and I started spending time together. Logan not only played the violin but was also quite a guitarist. He introduced me to the likes of Jean Luc Ponty, Mannheim Steamroller, and Pat Metheny. I liked the unique jazz flavorings of these artists.

Logan had a side job at a recording studio. It was interesting to see how involved it is to make recordings. We often went to his house (he lived with his parents) to listen to music together. Logan impressed me with his command of the electric guitar and all the sound effects gadgets he had. I thought it was pretty cool! It was fertile ground for another budding romance.

We never strained to come up with things to talk about. As our relationship unfolded, the dreaded ensuing physical expressions of our affections got more and more heated. By this time, after my shindig with Drew, I was learning to accept these affections with less fear. I found myself actually attracted to Logan sexually, which led to more intimate expressions between us.

In my dorm room, one of our passionate exchanges escalated to intercourse. It was the first time I experienced intercourse as feeling good. We got quite passionate with each other, and I actually enjoyed it. That was new to me.

Logan came to me with some shocking news. He had raw spots on his penis. He had never experienced such a thing, so it was pretty shocking for him. Little did I know, I had passed on a yeast infection to him. After growing accustomed to having them, I often ignored them rather than having to deal with the yucky, oozy medicine that went along with treating it. I didn't know it was something transmittable to another person.

When that happened, our little budding romance came to a screeching halt. He didn't want to have anything to do with me after that. My body betrayed me! I felt awful for having done that to him and expressed that. I vulnerably shared my ignorance, but it was more than he wanted to deal with. Once again, I felt like a freaky, raped mess.

It seemed like every time I had hope of having a romantic relationship with someone, something icky happened with my vagina. It just wasn't worth it. Intercourse was something I either had to endure, or it hurt or wasn't good for the other person because I was a mess. If this physical betrayal was always going to be part of the experience, it was something I could live without. I didn't need it, and I wanted nothing to do with it!

CHAPTER 21
SEX

S EXUAL ABUSE and rape are not just about sex. Sex is often the weapon in these circumstances. The bulk of the recovery has more to do with the emotional and soulful wounds that ensue. But sex is surely a part of it, or it was in my case. I had no exposure to intercourse or oral sex at the time of the rape. Upon this first exposure, I wanted nothing to do with sex. It was painful, and, in my experience, there was nothing enjoyable about it.

As I started dating and had intense experiences with loving, intimate touching, my curious nature wanted to understand more about that. I had a healthy understanding that sexual expressions could be loving expressions, but I didn't have any frame of reference for it.

As I shared details about this with the Rape Crisis Support group, I got some interesting information and advice.

"There are a couple of observations I'd like to share," Sherry said. "Part of dealing with our trauma is learning how to navigate triggers. Smells, memories, reminders, and touches can all act as triggers. When you shared your experience with Ian a while back, and now with Dennis, you spoke about how sexual touching is challenging.

"When our bodies are touched sexually, even during a rape, they can respond positively. It might even feel good. Do you remember having any physical feelings during the rape that felt good to you?"

"I don't. It was scary, in very unknown territory, and I just wanted to live through it, whatever that took. It hurt, and I just wanted it to stop. When he kissed me, all I could smell was his stale alcohol stench, and I choked back the urge to vomit. Nothing felt good about it!" I said.

"Sometimes, when coping with a dangerous situation, we focus on survival. However, even in those moments, without realizing it or making a note of it, our bodies will naturally respond to sexual stimuli. It doesn't mean you approve of the touch. It simply means your body is responding naturally. It's okay for your body to respond the way it is meant to, and you might not be aware of it. If you had any moments in the experience that felt good, I want you to know that it's okay. Even if you're being forced to do something against your will, if your body felt good, remember your body was responding the way it's supposed to."

This was a new concept for me to consider. As Sherry went on about these sexual feelings, I scanned through my memory of the rape and could not remember any moment when his touching felt good.

Sherry continued. "If you didn't have any positive feelings from the physical touching or the sexual act itself, that's okay, too. However you experienced it, your physical response to it is okay. You're here today, so whatever you did was the right thing. You survived, and it's all right."

I listened and did my best to make sense of what I was hearing. I did not recall any moment when the sexual gestures or touching felt good.

Is there something wrong with me because nothing felt good?

Sherry's words echoed in my head. *"If nothing felt good, that's okay. You were surviving."* Her words eased my concerns.

"I want to invite you to try something. Do this right now. Place your hand on your arm and gently caress yourself. How does it feel for you to be touched, gently and calmly, by your hand?"

"It's okay. My hand feels warm, and my touch is gentle. It feels okay."

"This week, as you are going through the day, I want you to try this. Take a moment indiscriminately to touch yourself kindly. A gentle caress. It doesn't have to be long. Maybe you gently touch your face, your hand, your leg, or your arm. A gentle touch, that's all. Allow yourself to feel the touch and make a mental note about how it feels. Give yourself some accepting, gentle touches. Once or twice a day, it doesn't have to be all the time. Give yourself a quick moment to be touched and simply make a note about how it feels. You're doing the touching. You pick the place and the time. Think for a moment about being touched and how it feels. We'll check in next week about it."

I accepted Sherry's proposal as an experiment. Through the course of the week, when I found a few moments by myself, I placed my hand on one arm and gently caressed it. I noticed where my skin was smooth and where it wasn't.

Another time, I looked at myself in the mirror and placed my cheeks in my hands. I outlined my facial features with my fingers. I felt the warmth of my palms on my face.

At another moment, while a teacher was talking, I folded my hands together and used my thumbs to massage the insides of my hands. I found places in my palms that enjoyed the extra tender loving care, especially between my thumb and forefinger.

When I settled into my bed at night, I put my hands on my belly and noticed the rise and fall as I inhaled and exhaled. Other times, I allowed my hand to rest gently on my legs as I curled up and got snuggly under the covers. One night, I held my shoulders like I was hugging myself.

At first, all this touching was strictly mechanical. I did it for the sake of my assignment. As the week wore on, I took moments here and there to casually but deliberately touch myself. I noticed how nourishing it felt to be touched. I was doing all the touching, but I knew how to touch myself, so it felt safe and caring.

These were simple moments, but with Sherry's suggestion, I learned what it felt like to receive touch. There were small moments, sometimes only a few seconds. My senses woke up to the tranquil moments of nurture. As I allowed myself to recognize what felt good and what felt good about it, I made mental notes to report back to the next group.

As the next group rolled around and everyone got settled, Sherry circled back to me and inquired about my exercise. I explained the different ways I touched myself and recounted my observations about it. As I wrapped up, I finished by observing out loud how nurturing it felt to be touched.

"So. Touching is not all bad. Think back to when Dennis held your hand. How did that feel?"

"At first, it felt like a thing I had to do. It was the socially acceptable thing to do. There were times, though, when it felt good to have my hand interlocked with his. I felt like I was his, and he was mine. It was a loving gesture between two people."

"Now, let's take this a little further. What did it feel like when he kissed you?"

"At first, it felt good when he held my face in his hands and pulled me toward him. Then, when the kissing got more intense, and he started French kissing me, it felt gross and slobbery. I tried to like it, but when he pulled my body closer to his, as he wrapped his arms around me, I could smell something that repulsed me. When was it going to stop? I didn't like the smell. It was a different smell, but it reminded me of the yucky smells when I was being raped."

"Our sensory memory is a powerful thing," Sherry said. "When similar smells, tastes, and feelings bubble up, the memory of the rape can easily come into the forefront of your experience. Even though you're not being raped at the moment."

"As you continue to experiment with touching yourself, allow yourself to identify what feels good and what doesn't. What smells good, and what doesn't. Be an observer and make mental notes about it. Then, when you feel comfortable doing so, try touching yourself all over; your arms, legs, your breasts; you might even try touching your vagina. Just observe what it is like and experiment with it. As you discover what feels good, then allow yourself to receive the touching— wherever that might be on your body."

I sat quietly, completely embarrassed. I did what I could to resist showing any outward sign of it. I didn't want anyone to see my vulnerability. As Sherry moved the conversation elsewhere, I sat with this new information and started daydreaming about what I heard. The thought of touching my breasts and vagina was a foreign idea that made me feel anxious. I was relieved there was no timetable for the ideas. I was perfectly happy to let these new ideas simmer for the time being.

CHAPTER 22
NEVER GETTING MARRIED

When I was a kid, and before the rape, I daydreamed about getting married someday. Immediately following the rape, all I wanted was for my normal life to resume. My dating experiences were pretty spread out and not all that frequent. When I did date, there were many occasions I walked away feeling like I didn't want to have anything to do with it.

Better than midway through college, I decided I would never get married. I was okay with that. Sex (specifically intercourse) brought up unpleasant memories that I desperately tried to run away from. I always experienced an increase in nightmares when I was involved in anything sexual. There were smells that made me want to vomit, and the discomfort I felt during intercourse never seemed worth it.

This was a time in my life when I became a survivor. I discovered a new "normal" that worked for me. I was doing life okay as long as I did my thing and kept to myself as much as possible. Who needs the complication of a boyfriend, let alone a husband?

I learned to live comfortably with myself. I had a good job as a technical writer and lived by myself. There was always a church job on the side. I played the piano for the choir and worship services, and my violin professor let me stay in the college orchestra so I could keep playing. I continued my volunteer activities and had a handful of friends to hang out with now and then.

My parents lived close by, and I involved myself with their daily neighborhood walks and a card game now and then. Mom and Dad organized trips to Jefferson, Texas (an old, historical town in east Texas). They started out as marriage enrichment fun weekends and evolved into fun weekends for anyone—marriage not required. I often took part in those to give myself opportunities to travel a bit and step outside of my normal routines. It was a safe way for me to do that and have a vacation.

About ten years after I earned my Music Education degree, with an all-level teaching certificate, I fell into a new church job opportunity. It was closer to home, and the church I was working for was slowly closing its doors. It was a second job that helped me make ends meet.

I interviewed for the position with the choir director. We got along well and had a lot in common. Our ideology seemed similar. Before I accepted the offer, I wanted to visit the church to see if the community and worship experiences were a good fit. My little sister agreed to go with me to check it out.

As we settled into a pew to partake in the worship experience, I pointed out the choir director. My sis made the observation that he looked like Michael Keaton, and we shared some giggles about that. He was cute! I absolutely fell in love with the church and the people and accepted the job.

Weeks turned to months, and I rooted myself in the community of this church. Jerome, the choir director, and I enjoyed working on the music together. He had an amazing voice, and we enjoyed sticking around after choir rehearsals or coming in early to run through some music together. During those times, we talked about different things. Many of our conversations were spiritual explorations. We shared many of the same beliefs and enjoyed stepping outside of Western spiritual topics to explore ideas that were more Eastern in nature.

He was married and had a four-month-old son. He often invited me over for dinner or to spend a weekend afternoon together playing with their youngster. We got to be pretty good friends, all of us. Having a small child, along with their jobs, limited their time to spend with each other. I offered to make myself available to take care of their little one. I wanted them to have some time together without their kiddo.

Now that I was older, taking care of their son gave me a chance to explore my desire (or not) to have a child of my own. It was safe. I didn't have to get married to determine if I wanted to have children of my own. I enjoyed taking care of their son, but I realized I probably wasn't cut out to be a full-time mamma. Fine in my book.

When they got pregnant with their second child, I proposed an idea. Because I would never get married, let alone have children, I wondered if they would allow me to be present during the birth. I had a curiosity about all of that and thought it would be an amazing opportunity for me to be part of a birth. Graciously, they agreed to allow me to be part of it.

It was amazing! I observed an indescribable magic about welcoming a new little human being into the world. What an amazing gift for them to allow me to be part of that! This new little bean did not know what it meant to be born into this world, the life he would have before him, the experiences he would have, or who he would grow up to be. It was a big, new, eye-opening experience for me. My eyes and heart were full of wonder, but it didn't change my deep desire to not have children or to be married.

I continued to offer my babysitting services to them so they could continue to have some much-needed time for themselves. About six months after their second son was born, Jerome discovered something quite shocking.

When he retrieved the checkbook from his wife's purse, he discovered some pamphlets about helping children through a divorce. Imagine learning that your wife wanted out of the marriage in this way. Jerome was speechless!

My frequent social engagements with them came to a screeching halt. The prospect of divorce always turns a relationship upside down, and there was no need for me to be around to complicate things. Being his friend, Jerome leaned on me to talk about this major turnover in his seemingly stable marriage.

In between our musical endeavors at the church, we talked often, and our friendship only got deeper. As he shared his turmoil related to the divorce, I took a risk and shared with him about my rape experience. It gave us some common ground to talk about our big uglies, and we each helped each other to navigate the ensuing growth that happens when big, disruptive life events take place.

Over time, we started spending time with each other socially. The proverbial exercise of that led to a deeper, more intimate relationship. Without realizing it, we started dating, and of course, that led to more intimacy in our relationship. That scared the living daylights out of me!

At first, this new intimacy expressed itself with hand-holding and gentle kisses. Eventually, it got more involved, and there was exploratory touching. I felt nervous about all that. My past kept me cautious and fearful. There wasn't an immediate jump to intercourse, which kept me willing to try things and weigh my emotional responses to things. He wasn't pushy about anything, but it was clear our loving physical expressions with one another were intensifying mutually.

I pulled back because I didn't want to jump into anything too serious too quickly after his divorce. I knew he leaned on me for support, and I didn't want to be the rebound person. We had a great friendship, and I wanted to keep that. He needed to explore being with other people before he jumped into anything remotely committed to me.

We talked about it and determined that before our relationship went any further, he needed to date some other people. I didn't want to get into a heavy dating relationship or other more intense physical expressions unless he was ready to be a more "serious" boyfriend. He agreed, so we kept our friendship open and on an even keel while he explored other fish in the sea.

Stepping back a little to my conversation with Sherry about learning to touch myself and discover more about what feels good and what doesn't, once I got out of college and lived on my own, I explored this idea a little further. I got comfortable with gentle, caressing touches. Touching my arms and legs felt good. I learned to cradle my face in my hands and experimented with looking into the mirror while I said loving things to myself.

When I got comfortable with that, I branched out and found a great massage therapist. I knew she would not be touching me anywhere that involved that which I held private and sacred. It was an exercise in trust, too. I learned how to surrender the weight of my body in a resting position while she moved and massaged my limbs, my hands and feet, and my head. It was a great way for me to learn more about the power of nurturing, healthy touch. Surrendering my body to this kind of touch allowed me to love myself while someone else touched me in a healthy and relaxing way. It felt oh so good.

After I got comfortable with massage and nurturing myself in this way, I was ready to experiment with more intimate touching. I read Alex Comfort's *The Joy of Sex* and *More Joy of Sex*, and that encouraged me to explore more about this orgasm stuff people talked about.

I got brave and started slow. To begin with, I started sleeping without any clothes on. No jammies, no underwear, nothing; totally naked. I made sure my trusty stuffed alligator friend, Alfred, was close by, and I enveloped myself with pillows. The cool sheets felt good on my skin. When I sleep, I lay on my arms and hands. This naturally introduced me to more private touching. When I turned myself in my sleep, there were times I'd touch my breasts, my face, my arms, and my legs.

Sleeping without clothes made me feel vulnerable, but as long as I had ample pillows and snuggled under my sheet and blanket(s), I felt safe. When I first started this exercise, I was apprehensive and didn't sleep well. The more I practiced, though, the more comfortable I became with it, and it became my new normal. I didn't notice any increase in the frequency or intensity of nightmares. It was nice to be introducing this without major drawbacks. Sure, I still experienced nightmares from time to time, but by now, they were infrequent, and the intensity of them grew less and less.

As I grew comfortable sleeping this way, I got a little braver and started caressing my breasts to see what felt good and what didn't. I usually did this when I crawled into bed at night, where I could be safe under my comfy bed coverings. At first, it was just a matter of holding a breast in the palm of my hand. Gradually, I experimented with small, caressing touches. I made mental notes about what felt good and what didn't. I noticed what was different between the left and right. As I discovered things that felt good, I listened to my body to notice any other feelings that arose when I did this.

When I got comfortable with that, then I started experimenting with touching my vagina. I started slowly, and as I learned what felt good and what didn't, then I became more exploratory. Eventually, I learned how to touch myself and actually elicited an orgasm. The first time that happened, it took my breath away. It felt good, but it also felt scary. Again, I practiced until I figured out what worked for me and what didn't.

Again, I didn't have any increased nightmare activity. I was learning how to be comfortable with my body. I even got to a point where I slept deeply enough that I actually had sexual dreams. The first one or two of those startled me, but I learned that this was my body's way of taking care of itself. Once I understood that, there was no need for me to control it. When I slept, I slept. If I had a nightmare, it was just part of the process. If I had a sexual dream, it was my body learning how to feel good.

Jerome and I stayed in touch with each other as friends while he took some time to date some other people. Our friendship deepened as we shared our lives with one another. While he dated a few other people, he didn't find the connection we had with one another.

Sharing our growing-up histories, we discovered our paths occasionally crossed. We never knew each other in our pasts, but it was interesting how our lives connected without us knowing it. We shared many of the same spiritual ideals and explored various philosophies and ideologies. Our conversations were rich and meaningful, and we enjoyed spending time with each other, in play, and at the church with our music jobs. I was more and more attracted to him.

The more time we spent with each other, the clearer our soulful connections became. Being with each other was natural and unburdened. We liked each other, and we enjoyed being with one another. We were "dating" without really knowing it. It was not uncommon for us to exchange "I love yous." Kisses were natural and equally enticing.

Our touching displays of affection were mutual, and the fear I usually had with that turned to eager exploration.

And then, the moment came when our loving physical expressions escalated into something more. I was nervous about where things were leading but also excited. He was attentive to be sure I was comfortable, and nothing felt required or demanding. His hands were warm, filled with tender energy. We undressed slowly, but it was clear where this was leading. He came prepared to be sure we had appropriate protection, but the ritual of putting that into action was a shared experience rather than one-sided.

When the point of intercourse began, it felt good at first. This was the first time I had experienced that. He kept everything gentle, and he stayed attentive to be sure I was comfortable. As that became more involved, I froze. My hands dropped to my sides, and it was like my mind passed out, and I left. Everything checked out.

With no judgment or demand, he simply held me. The intercourse stopped, and there were no subtle hints of anything being required or demanded. There was nothing threatening about how he went about anything. He just held me. A reflex of tears filled my eyes, and I gently wept. If he hadn't seen the moisture running down the side of my face, he wouldn't have known that I was even crying.

When my awareness came back to what was going on, I embraced him, and we simply held each other for several moments. As I came back into my body (that's what it felt like), I stroked his shoulders and back, and he resumed with soft, gentle touches and kisses.

"It's okay," Jerome said. "We can stop if you want to."

"Can you just hold me for a moment?"

He did just that, again, with no demands or judgment.

He must think I'm a freak! It feels good to have him inside me, and I know he loves me. There is nothing frightening about what's going on here. Why did I shut down? I want to share this with him. What's wrong with me? I don't want to freak him out or push him away. I love him.

Thank God he's willing to hold me. He's not running away or anything. It feels good right now to just hold each other.

When I got my wits about me, I kissed him gently. "Maybe we should stop for now. Can we get dressed and try this again sometime?"

"Of course. Everything is okay."

His reassurances helped me feel heard and seen. It was clear he wanted this to be a shared experience. He showed no sign of being weirded out by anything that just happened, which was a tremendous relief. We wrapped things up mutually and parted ways. I was okay but uncertain about what our next "meeting" would bring.

When we connected the next day, we picked up right where we left off. Nothing felt weird or strained. We were the same two people who enjoyed each other, loved each other, and got along well together. Nothing changed. Sure, we talked about it. Our dialog was supportive and exploratory, and we always fondly came back to one another.

As time went on, we tried this beautiful intimacy again and again, and it got easier. I still had moments when I checked out, but the intensity of that lessened. It was amazing he never pressured me. He never seemed to be turned off or bothered by these freakish episodes. We talked about it, shared our thoughts and feelings, and always came back to being ourselves with no interruption or concern. He always held me protectively and supportively, and I always walked away feeling understood and seen.

Fast forward to dinner at Sardines. One of our favorite places to enjoy some great Italian food, a nice easy jazz trio, and a good bottle of wine. The restaurant was small and intimate. We usually sat up on the stage area where we could chat with the musicians between numbers and sets. It was our hangout, and we loved the live jazz the old guys always brought to the table.

During one of our dinners, during a set break, Jerome and I joined hands and gazed into each other's eyes over the little spot of mood lighting on the wee table.

"Well, what do you think?" Jerome asked. "Shall we make this official?"

"What do you mean? Make what official?"

"We've been doing this for a long time. Don't you think it's time we make it official? Will you marry me?"

My heart skipped a beat, and all the breath I had in me escaped.

Oh, my gosh! He just asked me to marry him!

"Yes."

What did I just do? I thought this was something that might come. But I am never getting married! He really just asked me to marry him, and I said yes! Oh my gosh!

When he popped the question, life became instantly surreal. Everything moved in slow motion. "Yes," fell out of my mouth so easily. The prospect of spending my life with this person who had become such a great friend was real. It took my breath away. I was over the moon, happy with a joy I never felt before, but also suddenly worried about the other shoe falling.

Echoes of stories I heard from other rape survivors who walked into what seemed like a perfect relationship. Months later, these perfect relationships fell into complete terror. I didn't want to be one of those statistics. I had every reason to believe Jerome was sound, and there was no other shoe to fall, but how is a person supposed to trust that?

The duality of happiness and fear got the best of me, and I had to talk to someone. Someone other than Jerome. I thought giving it some time to settle would help my fear subside. NOT! Talk of setting dates and planning for this life-changing event took the forefront. When I shared my news with friends and family, I was happy and excited about our decision. The luggage of fear, however, never left my side.

Through my volunteer activities at the Women's Center (the Rape Crisis program), I had a unique relationship with the director there, Jane. She was a military chaplain, and I had such respect for her. In our conversations, I turned to her for guidance.

"Jane, I'm excited about marrying Jerome, but I'm also scared. He seems to love me dearly."

"What are you afraid of?"

"I've heard stories... How do I trust this? What if the other shoe falls? I don't want to step into this lifelong relationship and then find out it was a mistake."

"Alexis, you are an amazing woman, and I've seen you grow through your experience. You've shared about your relationship with Jerome, and he seems to be quite an incredible person. I know you well enough to know that if someone loves you enough to ask you to marry him, he must be a very special person."

"He is pretty special."

"It's okay for you to feel scared. It's a big decision. I think Jerome has found a really special lady. Not every relationship ends with another shoe. No one can predict the future, but you both have something really special with each other."

There was no talk about fear in this conversation. Jane knew me, inside and out, and she was a person who would not encourage me to move forward if she felt like there were indications of the proverbial shoe. It was a new journey of trust I was embarking on: trust in myself and trust in another person. Her observations about us felt true and wise.

~

The honeymoon we designed involved a road trip to several small towns starting in Galveston. What? Did you read that correctly? Galveston?

Fifteen years after my first introduction to the ocean, and being an ocean lover, I decided it was time to make some new memories. Jerome knew about my previous experience, so this was not a spontaneous surprise honeymoon stopover. Rape was surely a part of my past, and there was no running from the facts about where my captor took me. In my mind, this decision was very similar to my decision about the car. Galveston was a place, and I was sure there was more to experience there that had nothing to do with being raped. I would not allow my past to keep me from new life adventures! I loved the water and imagined sharing long, romantic beach walks and quaint seaside restaurants.

As we drove toward our destination, parts of the highway seemed familiar, but this time it was daylight; I saw some places I couldn't see before, but this was much more relaxed. I knew where I was going, and these were adventures I looked forward to. The dense trees of the hill country were amazing, and Jerome and I enjoyed both silly and serious conversations.

We drove over the big bridge from Houston to Galveston, and the ocean view was spectacular. It was amazing to see so much water and the vistas of the horizon across the sea. We stayed in an old Victorian home, and our room upstairs was complete with a nice porch area we could enjoy. We woke to the sound of seabirds and ocean waves. I thought I was in heaven!

We spent the day beachcombing and seashell hunting. I loved walking by the ocean, letting the waves roll onto my sandy feet. The smell of the sea, the sound of rolling waves; it was paradise to me. We fell in love with it and scrapped our other plans to spend our whole honeymoon in the Galveston area.

For one of our evening meals, we went to a highly recommended Italian restaurant. It was not very crowded mid-week for a beach town in early March. We enjoyed long conversations with the wait staff, who tended to our every need.

When we finished our meal, we were the only customers left in the place and enjoyed savoring some wine and conversation. We talked about things to do in and around the area. It's always fun to talk with the locals about their favorite hangouts to learn about the less-publicized things to do in a place.

Our conversation eventually turned to urban legends and listening to tales of adventures long past. It was fun to learn about some of the history of Galveston, some lore, and some facts. Before I knew it, someone was telling a story about a shocking discovery in one of the local gas stations. They talked about the volume of blood all over the bathroom floor and a note left about someone who was in trouble. My heart skipped a beat as I realized they were sharing a piece of my story. Fifteen years later, people were still talking about it!

I told them what happened to me, and they were shocked to find out it was my story. It was unusual to hear complete strangers talking about my experience. They didn't know me from Adam. What made this come up in conversation? Whatever the reason, it was interesting to hear other people sharing this story about my past. Someone finally heard my plea for help, and that's what started a chain of events of people trying to find me. I made it home undiscovered, but it was some relief to know that people cared enough to look for me once my message was discovered by the gas station attendant.

Jerome and I made several more trips to Galveston over the years.

We never had another conversation like this with the locals, but we created some amazing memories in this little Texas coast town.

Thirty-plus years later…

The shoe has never fallen. Sure, we've had our difficulties, some larger than others. History reveals, though, that we always come back to each other with an openness to talk about anything that's going on. In the beginning, he was the first to start those conversations, but as I have learned to be more comfortable with myself and my feelings, it's a more mutual sharing. Jane was right. Jerome is a very special person, and I'm fortunate to be sharing my life with someone such as him.

CHAPTER 23
NIGHTMARES

BECAUSE I KEPT myself busy and tried to sleep as little as possible to avoid dreaming, this trauma I experienced festered like an open wound. When you hike up a mountain and get a blister on your foot, you can only ignore it for so long. Eventually, it will become so painful you have to pay attention to it. Nightmares were my blister.

Right after being kidnapped and raped, I dreamed about the events that took place in the car and the 23 hours of horror I endured. They were very specific about the events that took place. They were so intense I often woke up breathless. Sometimes, though, I woke up because I wanted to scream, but nothing would come out. I was so frozen with fear in my dream that I couldn't make my vocal cords make any sound. I opened my mouth to let the sound out, but nothing came. The intensity of it, though, woke me up. I thought I screamed myself awake, but no sound was coming out.

I was so desperate to forget and pretend it never happened. Giving myself an inch to process the myriad of feelings that went along with it felt like popping a blister that would ooze goop for days! I thought if I opened the wound, the pain would never go away. When I finally cried, I cried and cried and cried and didn't think I'd ever be able to stop. It was uncontrollable, and I wanted to be in control! He took all the control from me that he could have. No more!

My emotions and my spirit had to figure out how to process the experience somehow. If it couldn't get any daytime attention, it would come out while I slept. Its determination was every bit as intense as my will to make it all go away.

In one of my dreams, I was sitting at a traffic light. I was driving. While I waited for the light to change, a guy used a gun to break the window, and then he pointed the gun at me. He demanded that I get out of the car and go with him. I couldn't drive off because there were cars in front of me. When I tried to move to get out of the car, my body froze. I couldn't move.

"If you don't come with me, I'm going to kill you."

The assailant in my dream would not take no for an answer.

It was the face of my captor, and I knew if I got out of the car, he was going to rape me again. I didn't know if I could ever get away from him.

"I'm going to kill you right here if you don't move."

When my body froze and I couldn't move, I resolved that letting him kill me was better than having to endure whatever was going to happen.

"Just kill me, then!" I said in my dream.

He shot me in the head, and I felt the bullet go through. It stopped in the center of my brain, and then my head exploded. I saw a myriad of colors, and then my life started flashing before my eyes. In my dream, I died. I actually died. I woke up when I realized I couldn't feel anything anymore. Even though I woke up, I thought I was dead. It took several minutes for me to realize I was awake and it was only a dream.

Once I learned nightmares were my body's way of processing the experience, I forced myself to sleep. When I woke up from a nightmare, I chanted to myself it was only a dream. It wasn't real; it was just a dream.

After I got married, Jerome often held me while I slept. One night, I slept with my back to him, and his arm draped over me while he held me. I dreamed again that I was driving, and someone broke my window with a gun, and he was intent on killing me. It was the exact dream I had before. This time, though, I was not about to die. I chomped down on his arm, and he dropped the gun. Jerome screamed, "Ouch!" I awoke to find out I bit my husband!

I still have nightmares. They aren't as intense as they once were, and they are certainly not as frequent, but I still have them. I often wake up telling myself that I'm okay and that it's only a dream. Sometimes I still wake up breathless. When these dreams occur, I know I'm still processing something. I've learned to give myself the freedom to explore what's going on, instead of fighting to run away from it. I've learned so much!

While I've been writing this book, disturbing dreams have stirred. I had one a few weeks ago where I had my period, and I was in some sort of place where I was being held captive. I sat on the commode trying to get my cramps to stop, and a lady was trying to get me to hurry. The more persistent she was for me to hurry, the more intensely misunderstood I felt. (It's a dream, remember.) I woke myself up in a cold sweat, saying out loud, "Just kill me. Just go ahead and kill me."

And then, just the other day, I've never had a dream like this before... I guess my dreams evolve as I do. Unfortunately, I don't remember the circumstances, but I woke up laughing uncontrollably. I could not stop laughing. When I woke up, I was actually laughing out loud! I didn't think I'd ever stop laughing! I laughed all day.

CHAPTER 24
HE GETS OUT OF JAIL

WHEN I GOT HOME one evening after a support group, I received an ominous greeting from my mom. I could tell by the energy in the room that something was stirring.

"Your dad should be home shortly, and we'd like to visit with you about something."

This means something is up. I wonder what's going on now.

On cue, as the daily reports wound down, Dad walked in.

"Hello, Alexis. How was your day?"

It wasn't too common for me to be sitting in the living room with Mom chit-chatting about my day. While I rattled on about my day, Dad got comfortable to join the conversation.

"We have something we need to tell you," Dad said. "We got word today that the person who raped you got out of jail."

My heart dropped into the pit of my stomach.

He got 12 years with his guilty plea to the kidnapping charge and an additional three years from a prior sentence. It has only been two and a half years! How can he already be getting out?

Without missing a beat, Dad continued. "He got out early because of good behavior. The parole board rewarded his good behavior and released him early. Prisons are crowded, and I guess they let people out to make room for other prisoners. Knowing that he threatened you, we felt like you should know what's going on. How do you feel about that?"

"Well, Janice and everyone said only about 20% of the people who get released ever come back and follow through on their threats. Hopefully, that's true! I don't like the idea that he's out, but we live in a different place, and I'm not in the same school."

"It's a surprise for all of us. I also wanted you to know that I talked with a friend of mine who is in the FBI about all of this. He told me he put the fear of God in him before he got out of jail. Told him if he came anywhere close to you, they would kill him on sight!"

"Wow! I'm glad about that. That feels better, knowing someone is out there thinking of my best interest. I don't want to live in fear, but I also know there aren't any guarantees. Hopefully, the threat is enough to steer him clear of us here in Fort Worth. I guess I'll just carry on with my school and work, and hope for the best."

"That sounds like a good plan," Dad said. "I want you to know that we're here if you ever want to talk about it or if you have questions about anything."

Dad's words eased my fear. They echoed lovingly in my head.

"Thank you for letting me know about this."

"It will all be okay, Alexis. We have statistics on our side, and I'm grateful for that!"

"Please share my thanks with your friend, Dad. I just want all of this to be over! I know I'll be looking over my shoulder for a while. Hopefully, though, he'll heed the warnings and stay far, far away."

I had mixed feelings about the threat from Dad's FBI friend. It felt good, on one hand, that someone outside of our normal law enforcement circle was on my side. The thought of someone being killed, rapist or not, was unsettling. I hoped it wouldn't come to that!

Janice said the chances of him coming back to follow through on his threat are really low.

I let those words echo in my brain as I returned to the limited sanctity of my makeshift bedroom. My thoughts were like a hamster running on a wheel, spinning with lots of new information. I plopped myself on the hide-a-bed in my bedroom and let my thoughts run for a while. I wanted so desperately to pick up my journal and write, but that was no longer safe to do. Not while I lived in the same house with my parents.

The all-too-familiar trembling I experienced during the rape crept in.

I'm at home. I'm safe. Why is my body shaking? I'm here in my room. No one is here to hurt me. Stop it!

My body went back to its fear response, like a dropped plate falls to the floor. The more I tried to stop the shaking, the more intense the trembling became. I stretched myself out on the couch and made myself breathe.

As the trembling subsided, I turned my mind to all the homework I had to get done before tomorrow. I sat up and pilfered through my stack of books, pulled out a notebook, and buried myself in my studies. My handy-dandy distraction technique of choice: to stay busy. It helped distract the roar of scary thoughts taking hold. Music and studying was like being in a candy store for me.

With the urgent homework completed, I readied myself for bed. I gathered all my pillows, my trusty alligator friend, Alfred, and Fume, the misfit stuffed mouse, and crawled into bed. My pillows and friends made me feel safe and held. I rocked myself to sleep, thinking about sharing this news in the safety of my support group.

Over the next several days, I kept my thoughts on school and work, and the practice room became my best friend. Practicing the piano or violin always made me feel better. The music served as a comfort. I put all the whirling emotions I had about his release into expressive musical phrases. Music was always my solace: a place to express the turmoil that brewed inside. Without the freedom to write in my journal, this was the next best thing.

Knowing he was out of jail, even though he was 200 miles away, I looked over my shoulder everywhere I went. I scanned my surroundings for any sight of him. He was never there, but it seemed comforting to look and find nothing. I kept Janice's reassurances in the forefront of my thoughts while I made myself aware of my surroundings and who was near me.

~

The FBI threat, or the natural course of the universe, has protected me all these years. I've never seen him. I've seen people that look similar to him, which is always cause for a double take. But I've never seen him.

With the FBI resource long gone, I don't have this kind of resource available to me anymore. This leaves me feeling a little unsettled sometimes, but it is a background rumbling that doesn't take up too much room. With no sense of regularity, I do some Internet searching now and then to see where he is located. Thankfully, to date, he remains far away from me.

PART THREE

WHOLE PERSON

CHAPTER 25
BUT WAIT! THERE'S MORE!

I'M A SURVIVOR; there's no doubt about that. I survived being kidnapped and raped. But is there more to life than just surviving it? If I'm a survivor, am I still surviving something? Is it still somehow in control of how I function, and does it influence who I am in the world? I think yes. Is there an integration point with the healing and recovery where the experience is now a part of who I am, and it is part of me? Yes, I've found this to be true.

Is it ever over? Is there a point in any trauma recovery that it's just over and done with? I don't think so. This experience is part of what makes me who I am. Because this experience touched every part of my existence, I'm still learning about it. As I get older, I continue to learn more about life. My experiences influence how I perceive my new learnings and how they fit into the whole of who I am.

It is an important step to become a survivor instead of being a victim. The survivor perspective gets you to a functional living state. And that's important. In my process, I got to the point with the survival part where I got more inquisitive. "If I'm a survivor, aren't I still surviving something? If I'm surviving something, isn't the thing I'm surviving still functioning as an important part of my life?"

I thought there had to be more. There had to be another level.

When do I get to just be a whole person? Do I have to be a survivor? (That determined part of me that refuses to let this experience dictate my life still shows its face from time to time.) That's when I started integrating this experience into the whole of who I am.

Integration of the experience means, to me, that it is a historical event that happened in my life. There are many events in a person's life. I have played a piano concerto with an orchestra, won billiards tournaments, and been a successful project manager. I've been a step-mom, a wife, a sister, and I've walked up mountains and lived in the woods in a tent. These are all life events. Rape and kidnap are also experiences I've had. I also experienced a broken bone, had surgery, and got married. These are all events and experiences in my life.

Every day that I live, I'm learning and living. New experiences happen, and they become part of who I am and what makes me who I am. We all have this. The experiences you've had in your life are unique to you. How you experienced them and the impact they have had on your life are unique to you. We all process and deal with events in our lives differently. Isn't it great that our world is full of people with unique experiences? And we can learn from each other when we share our stories.

I still experience growth moments because rape and kidnap are part of who I am. These moments are not debilitating or as intense as they once were, but I still have them. I still experience an occasional nightmare, and I still have memories of the experience when I smell certain things.

I invite my life to be free of these things. Wouldn't it be nice to live life without another nightmare about being raped? I've had many, many nights without them. The longer I live, the more nightmare-less nights I have. That's the good news. Will I still have them ten years from now? If history is an indicator, probably. I continue to learn new ways to deal with these hurdles, though. And thank goodness, there are some amazing people out there who can help when I come up against a tough spot.

Will certain smells remind me of the experience? Yup. They sure do. It's fortunate for me it is a smell that only happens in certain circum-stances. I've learned how to acknowledge it and realize where it's coming from and remind myself that I'm in a different place now. And I limit the opportunity for me to be exposed to it. It really has more to do with how I choose to be affected by it and respond to it. That's what makes a difference to me.

These scenarios I've described are some ways that this experience has evolved from victim to survivor to integrating the experience into the whole of who I am. I can talk about these things with ease because I know what they are all about and where I am with them. It's not something I go around telling everyone about. Not everyone I know knows this about me. When a conversation can deepen or it can help someone else with their own process, it's a rich experience to share. It is a part of who I am.

CHAPTER 26
GIVING BACK

I GOT PRETTY good at holding myself together after a couple of years. My coping mechanisms worked. They evolved, but they worked. The Rape Crisis Support group I involved myself in proved to be a stable source of support and learning for me. One of the professional counselors I saw, who was an Episcopal priest, helped me see the many ways I learned to take care of myself. His words, "…*seems to me you did everything right. You're here talking to me…*" was a catalyst for propelling me forward.

Once I achieved stable ground, I wanted to give back. I realized the value of kind, non-judgmental support and wanted to offer that to others. The most logical place for me to start with this was our local Rape Crisis Center. They, of course, helped me in a big way, and I wanted to give back. I signed up to carry a pager on weekends, to meet people at the hospital when they were going through the rape exam. I was there to listen and support.

It meant a lot to me to have this support when I went through my experience. Jenny helped me feel glad to be alive, and I felt like she understood me while I unveiled the details of my experience. I wanted to support others going through that process. It's scary right after such an event. Having someone around to go through those immediate motions can be an anchor to grasp onto while things feel so profoundly chaotic.

I did that for several years. I supported people of all ages. My place was to be with them while they went through the raw experience of telling their stories to law enforcement officials. I was an invisible hand to hold while they went through the rape exam. It felt good to be a part of the lives of these people as they were in the early hours of their recovery and survival.

But something tugged at me. Rape is a very two-sided issue: victim and offender. I took my curious mind to Jane at the Women's Center.

"Jane, I've been thinking. The support we offer here at the Women's Center is a very important part of the equation. I wonder, though, if there is an opportunity for us to interrupt this cycle of victimization by talking with sex offenders. How can we teach them about the impact of their decision to hurt people? Are you aware of any programs that offer something like that?"

"Wow! You bring up an excellent point. I don't think there is anything like that here in Fort Worth. Let me reach out to some folks and see what might be available for that."

There was much discussion about this in the coming weeks. It was important for an experience like that to be safe. There had to be some ground rules put in place for both sides to assure safety and confidentiality for all parties involved.

There was a program through MHMR (Mental Health Mental Retardation) of Tarrant County for sex offenders who were on probation or parole. Jane talked with the group facilitators, and they agreed to try it. A dialog between survivors of sexual abuse and offenders. An hour and a half, one session only. Offenders and survivors gathered separately in different spaces. There were four or five survivors who agreed to take part in the groups, and there would only be 10 to 12 offenders present.

When it was time for the group to start, offender facilitators escorted their clients into the room with survivors. We started with introductions. Offenders kept their introductions short: first name and a brief, non-detailed account of their offense. Then, survivors introduced themselves, their names (or made-up names), and a brief account of their victimization. They did not allow physical contact, and they seated survivors so that they were not next to offenders.

From there, the floor was open to discussion. It was tense! No one knew what to expect or how things would go from there. There were some underlying objectives for the dialog. Offenders needed to accept responsibility for their offenses. Survivors needed to share what they were comfortable sharing about the impact of being raped or sexually abused. The idea was for the offenders to learn about the impact of their actions on other people.

When the group was over, offenders left first, quietly—with no ingratiating "thank yous" or comments. They were to leave without gathering in the parking lot for post-group discussion. Survivors hung around for a few moments afterward to process the experience and their feelings while the offenders dispersed. It was important for the survivors to leave the facility without being watched or followed.

It's hard to describe the energy of the experience other than extreme intensity. Offenders were afraid of being berated about their wrongdoing. Survivors were fearful about being re-victimized (not physically, but verbally). We talked about how difficult it is for survivors to trust, the immediate effects of nightmares, and the raw vulnerability of rape and sexual abuse. Relationships were always a suitable topic, familial or otherwise. It was easy, especially the first few times we did this, for survivors to capitalize on how dangerous offenders are for doing such a thing.

The more I did this, the more I learned about how to transform the discussion into a more productive direction. My observation about berating offenders showed how stifling it was for the conversation. They quit being curious about things and the discussion became very one-sided. I came to realize that offenders are not bad people but people who have done bad things. It's a subtle difference but a very important one. That little change in the conversation moved the needle and changed the direction of our conversations.

I learned a lot about myself talking with offenders. New patterns in my victim/survival surfaced, and it became a playground for learning, at least for me. Once I adjusted my language about things from bad people to offensive actions, a new level of understanding unfolded.

Giving the offenders credit for being a person capable of learning shifted the entire playing field.

Allowing offenders to see my vulnerability was also a good dynamic to learn about. Vulnerability is a powerful emotion to show in this circumstance. Offenders are controlling. Demonstrating how vulnerability doesn't destroy me opens the door for them to get in touch with the parts of themselves that are vulnerable. That's when the magic happens. It breaks down their desire to control the conversation and brings a wealth of topics for us to talk about.

Slowly, I learned that if there was any hope of impacting change in this forum, it was to get them to talk about feelings. In order to do that, I had to do the same. I gave myself permission to do that, and the group dynamic completely shifted. When offenders are in touch with their feelings, they are much more open to seeing other people as people. When they can see a person rather than a thing to conquer or get what they want, they get into a mindset that allows them to act more appropriately.

The tricky part is getting this group of people to talk about feelings. I got creative and came up with a perfect example for them to experience while I was there so we could talk about it. Before the group started, I had them write one word on a piece of paper that described something that was important to them. I collected all their words and put them in a basket without reading them. Then, I had someone pull a piece of paper from the basket. Without reading it, I tore the paper into four pieces and asked them how that felt.

They felt so very betrayed. Shattered almost. We talked about the feelings they experienced. I talked about that was exactly how it felt to me to be raped. Someone pulled my life out of the basket and tore it to pieces. After some discussion about that, I would then try to tape the piece of paper back together. I always have trouble doing that. It never goes back together the way it was before I tore it. I ask them if it's the same. Is the piece of paper ever going to be the same after tearing it? Of course not! It's easy for them to see and gives us a great deal to talk about. But now they are invested in the conversation. I took their important thing, disregarded it, and tore it to pieces. Then, we can also talk about how hard it is to put the pieces together.

The program of conversations between offenders and survivors expanded. The MHMR program ran its course for a couple of years, and then something interesting happened. Local private sex offender treatment providers started implementing victim empathy modules into their curriculum. Offenders could not attend a survivor group until they were at a point in their treatment to take responsibility for their actions. It wasn't effective until they got to this place. I'm still doing this today.

I knew I'd been doing this for a long time when I started seeing people I knew on the offender side of the conversation. The first time this happened, it was a guy I knew when I played in the Youth Orchestra in high school. My first instinct was to clam up. I let others jump into their conversations while I gathered my wits about me.

It is one thing to talk with a sex offender you don't know. There is a delicate sense of separation between offender and survivor. It is quite another to be having these conversations with someone you know. When I gathered up my wits and spoke, I pointed out that we knew each other. I thought the group facilitators were going to come unglued. Their primary concern was my safety, of course, but I didn't want to run away from this. I was in a unique position to make a very personal connection with him.

A few other times, I recognized people I saw in my neighborhood stores. I even came face to face with one person who was a favorite server of ours at Sardines, where my husband proposed to me. He took care of us for years! Imagine my shock. Another time, I came across someone who went to my church. In every case, I made sure they knew who I was and that we knew each other. I thought it was important for them to know that I knew their little secret. I always respected their confidentiality outside of the group, but it made me feel safer to make that kind of connection with them.

This all led me to think about what it might be like for me to have the same conversations with the person who raped me. The thought of being face-to-face with him scared the piddle diddle out of me. I learned that after his release from prison, he went back on a charge of indecency with a child. Finally, he got a sexual abuse charge. They released him into a halfway house in West Texas. As far as I knew, he was not local, and the chances of me coming face to face with him were slight to nonexistent.

My work with offenders strengthened my trauma resilience journey into something far beyond just being a survivor. I came to be a whole person with rape as one of my many life experiences. The experience did not define me, but it deepened my understanding of myself and how I relate to the rest of the world. I'm not sure I would be the person I am today without the journey of this recovery.

During a spiritual retreat, while taking communion, it hit me like a ton of bricks. This person who forever changed the landscape of my life gave me a gift—a life gift. What he did to me was horrific, and it is not something I would ever wish upon another soul to endure. Because I had this experience, though, I made the choice to learn more about myself and what makes me tick. I got acquainted with a new person. I've changed from the person I was when I came into this life.

Would I be the same person today if this was not in my experience library? I don't know. Can I learn what I've learned through other means? Yes. Would the color of this picture be the same, though, without the experience? I'm not so sure.

As I took the sacraments of communion, a wave of immense gratitude and love came over me. I pictured the person who raped me in my mind and came to a moment of forgiveness. I have no desire to be face-to-face with my rapist again. There is no need for me to say these words to him in physical form. What mattered to me was the acceptance I felt toward myself and my past. It was a profound healing moment for me.

Empathy is an interesting thing to teach in any circumstance. Offenders are not well-versed in their emotional health. Before one can feel empathy, I think they need to connect to their own hearts—and by that, I mean feelings. The paper trick helps elicit a feeling we can talk about. But how do I help them learn how to care? Can an offender learn how to care? I believe they can. But how do you invite them to go there?

This is my experiment. Perhaps you could try this out loud with a friend and drop the caring part if that feels more comfortable to you. This is how the conversation goes when I speak with offenders.

"Don't think about a purple giraffe. What are you thinking about?"

"A purple giraffe."

"Now, think about a brown giraffe. What are you thinking about?"

"A brown giraffe."

"Don't think about a purple giraffe. What are you thinking about?"

"A purple giraffe."

"Do you see how your mind doesn't hear the word 'don't?' Now let's talk about caring. Do you want to care for people or hurt them?"

"I want to care about them."

"When you tell me you don't want to hurt people anymore, what are you thinking about?"

"Not hurting people."

"Where's your focus? What are you thinking about when you say, 'not hurting people?'"

"Hurting people."

"Our minds are pretty powerful, aren't they? You're telling me you want to care about people, and then you turn around and say, 'I don't want to hurt people anymore.' Where's your focus? What is your brain hearing?"

"Hurting people."

"If you want to care about people, what can you say instead so that you focus on caring?"

"I want to care about people."

"It takes a little energy to be forward-thinking enough to set yourself up to care. You have to keep your care switch on. If you want to care, think about caring. Is it worth the effort to care? Can you do it? Because you've hurt people, you've learned how to forget about caring. I believe in you, though. If you can think about purple giraffes, I know you can think about caring. You are far more skilled than you realize."

Well, this is just a sample, but you get the idea. Our minds really are powerful. From a victim/survivor/person perspective, our minds are just as powerful. If we want to live comfortably with the experiences in our lives, our minds can help us. We need only be deliberate and intentional about how we choose to think.

That's a pretty powerful lesson, isn't it?

After several years of having these conversations with adult offenders, word got around. I started getting invitations to speak at a local medical prison facility. They had an Empathy Training program at their facility, and they asked me to come and speak. The people incarcerated at this facility were there for a variety of offenses, but the message was still the same. Purple giraffes and caring are a universal language applicable to anyone, incarcerated or not.

I wonder what it would be like to have these same conversations with adolescent offenders.

I asked the adult treatment providers if they were aware of any such programs for kids. There weren't any. After some networking, I found a couple of programs open to trying it. What I found is that adolescent offenders are still moldable. They have a natural curiosity that adult offenders don't have. It's a different audience because they are younger people, but the same conversation still applies. Purple giraffes and caring are still a universal language.

I extended my work to local and non-local adolescent prison facilities. I started by speaking with sex offenders in these facilities. After a while, though, they rotated me around to speak with other inmates who were there for other types of crime. It is a sobering experience to speak with a 12-year-old person who has already taken another life. But alas, the purple giraffe and caring still apply—young or old.

All this talk with offenders. Is it worth it? I know a good many people will never make the choice to change. If I can spend an hour and a half with someone, though, and one person learns to care, it's worth it to me. I'm willing to talk about the darkest, most horrific experience I've ever had if it will help someone take the risk and learn to feel—learn to care. Yes, I'm still doing this today. I'm still talking with both adolescent and adult offenders in prisons and out.

CHAPTER 27
SUGAR-COATING THE UGLY

THE CONCEPT that there are rich lessons to be learned from our life experiences is interesting. There are those who respond to this idea with a negative connotation. Somehow, the "good" that comes from such an experience lessens the profound horror of the experience. If I'm speaking from my experience, I see it from a different perspective. My big ugly is my big amazing. Not that I'm grateful for the experience, but I'm grateful for my choices.

There is nothing good or pretty or amazing about being raped and kidnapped. It's horrible! In my mind, there's no reason for another human being to do that to another person. It is senseless and cruel.

We have a choice, though, about how we choose to deal with it. Some people will forever feel victimized by their experiences. Others will pick themselves up and survive it—life will go on and it will become a past. For me, this historical part of life is now a part of what makes me who I am. No matter what sort of path you choose to come to peace with it, I'm so very glad you're here and that you are alive.

Dealing with this kind of trauma is vast and complicated. There are about as many ways to handle it as there are people in this world. One way is not necessarily better than another. They are all different. This story is about the hills, valleys, and mountains I've climbed to be where I am today. I honor whatever process works for you. You are you, and I want you to do you.

Maybe I've talked about some things that you can relate to. There are probably parts of this story that you don't relate to. That's all good. Perhaps sharing the way I navigated this burning building will give you some ideas or, at the very least, hope in navigating yours.

There is nothing about this journey that is easy or delightful. I made a very conscious choice to examine my innards. It has become a curiosity for me. I have a nightmare, and I want to understand what it's about. When I smell a revolting smell that brings back a memory, I choose to look at how far I've come. When my dreams express themselves as terror, I know my soul is still processing this experience, and the whole of me is still a work in progress.

I would not be where I am today without the many forms of support and guidance I have received. Some of it was more helpful than others. I tried fervently to deal with it all on my own, and I learned that I could not do it all by myself. It took extreme discomfort, but I eventually hurt enough to find a better medicine. Because I did that, I have learned some amazing tools to help me navigate the way out. A way to the other side of the dense and dark forest. That is the part that I am most grateful for.

If you are afraid to ask for help, I get that! I urge you to find supportive resources to help you navigate the chaos. Sometimes, a willing hand is just what you need to steady yourself. People come together to rebuild communities after devastation. It's okay to have a community to help you through the wake of trauma.

I tell you this not to sugar-coat the ugly but to paint a picture that might help you paint your own picture of what life on the other side of rape can be. I made some choices that made things better and others that made things worse. There's no denying that. Where I excelled was when I found resources that understood and honored me. They let me feel without criticism or judgment. They helped me understand what I was feeling and why. When those resources shared information and gave me opportunities to try new things, I learned what works for me and what doesn't. It's true that some approaches help the process, but others aren't a good fit.

It's a dance. There are no instructions, and there are no right or wrong ways to find your path. This picture is not black and white. There are so many, many shades of color. I encourage you to move to the rhythm that resonates most harmoniously with your instrument. Find the sweet spot that allows you to feel whole.

CHAPTER 28
A WORD ABOUT INTUITION

JUST BEFORE BEING KIDNAPPED, my intuition let me know something wasn't right. Because I was nervous about my date, I completely overrode the wisdom coming from my gut. This choice taught me how to question that inner voice, which led to a spiral of not trusting it. Relearning how to trust it—well, I'm getting better at it, but it is still a work in progress for me.

Two amazing people who happen to be authors have helped me in this process: V. Vernon Woolf, Ph.D. (*Holodynamics*), and SARK. I'm sure there are a ton of other authors out there who've written about this, but these were the two who propelled me forward on this journey.

SARK calls intuition our inner wise self. What a fabulous description of it! That little voice inside of us is wise. Tuning into it and learning to trust it is my challenge. Dr. Woolf calls it our full potential self. It's that picture of you that is your fullest potential. Close your eyes and allow yourself to be in a place of peace. Then, imagine your full potential walking toward you. What does it look like? Mine looks like a radiant form of light that is shaped like a human.

This inner wise self, full potential, intuition, or whatever you choose to call it, is always available to us. All we need to do is ask it to be present in our lives with us. SARK recommends writing letters to yourself from your inner wise self. She recommends asking it specific questions about anything you're wanting guidance about.

Dr. Woolf's idea has more to do with a maturity or mind model that includes six parts of ourselves. These six parts are physical, personal, interpersonal, social, principled, and universal well-being. I've taken what I've learned from both people to find a solution that works for me. I'll share some of that with you. And I invite you to use whatever works best for you.

The first step for me was giving my full potential an identity. I call her FiPS (Full Potential Self). At SARK's suggestion, I regularly write letters to myself from FiPS. I visualize her in my mind, pick up my pen, and let her share what's going on inside of her. She speaks to me with such adoration, which is loving and kind. I ask her questions like:

How can I create more _____?
What is easiest for me to receive regarding _____?
What is one path for me to explore more about _____?
What will further support me as I create _____?

These questions all came from SARK, and I still use them (or derivatives of them) today. The wealth of information I receive is amazing. And when I heed her advice, it is amazing to me how often her guidance is spot on. It doesn't always happen overnight, but it creates a "field" for things to materialize, and I've learned to trust what comes out of her.

The amazing part of this is my inner wisdom/full potential/intuition is me. It is a part of me. This voice teaches me how to trust myself and my inner guidance system.

FiPS is multi-dimensional. She has a physical representation that is full of vitality, abundance, health, strength, and energy. The personal part of her fosters creativity, confidence, and self-assertion, helps me feel like "I'm okay," and aids in self-discovery. Her interpersonal parts assist me with intimacy, friendship, "we are okay," mutual respect, and rapport. The social part guides me with synergy, teamwork, open trust, camaraderie, and cooperation. Her principled part helps me with integrity, "I am," owning it, fair-care-share, and openness. Last, the universal part of her guides me about oneness, knowing, empowerment, loving, and being attuned.

This is straight out of Dr. Woolf's maturity model, as defined in *Holodynamics*. With these dimensions, the guidance I receive from my intuition comes from a whole and peaceful place of full potential. Imagine having a regular dialog with that special part of yourself. Writing letters to me from this part of myself is extremely enlightening. The longer I've done this, the more natural it is for me to consult with this part of myself for literally everything!

Here's a recent sample letter to me from FiPS:

Adorable, Accomplished Writer Alexis...

You're a published author, my dear! You've given the world a beautiful gift. I'm wiggly with excitement!

Focus Points:

How can I create more momentum in my Daily Calm and chair yoga routines?

Give yourself some writing breaks. Use those to think about other things and do your chair yoga before you park your butt on the couch to watch TV. You've got this! Just do it! Your heart and I will thank you.

What is easiest for me to receive regarding Daily Calms and chair yoga?

Daily Calms feed your soul and open your heart to new ideas. Embrace them and walk with them. It will soon become automatic as your walking has. Chair yoga helps your body to stay in motion and keeps you flexible. You always feel good when you do it. Let it be part of who you are. You will love yourself, as I do, for it.

What is one path for me to explore more about Daily Calms and chair yoga?

These are both activities that keep us connected and working together. Just do it! It only takes a few minutes, and those minutes are full of juicy goodness. Here's a reminder: Phone games will wait for you. Be diligent in your focus on caring for yourself. Amazing gifts are waiting patiently for you to discover them.

What will further support me as I create space and energy for Daily Calms and chair yoga in my life?

These are things that strengthen your inner sparkles. People will feel good around you without really knowing why. And that's okay. They don't really need to know. What matters is that you're doing you. The rest will follow. Be diligent and stay flexible. It works wonders!

I love you so very much, Alexis. You are an amazing person—

Your Full Potential Self

I have gone long periods of time where I didn't do this: writing letters to myself. I've found, though, the more I do it, the more integrated it is into who I am. It's becoming more natural. Experiment with it yourself. You could write yourself a letter and actually mail it to yourself so you can read it later. It's fun to play with, and it is such a powerful tool for getting back to your beautiful, authentic self.

After I finish this memoir, I'm going to write a series of children's picture books about this very thing. Helping kids learn how to tap into their intuition. Can you imagine what your life would be like if you learned this skill as a child? Well, that is an adventure for the future.

CHAPTER 29
VULNERABILITY

RAPE EXPLOITS one of the most sacred things in a person: vulnerability. We're all fragile when we enter this world. We are at the mercy of our very undeveloped spirit and the influences of those who care for us to develop into who we want to be. As we grow older and more independent, the breadth of our vulnerability shifts and becomes a much broader scope.

When we're older, life throws us new curve balls. The things we've been through and what we believe can affect how we choose. Uncertainty increases vulnerability. Uncharted territory causes fear, and what I trust and don't trust influences my choice. The smaller the real estate for my footing, the more vulnerable I feel.

The flip side is also true. Confidence decreases vulnerability. I approach my choice with more certainty about the outcome. There is less fear, and there is an underlying current of trust about the choice I'm making. The larger the real estate is for my footing, the less vulnerable I feel. A road feels more stable than a ledge.

I have a friend who describes part of her trauma recovery as balancing on the head of a pin. It is a perfect description. I can relate to that. A blind date, for me, was like balancing on that pinhead. I had very little dating experience and was very uncertain about the whole thing. Things are so uncertain after being kidnapped and raped. There is nothing certain about getting married. You get the idea.

Vulnerability is something we all have in our lives, regardless of living with traumatic experiences. It is intensely harmful when someone chooses not to see another person's vulnerability and capitalizes on it or takes advantage of it. I can't control what another person is going to do, but I can be conscious about how vulnerable I allow myself to be in any setting, socially, at home, or with friends and family.

I like to give my vulnerability a voice so I can learn from it. It often has some interesting lessons for me to learn. These golden nuggets offer a wealth of information, and giving it a new look has helped me find a larger confidence in myself that I never knew I had.

When I'm open and vulnerable with loved ones, it brings us closer together. How magical is that? My vulnerability allows other people to see the delicate, human part of me. When they see mine, they are often willing to share their vulnerability with me, and it just deepens the whole relationship experience. It is a hard thing to do, but taking baby steps with it can uncover some big life magic.

Offender dialog is an extremely vulnerable experience for me. I'm stepping into a room full of men and/or women who have turned off their care switches and made choices to hurt people. Talking about rape is one of the most vulnerable parts of myself. Exposed vulnerability, though, makes me human and shows them that the feelings I express don't hurt me. They are a part of me and who I am.

When I share myself with them, they are much more receptive to sharing with me. It allows them to see firsthand the impact of their uncaring choices on other people. I want them to get to know that part of themselves. It's easier for them to make caring choices when they are in touch with that part of themselves.

I've had some doozy conversations with these people! It never would have happened without my willingness to be vulnerable with them. I'm choosy about how I do that and to what degree. I've cried in front of them, I've gotten angry, I've even shut down and gotten totally quiet. These are all genuine feelings. Taking the risk, with the right safety in place, gives us a chance to talk about these emotions, get to know them, and understand more about them.

After I give myself a moment to process these feelings, I always talk about them with the group. It helps them to learn how to feel and understand these feelings and that it's okay to talk about them. Dealing with vulnerability is easier in private, for sure. But if the opportunity arises, and it feels safe to do so, it is an excellent tool to get to the meat of different topics. Recognition, feeling, and learning about emotions—it's a powerful vehicle for us to connect to the heart of who we are.

CHAPTER 30
INTEGRATING THE EXPERIENCE INTO MY LIFE

BIG, ugly traumas that happen in our lives change us. My personal perspective on this: the path of life I followed before being raped drastically changed when someone decided I didn't matter. Think about this for a moment. If you walked out into the world today and lost one of your legs, how would your life be different?

Perhaps you've experienced this firsthand. To me, everything about life would be harder: getting out of bed, learning how to walk again. If I got an artificial limb, I'd have to put my leg on to be functional. If I didn't get an artificial limb, I'd have to learn how to navigate this life with one leg. Everything would change!

That's how I feel about being raped. Everything about my life has changed. I didn't lose a limb, but rape forever changed the soul of who I was when I was born. It impacts the relationships I have and my family dynamics. This experience has changed how I see the world and the people in it. My emotional responses to things are forever impacted. If you're reading this book and you never knew this about me, you have a different perspective now that you know this about me.

I would give anything to wake up in the morning without rape being part of who I am. What a gift that would be. But I can't make that happen. Tomorrow, when I wake up, this experience will still be a part of who I am. The scar I have on my knee from falling off my bicycle when I was young has forever changed the landscape of my knee. Rape is a trauma that can impact someone physically, sure. For me, the most profound impact of this experience is invisible to the naked eye. The scars are in my heart—my soul. Unless I tell you about this experience, you'd never know that it happened. It is a part of who I am and will be until the day I die.

This scar on my knee has not prevented me from living to my current ripe old age. Rape hasn't either. There was a time in my life when I would have preferred to die. I thought if the guy who raped me would have killed me, that would have been so much easier. I don't feel this way today, but I did once upon a time. Today, I'm living life, and rape is a part of who I am.

The road to get here has not been easy. I had to get to know who I am with this experience. The experience of getting here has helped me to understand who I am and how I deal with the world around me. I've had to learn how to use the new soul I've crafted.

I've learned that people who hurt others create a vast chasm between their hearts and their feelings. When I talk with sex offenders, I ask about caring. If they care about the person they want to hurt, could they still hurt them? Often, the answer I get is no. What this tells me is that there's a disconnect between their hearts and their actions. I think if people were more connected to their hearts, many of the cruel and thoughtless things people do to others would diminish. Can you imagine what the world would be like if everyone cared for each other? If we lived from a perspective of love and care?

This has propelled me into a new journey of helping people connect with their hearts. Our emotions are the inner workings that help us function. Like our hearts beat without thinking, or we breathe, usually without conscious thought, they are inner workings that keep us living in this world. I think our emotions are the same way.

We experience a vast array of emotions every single day. We have happy moments, sad moments, moments of dire frustration and anger, and we experience love in so many forms. Our emotions shift in a matter of seconds. Understanding this about ourselves helps us learn how to make choices and how we make choices. If we are making angry choices, the results of our actions can be so destructive. If we are making loving, caring choices, our actions can be amazingly powerful in creating the life most of us strive for.

Understanding how we feel and how we want to feel could be a new superpower. It takes awareness, though, to pay attention to what's going on inside. Sure, it takes more energy to do that, but the rewards are amazing. Emotional awareness can help us respond to things more effectively. When we react without realizing what's going on inside of us, our actions can be counterproductive.

When I feel depressed, angry, or frustrated, taking a step back to realize what's going on inside helps me understand where I'm growing. It gives me an opportunity to choose what I'm going for. What if the emotions we perceive as negative were opportunities for us to grow ourselves into who we want to be? What if they are pining for our attention because they are leading us to a garden of wonder?

When you see a tree, how do you figure out you're in a forest? Looking at the tree from a different perspective allows you to see the forest. When I do the same thing with my emotions, the garden of who I am becomes more visible. Living from a place of fear gives us an understanding of the world that is fearful. Living from a place of curiosity about fear gives us an opportunity to learn more about it.

This is one way that I experience the world differently now. It takes conscious thought and effort to do this, but I've learned that the emotions I think are negative are often chock-full of gifts. I'm going for the gift perspective.

I never could have talked with sex offenders the way I do without my personal experience with it. Would I prefer not to have that expertise? Sure! But because I do, I have a choice.

Back to my knee. The scar is still present, but I'm a better bicycle rider now. With rape, I choose to keep learning. As I say, I don't think there is ever a point that it will be over, but the way I process information and feelings about it has made me a different person. It's a part of me now, just like the scar on my knee.

WHAT DO YOU THINK ABOUT YOUR GOD NOW?

My assailant asked me this question during one of our conversations. I didn't know what I thought when he asked me this question. As I rode through the course of the trauma and my recovery, I got to a point where I was angry with God. Why would this loving God I've been told about all my life allow something like this to happen to me?

I grew up in a Christian environment. My dad was a preacher. I couldn't run from that if I tried, at least as a youngster reliant on my parents to help raise me. After this experience, though, I cannot deny the anger I felt toward God. I remained involved with the church, but yes, I was angry! I felt confused about this whole "loving God" idea.

After I wrestled with this, I came to realize that God didn't do this to me. He didn't allow it to happen. Someone made a choice to hurt me. That wasn't God. It was a person who did this to me, not God. I was on the path of this person's choice. It wasn't God; it was the person who held a knife at my side.

Once I came to understand this, my anger toward God subsided. Thank goodness this powerful spiritual force has the grace to allow me to be angry when I need to be and love me all the same. Isn't that a powerful lesson about love? People do things to us that will make us angry enough to spit nails. It's okay to feel that anger! It's appropriate. We can be angry and still act from a place of love. That is the lesson I've learned from this. Thank You, God, for being a teacher and for Your willingness to allow me to feel anger about You.

Big, ugly traumas that happen in our lives change us. Are there more friendly ways to learn the lessons that come from our traumatic experiences? I believe so, yes. When we fall victim to the uncaring whims of other people, we still have a choice. We can choose to be a victim of our circumstances, or we can survive them and continue to move forward. Note the loss of a limb I talked about earlier. Is life harder? Of course, it is. Can we still live and be whole? Yes, we can. Is life forever altered? Yes, indeed.

We can have moments of crippling weakness, and we can have moments of great strength—physically and spiritually. It's our choice. Aren't you glad we can choose?

CHAPTER 31
THE WHOLE ENDING

LET'S talk about the idea of the whole ending.

I said it's never over.

What do I mean by this idea of a whole ending?

What does the "end" mean if there's no finish line? The effects of rape still rumble around in my existence. To date, a finish line eludes me. The milestones achieved in this process sometimes feel more final, and at other times, they feel more resolute than complete. I'm still living. Who knows what my experience of this history will be upon my last breath?

Traumatic experiences are extensive and life-altering; they forever color how we see the world and our place in it. The longer I live, the more my understanding of this experience evolves. It's been over 40 years since someone held me at knifepoint and my determination to take back control of my life is still in force. I'm no longer afraid of growth, or the process of growth, but look upon it with curiosity.

Internal growth is happening all the time. We each choose how aware we want to be about the process of internal growth. In my experience, awareness keeps us caring. It is true, though; sometimes it is more painful than others, and there are times it's inconvenient as hell. Consider the light bulb (awareness) when it is on. Scary and dark moments make us want to run away or hide. Magical moments, ahas, and moments of relief, peace, and amazing beauty make us lean in. (The big ugly might be essential to recognize the big amazing.) I've learned to experiment with curiosity instead of being afraid.

My footprints don't look like other prints already settled in the dirt. We're all navigating life in different shoes. Because we are all unique, we all process things with our own brain and emotional chemistries. We react and respond from a place that feels right for us. Our beliefs influence this.

Putting this part of my life story into words is exercising my dance with vulnerability. I don't know how you are going to respond to reading this story. Your experience is yours to have. To those who know me, how is this going to change the fabric of our relationship? In my experience, sharing this story with others has changed many of my relationships. Sometimes, it's for the better, and other times, it can be very disruptive.

I share this experience with my hands open and my heart extended to yours. If sharing my journey can help someone else to walk through their own experience, I share it freely. Maybe my process can inspire you. There is hope, and I encourage you to find your big amazing!

The whole ending is more about the journey I continue to experience about becoming a whole person. That's what I mean by a whole ending. I'm resolute in my processes now. I feel whole and roll with life as it continues to unfold.

As for looking forward, I don't know what the next month, what the next year, or what the next two years will bring, but I know now that I can manage it. This experience has become more of a curiosity than a trauma. That's saying something! Taking an approach of curiosity with it makes it more like finding new pieces to the puzzle. Sections of the picture come into clearer focus and no longer require the same attention. I can see a more complete picture, and the picture is much more beautiful now.

POSTLUDE

PRODUCING this story in its current form has been a journey for me. Putting these experiences into words and ultimately into this story has been a process. From learning moments, emotional moments, and (of course) the hours of spilling words onto paper (or virtual paper).

I want to take a few moments to express my fondest gratitude to a few folks.

First, the people at Miramare Ponte Press have graciously coached and supported me through writing, editing, and publishing this story. Marcy Pusey and her team are a perfect fit for this type of endeavor.

My writing tribe through the Unchained Writer community has spent countless (virtual) focused hours with me as we each create our own stories for publication. Joseph Michael is on to something, and I'm beyond grateful to him, his team, and the fellow writers in that community. It's a magical place.

Finally, I want to thank my husband, who has graciously respected the time and space I needed to put my experiences into words so that others might find support and hope in their own trauma-resilience path. I want to leave you with these words from him:

For my lover, my wife, my friend,

I stand aside, watching her be methodical, with self-induced guides, to live the whole day as it is her last. She sets timers, writes journals, follows daily rituals... each bringing meaning to her living.

She pours her heart out on paper while no one is listening, yet as if everyone will at some time experience her words in ways that will deeply affect their lives. Her intent is sure, her desire is pure, and her heart is full.

There is no "I wish" or disdain for missing any task or activity that may have fallen aside along her path. In contrast, there is "I will" when it comes to those asking for her hand to walk with her.

I am so full in being a bystander... just getting a wisp of her brilliance and light. There are so many ways I could express the "complete" in which her decisive walk has enlightened me.

She sees color where gray is encompassing. She sees fun where unfriendly looms. She sees helpful where grouchy is loud. She sees the best in herself when others can't seem to.

But out of all that I witnessed... if I was forced to find one aspect or one word to describe who she is and makes me so smile, it is her unwillingness to accept mediocrity in anything she does.

My only wish in my life is that you get the opportunity to meet her someday and experience just a sliver of the beautiful abundance she exudes.

RESOURCES

International Trauma Center
807 Hale Street
Beverly Farms, MA 01915
Contact Dr. Robert D. Macy
617.699.9939

National Sexual Violence Resource Center
https://www.nsvrc.org/find-help

Suicide & Crisis Hotline
Call/Text: 988
Or text "TALK" to 741741
https://988lifeline.org

OTHER BOOKS BY ALEXIS FAERE

These books are available on https://AlexisFaere.com, on Amazon, and where books are sold.

Whispers of Love: 365 Wonder-Filled Prayers for Grandma

Graceful Whispers: 365 Wonder-Filled Prayers for Grandpa

Emotion Prompt Journal Series:

Stayin' In Touch

Stayin' In Touch: Positive Emotions

Stayin' In Touch: Negative Emotions

Stayin' In Touch: Peaceful Emotions

Stayin' In Touch: Corporate Emotions

Stayin' In Touch: Elder Emotions

Stayin' In Touch: Parental Emotions

Stayin' In Touch: Friend Emotions

Stayin' In Touch: Gratitude Emotions

Stayin' In Touch: Grief Emotions

If you'd like to connect further with Alexis Faere, you can reach out to: contact@alexisfaere.com.